MW01469788

RETIRED . . .
AND LOVING IT!!

AN AUTOBIOGRAPHY/MEMOIR OF A FORMER FLORIDA GOVERNMENT LAWYER WHO'S HAD A VERY REWARDING CAREER (EVEN IF I SAY SO MYSELF)

RETIRED . . .
AND LOVING IT!!

GEORGE WAAS

AuthorHouse™
1663 Liberty Drive
Bloomington, IN 47403
www.authorhouse.com
Phone: 1-800-839-8640

Published by AuthorHouse 08/21/2012

ISBN: 978-1-4772-6257-3 (sc)
ISBN: 978-1-4772-6255-9 (hc)
ISBN: 978-1-4772-6256-6 (e)

Library of Congress Control Number: 2012915186

CONTENTS

Acknowledgments

When I finally decided to write this book, I had my family in mind; specifically my wife, children and grandchildren. I never learned much about the lives my grandparents led, and my parents were never open to volunteering much information about their lives, especially their younger years before they had me.

I'm told life was different back then; there wasn't much communication among family members about matters of such a personal and intimate subject as oneself.

Now, with communications so much easier, and with so many more means of providing and preserving information, I decided to write about me—my early childhood, my family, my professional life, my thoughts; literally everything that makes me, well, me.

I believe we all want to leave something for our children, their children, and on and on. A life well-lived and a solid reputation certainly accomplish this. This book will give my wife, children and grandchildren as complete a description of me as I can give. It will also allow my grandchildren's children to read about me as told by the best possible source with no filter; every word here is mine and mine alone except the few items as noted in a couple of chapters.

Why would I want to do this? I'm not rich or famous. Well, of course I am. I'm famous in the eyes of my family, and rich with their love and support. That's really all that matters.

So, with more thanks than I could give to my wife, Harriet, my daughters, Lani and Amy, my granddaughters Hailey, Kelsie (Lani) and Avery (Amy) and my grandson Connor (Amy), this is my story.

To my other family members, friends and colleagues who've helped mold me into me, thanks for your efforts. I appreciate all the good things people have done for me over the years. Any failures are mine and mine alone.

And to those of you who read this, I hope you enjoy my story . . . . and hope that it will inspire you to tell yours.

Retired . . . . And Loving It!! An Autobiography/ Memoir Of A Former Florida Government Lawyer

by George Waas

The R word finally hit me like a ton of bricks in January 2010. Retirement. Although my retirement date of June 30, 2010 was well known to me for five years, I hadn't given very much thought to it until I had reached less than six months out. As I began to think about it, however, and the change of life it meant to me, I had the first panic attack in my life, requiring counseling I never had need of before.

My father instilled in me a strong work ethic, telling me not "to talk a good game." He made it clear that words without action are meaningless. So, I equated action with work, work with productivity and productivity with usefulness. In short, being useful and productive meant working. Retirement was, to me, the opposite of action and productivity. I feared becoming useless. Imagine the feeling of anticipated uselessness! That's precisely where I was. How I dealt with this is explained later.

The first question you might ask is why would I write an autobiography/ memoir. I'm not a former high-ranking public official or high-profile athlete, singer or movie star. I haven't survived after years of abusing alcohol or drugs. I didn't rob, maim or kill. I'm not famous or notorious; just an ordinary retired lawyer who toiled in the public sector for over 32 years and was fortunate enough to be named outstanding Florida government lawyer in 2000; appeared in several Marquis Who's Who publications, including Who's Who in America; twice named as an outstanding government lawyer and legal leader by Florida Trend

Magazine in its annual Legal Elite publication; and handled high-profile cases that took me to the United States Supreme Court and appearances on national, state and local news. Ok, so I'm important to my family and friends, but it's not like I'm famously known by millions. Heck, I'm probably not even known by more than, say, hundreds. But I've led an interesting life (by my standards), had some wonderful experiences, and I do have a few pointers on how to deal with retirement following a reasonably active professional life.

My recollection of events leading up to retirement made me focus on my years in the workforce, my family, my activities before—and now in—retirement, my professional and fraternal accomplishments and how I might spend at least the first few of my retirement years. Now, after the passage of a couple of years between my toiling in the workaday world and retirement, I began reflecting on the paths my life has taken so far; its many twists and turns. I thought about the meaning of retirement for me, and how I've handled it—again, so far—and decided to put it all in writing. Hence, you have my motivation to write this autobiography/memoir. I don't believe this is an uncommon motive. So instead of asking "Why?," I asked "Why not?" There's really nothing to lose by telling your story.

I must begin this endeavor with a confession. My original plan was to write the Great American Novel. I think all writers want to do this as part of their legacy. But after reading dozens of novels—I particularly enjoy Da Vinci Code-type books—and visiting several bookstores, I realized that lots of writers already had written the Great American Novel, or at least believed they had. I also realized that works of this nature require a tremendous amount of research and great attention to detail. I am not a patient person, and I had retired from a profession that demanded voluminous research. Why would I want to write a book requiring what I retired from doing?

I wanted to write on a subject I knew something about, and I wanted to write it relatively quickly without doing much research. Not that I'm lazy; I just wanted to write something that had meaning instead of a work from the made-up world of fiction. What better subject meets these conditions than me? No significant research is involved; just a little here and there—you'll know it when you read it—and a reasonably good memory is all that's required. So, I drafted a four-page outline, sat down at my computer, and started typing. As I proceeded from draft to draft, I made additional notes on a pad I keep next to my computer. I had my first draft done in less than one week, and my second draft done in three weeks. The words were pouring out of me at the rate of 4,000 to 5,000 a day on some days. As a thought or idea would come to me, I'd write it down and include it in my narrative. I found that, quite frequently, one word or a brief phrase would lead to hundreds of words that I included in the text.

A memoir usually doesn't start with one's family background; an autobiography might. This really doesn't matter, because mine does. Since we are all products of our ancestors, I'll begin by telling you about my family history—at least as much as I can recall, since my youth, combined with my parents' and grandparents' non-existent discussions about their families, give me precious little history. Then, I'll introduce you to my wife, children, grandchildren and pets. (Yes, pets. They are very important to one's well-being, as I found out rather late in life.)

Then I'll discuss my life so far; my last job; some personal observations I picked up along my journey; my anxiety facing retirement; personal health issues; positive thinking, values and leadership skills; and wrap it up with some not-so-final thoughts.

MY FAMILY BACKGROUND

A good place to start this discussion is at birth. I was born on July 12, 1943 to George Waas and Anna Weintraub Waas in the Bronx, New York City. My maternal grandparents, Bernard and Mollie Weintraub, were born in Poland and Russia, respectively, and lived in Kiev until moving to New York City during the mass migration of Jewish immigrants in the early 20th century. Thanks to my daughter Lani, who is doing a family search on Ancestry.com, I recently found out Grandma Mollie's parents were Nathan and Sabina Tabachnick from Russia. My maternal grandparents had five children; my mother Anna was the oldest, born on March 13, 1918. She had four siblings, three sisters and a brother. I have no recollection of my maternal grandfather, as he passed away suddenly on my third birthday at age 54. I remember that in the late 1940s, my parents and I lived with my maternal grandmother in New York. I remember her as a strong woman with a strong accent that she didn't pass on to her children, who prided herself on caring for her family. She loved to cook meals for her children and her several grandchildren.

I have a far better memory of my paternal grandparents because, for a two-year period beginning in 1958, my dad, my brother Barry and I lived with them in an efficiency apartment in Miami Beach. My dad moved his parents from their apartment in Newark, New Jersey, to Miami Beach in 1957 and, shortly thereafter, moved there himself (my parents separated in the early 1950s and divorced in 1953) and then moved my brother and me within three months after he moved there. (To this day, I'm thankful that my mother gave my brother and me her blessing to move to Miami Beach in January 1958. My health wasn't great—severe childhood allergies—and the move was looked upon by my dad, his parents, and my maternal aunts and uncle as a path to a better life for my brother and me.)

I didn't see much of my mother after the move to Miami Beach. She would visit once a year, and my brother and I would call every so often, but she didn't want to leave her family and friends; New York was all she ever really knew. In 1977, when her health started to decline, my brother Barry, who was living in Maryland at the time, found an apartment complex in Laurel and my brother and I went to New York, packed up her belongings and moved her to Laurel and a new life. We visited with her every couple of years. As her health deteriorated, she eventually was moved into a nursing home in Maryland in 1993 and passed away in 1996.

My paternal grandparents, Leopold (who went by the name Leo) and Bertha Jones (pronounced Yonas) Waas, were born in New York City on October 15, 1884 and July 2, 1885, respectively. Again, thanks to Lani, I discovered that my paternal great-grandparents were George and Julia Kingsburg Waas, born in Middlesex, England; my maternal great-grandparents were John D. and Melissa Jones, born in New York City. I could show what a great job Lani did by going back eight generations, but I've made my point. (Actually, not quite. Lani told Harriet and me she will continue with her search, so I certainly look forward to learning more and more about my family from generations past.) My grandfather was a jeweler; my grandmother a homemaker. They were of English and Dutch background. (You can pretty much tell whether a person has a Dutch background—just look at a person's last name and if you find the same two vowels next to each other, usually near or in the middle of a name, you've found a Dutch name.) My grandfather had three brothers and two sisters; my grandmother was an only child. My father was born in New York on May 18, 1909; his brother—my uncle Ed—was born in 1913. Both grandparents were very strong-willed, yet kind and loving. During the two years I lived with my grandparents, not a day would go by that grandpa didn't greet me with his booming "Hello, my boy!" whenever he would see me. I can now carry on this greeting with my grandson. My grandpa was a minor league baseball player in the early 1900s. He pitched for the old minor league Baltimore Orioles under a different name; I believe it was Waco. I remember him taking my brother and me to the ballpark in Miami Beach where he would throw batting practice to us. He had the most wicked curve ball that neither one of us could touch—and he was in his 70s at the time. He must have been quite a pitcher. A broken hand ended his career before he had a chance at the major leagues.

For about a year, my dad, brother and I lived with my grandparents in what was euphemistically called an efficiency apartment. What was efficient about it is that it consisted of three rooms—a small kitchen/ dining area, a small family room/bedroom with a small closet, and a small bathroom. At night, my dad would put a mattress on a coffee table and one on the floor. I got to sleep on the coffee table; my brother got the floor. For about a year, five people lived in about 400 square feet of space.

Then, my dad and brother moved down the hall into a smaller efficiency that had no kitchen/dining area. I was just happy I didn't have to sleep on the coffee table anymore.

Because of my father's struggle to raise us while trying to find work, my grandparents assumed much of the parenting responsibilities for these critical formative years for my brother and me. My first job at age 14 was as a jeweler's apprentice for my grandpa, and for a jeweler grandpa worked for who had a store near where my grandparents lived on Jefferson Avenue. (The name of the small apartment building in which we lived was the Elaine Apartments. My oldest daughter's name is Elaine. When my wife and I named her, I had completely forgotten the name of the first place I lived after moving permanently to Miami Beach. Just a coincidence, I suppose.) I used to carry jewelry, including diamonds and rubies, in my pocket to and from the Miami Diamond Center. My grandpa must have assumed that no one would figure that a teenager riding the bus would be carrying thousands of dollars worth of rings and gems from Miami Beach to Miami and back. I was a perfect gem transportation courier.

I worked for this other jeweler at his shop only on Saturdays, washing and polishing rings, using special chemicals for this purpose. My fingernails turned a reddish brown that lasted quite some time after I stopped working as an aspiring jeweler in 1960. One day, a young man came in, shook my hand and gave the jeweler and me a card that identified himself as Doyle Conner. He was the speaker of the Florida House of

Representatives—the youngest in Florida history—and was running for state agriculture commissioner. He was elected and served for 30 years. This was my first brush with a political figure.

My grandpa passed away in 1963; my grandma in 1970. Today, I proudly wear the ring my grandfather made for me when I turned 13, as well as the ring he made for my father which was passed down to me when my dad passed away.

My father met Reona Shapiro in 1958 and they married two years later, after which the four of us moved into a two-bedroom apartment in Miami Beach. My father was a hotel manager, managing such hotels as the Fontainebleau and Eden Roc, as well as hotels that now are a part of the Art Deco section of south Miami Beach, including the Clevelander. He used to tell me stories of the times he helped President John Kennedy with his back brace, and how Frank Sinatra and other members of the Rat Pack (Dean Martin, Peter Lawford, Sammy Davis, Jr. and Joey Bishop) would hang out in, and literally take over, the Fontainebleau hotel restaurants and bars. The 1960s was a great time to live and work in Miami Beach, and my dad thoroughly enjoyed getting to know these famous men, and how thankful he was that they would take their time to get to know him. My dad used to tell me the story of the time a hotel guest loudly complained to my dad when Frank Sinatra came over and asked my dad if he needed any help. My dad said everything was under control, to which Sinatra said "ok, just let me know if you need any help in taking care of this." My dad said he didn't want to pursue the matter any further, and the complaining guest quickly took his leave.

As I look back, I realize how much trouble I caused my stepmother early on. I think it's unfortunate but natural for children who have gone through a divorce to vent their anguish on the "replacement parent." My stepmother never tried to take my mother's place, but in my mind, this is what I thought. "Re" (this is what everyone called her) never married until she married my father, and never had children of her own. She was 50 at the time of their wedding; despite all of this, she did everything possible to make us a family and give my brother and me a warm, comfortable home. She even co-existed with my grandmother when she came to live with us after my grandfather died. I didn't realize it then, but it takes a remarkable woman to share a home with her mother-in-law. And Re did this for almost seven years.

My dad and stepmother eventually moved to Fort Lauderdale after he retired from the hotel business in the late 1970s. He passed away in 1988. From that time until Re passed away at age 92 in 2003, I visited her every time I traveled to south Florida on business. I would take her to her favorite restaurants, and she would proudly introduce me to her friends and neighbors. She was a great and proud lady and quite influential in my life.

My father served in the Army during World War II, but he liked telling me how he almost missed it. He was discharged on December 5, 1941--only to be recalled three days later. Pearl Harbor. It was during his second stint when, while stationed at Ft. Bragg, he was accidentally hit in the mouth by a rifle butt that took out all his front teeth and so damaged his mouth that he needed full replacements. I often wondered why, as a relatively young man, he had all false teeth. I was 10 when he first told me this story.

My dad wanted to be a showman-a comedian-but grandpa was adamant in believing that no one could earn an honest living engaging in such foolishness, and that my dad should go to work for a hotel if he wanted to make a decent living. So, it was the hotel business for him. After we settled in Miami Beach and my dad started working for hotels, I worked with him on different occasions during the summers as a cabana boy, pool boy, bellhop and telephone switchboard operator. Back then, switchboards used plug-in cords to hook up rooms with callers. If the operator used the wrong plug, the guest didn't get his/her call; another guest did. Needless to say, my dad would get complaints from hotel guests who were upset at not getting their calls, or being connected to people they didn't know. I got some big tips as a bellman, cabana boy and pool boy, but the biggest tip I got was from my dad who told me not to go into the hotel business.

My dad was a character in every sense of this word. As a child, he would come to my elementary school and tell the principal that he had to take my brother and me to "Dr. Yankum Studyum" because we were sick. It turns out that this was really Yankee Stadium and we'd see baseball games in the afternoon. How many fathers take their sons from school to go to ballgames? After my parents separated and my dad moved into the hotel he happened to be managing at the time, he would have my brother and me take the train from our apartment in the Bronx to Manhattan (you could do this as a 10-year-old in New York City in the 1950s) after school on Friday, and meet us at the station near his hotel. He would take us out for dinner, have lots of candy and ice cream for us in his hotel suite, and then on Saturday, after a breakfast of a dozen cinnamon buns (six for me, six for my brother and dad—I was a big eater and a fat kid back then) we'd go to the circus, rodeo or hockey games and other sporting events at Madison Square Garden or the Polo Grounds (home of the New York baseball Giants), or visit "Dr. Yankum Stadyum." On Sunday, dad would take us to the train station for our trip home. We did this weekend routine for more almost five years.

Another thing my dad would do is "get me" into the boxing bouts at St. Nicholas Arena. St. Nick's was a famous venue for boxing in the 1950s, and he convinced me that I had to be 18 to get in. My dad, who through his hotel work had connections with the arena management for complimentary tickets, would tell me I had to wear a big overcoat and disguise my voice so the ticket taker would think that, although I was 12 or 13 at the time, I was really 18. Even though my admission was all pre-arranged, I had to tell the ticket taker my name and address. I took this responsibility very seriously, wrapping myself in my too-large overcoat, lowering my voice and making a big frown all to show that I was 18. Only years later did I find out how much laughter this brought to my dad, as well as the St. Nick's staff. What surprised my dad, however, was my yelling at the fighters to "hit him harder; knock him out." I guess my dad didn't expect me to cheer for such violence. He probably thought my cheering on the hockey players who got into fights was just an anomaly.

There was one occasion where my dad used his humor to deal with a serious situation involving me. After my brother and I moved to Miami Beach, I developed emotional problems having to deal with an entirely new environment. I continued to complain about being homesick, but my dad knew it was just a matter of adjustment to a new environment. So, on one particularly bad day for me—bad grades on two tests—I wailed about missing New York. My dad took me to an airline ticket office in Miami Beach, went in and came out with a ticket, saying "Here's a one-way ticket back to New York. Do you want to go? The plane leaves in a couple of hours." I said I didn't want to go back; that I would try harder and do better. He promptly tore up the ticket, took me back to our efficiency apartment—and almost immediately, I began to feel better and do better in school. Turns out the ticket was only an empty envelope that he found on the floor in the airline office. When he told me this years later, I laughed but also realized the sacrifices he made to give my brother and me a much better life than the one we most likely would have had had we remained in New York.

Whatever sense of humor my family and friends attribute to me no doubt came from my father. He was the funniest person I ever met. He did pantomime, which is physical humor without spoken words; how would act out scenes playing multiple characters. He managed to combine his hotel work with show business on occasion, doing shows at a few of the hotels he managed, using the stage name of George Allen. After he passed away, I went through some of his papers and found, to my delight and surprise, that my dad's involvement in show business was far more extensive than I was led to believe. He started in burlesque with entertainer Robert Alda, whose son, Alan, is a great comedian/actor in his own right, most famous for his role in M★A★S★H. He also worked with comedian Phil Silvers, Guy Lombardo and Sophie Tucker. During World War II, my dad played in a show entitled "This is the Army," put together by Irving Berlin. In the 1950s, he appeared in a Broadway show entitled "I Married an Angel" and then started entertaining on cruise ships for the Costa Cruise Line. He did shows on the Condominium circuit in Fort Lauderdale until the early 1980s. How I wish I knew this before he passed away.

As for the name George Allen, so many Jewish entertainers changed their names during this era. We know so many Jewish comedians by their stage names: Jack Benny, George Burns, Milton Berle, Danny Kaye, Jerry Lewis, for example. Their real names are quite remarkably different because they identify their religious background, and any performer with an easily identifiable Jewish name was urged to change it. One day, we were walking past Pumpernick's Restaurant, a famous gathering place in Miami Beach, when a man standing in the doorway yelled out "Georgie. Georgie Allen." Turns out it was Milton Berle, one of the great comedians of the 20th century. He told me my dad was the funniest man he ever met. Did that give me a swelled head!!!

My dad never lost his great sense of humor. Even at the most difficult times in his life—divorce, loss of family members, employment difficulties—he always tried to find that nugget—however small—of humor that would allow him to tell a funny story. I learned that some of the greatest comedians led very troubled personal lives. I can only surmise that humor allowed many of the most famous of comedians to survive economic depression and war, and other personal tragedies. Humor was their outlet from disappointment and despair. I know my dad used humor the same way; and I've thankfully inherited his attitude in dealing with difficult events. I now see this in my daughters and grandchildren. Thanks, dad.

Recently, my daughter Lani did an ancestry search and discovered that my father's full name is George Leo Waas. Until Lani's research, I didn't know my dad had a middle name; he never used it, and I never saw a single piece of paper that had his full name on it. I am not a junior, however, and my middle name is not derived from my father or grandfather Leo. In the Jewish tradition, a male child is not named after a living relative; if he is to be named after a family member, he is named only after someone who's deceased. To name a child after a living relative is to, in effect, wish that that relative were deceased. I am named after my great-and great-great-grandfathers (George and Lee, respectively). I've been told that I'm more like my grandfather than my dad in demeanor and personality. Over the years, family and friends who knew both say I get my doggedness, tenacity and determination from my grandfather; my sense of humor and warmer side from my dad. To make a living in journalism and law, you need doggedness, tenacity and determination; to be a caring parent and grandparent, you need a solid sense of humor and nurturing ability. Perhaps these relatives and friends know me better than I do.

MY WIFE, CHILDREN, GRANDCHILDREN, ETC.

Now, let me introduce you to my family, which I'll begin with the title

Harriet

Harriet was born in Miami on July 6, 1949 and lived with her parents until she moved to Tallahassee to enter Florida State University. She entered my life one September day in 1969 while we were both students at FSU. I was attending a social event, talking to a girl, when Harriet walked over to us, and took over the conversation I was having with this other girl, causing this girl to leave. Impressed with her persistence (and noting that she was a cute as a button), I took her dorm phone number and called her a few days later. I didn't have a car, and this gave me great concern over asking her out. Left over from my high school days was the belief that without a car, I wouldn't have a chance at getting a date. As a result, I dated very little in high school and college. Nevertheless, I summoned the courage and called her, and I did ask her out, and we went on our first date. We walked from her dorm to a downtown movie theater and at no time did she complain. In fact, she enjoyed walking and talking about nothing in particular. I found myself becoming nervous as we dated more and more. I never felt this way before, since I'd never come close to anything of a, shall I say, more permanent relationship. What I didn't know until much later is that after we met, she called her parents that same day and told them that she had met the boy she was going to marry. Once we got engaged, she told me this story. Of course, it didn't matter then, but it was quite a revelation and leap of faith.

After a few weeks, I made the stupid comment that perhaps I should "play the field." To her credit, she didn't show any emotion; rather, she said that if I wanted to date others, she would do likewise. This is not the answer

I expected or wanted to hear. I could date, but she couldn't. (Now how silly is that!!) I suppose love can be both blind and stupid. (Interestingly, Harriet's recollection differs from mine. She says I made my "play the field" comment after we were engaged, upon which she offered to return the engagement ring I gave her. The passage of time does indeed affect memory, but this is my story, and I'll stick to my understanding of what happened. I'm including Harriet's because she wants me to, and I'm interested in keeping the peace. Either way, what really matters here is the story that I did get "cold feet" but that my nervousness eventually worked itself out to our mutual satisfaction. Besides, as the saying goes, either version is close enough for government work.)

What I didn't know then is that she called her parents after my "play the field" comment and bawled her eyes out. Her mother told her it's just nerves and if he truly cares, this will pass. And it did; in just a few days. I felt nervous around her, but missed her when I was alone. This is a sure tell-tale sign; but I didn't realize it then.

I must say a few words about Harriet's parents. From the moment I first met them, I believed that Martin and Hildegard Issner were the kind of in-laws every son-in-law should have—caring and great to be around. Both were German immigrants and Holocaust survivors. He wanted to be a doctor, but Hitler prevented this. Martin, who I called dad after Harriet and I married, was born in 1912; he stood about 5'7" and was as big around as he was tall. His heart was also as big as he was. I will never forget his generosity and love, and he could make the best barbeque I ever ate. He managed a couple of service stations in Miami and, at age 65, went to work as a security guard. I remember him lying on his couch with the telephone beside him watching the stock market on TV. He would frequently call his broker and give orders to buy and sell. He self-educated on the stock market and, although he arrived in America with virtually no money, made a rather significant nest egg for his family via the market. He was a good and decent man. A chain smoker, he passed away from lung cancer in 1979 at age 67.

Hildegard was born in 1916 and was a homemaker who sold Avon on the side. A few years after Martin passed away, Hilde met and married Herman Wilzig and moved to Tamarac, Florida. He passed away from

Alzheimer's Disease after a few years. After she turned 90, Hilde was interviewed as part of the Steven Spielberg project to record personal histories of Holocaust survivors. That interview is now preserved as a permanent part of the Holocaust record as told by those who lived through its horrors. After Hilde's second husband passed away, she remained in her Tamarac home until she turned 93, when she moved to Michigan to be close to her son and my brother-in-law, Jim, and his family. She now lives in a memory care facility and turned 96 on July 24, 2012. From the day we first met, I called her mom, and still do so today. She is a most generous, loving, caring lady. Although only 4'8", she was and is a giant to her family-including me.

Harriet and I dated steadily shortly after we met, eventually leading to a New Years Eve 1970 engagement and, on July 18, 1971 marriage in Miami. July 18 is significant to us because if you add July 12 (my birthday) to July 6 (Harriet's birthday) you get . . . . well, I made sure there would be no way I'd ever forget our anniversary.

Our engagement took place literally by accident. While I had been thinking about this for awhile, one evening we were in the ballroom of my dad's hotel dancing, when I said "It would be nice to have you around." Harriet said "Is that a proposal?" "Well, I suppose it is," I said. And that was that. I had no ring to give her then, but I took care of that rather quickly, gathering together all I could to buy a small diamond ring. One night, I hid the ring under my couch in my apartment and did the usual "on your knee" plea. That formalized our engagement, and satisfied Harriet that I did it "the right way."

Over the years, I've asked Harriet to let me buy her a more suitably sized diamond ring. She steadfastly refuses, saying the one she has means so much more precisely because I had so little money back then. I did eventually buy her diamonds, however. After our 35th anniversary, we went on a December family cruise and returned to St. Thomas, V.I.—the place of our 1971 honeymoon. We took a taxi to the same hotel we stayed at, and in a dining room where we had dinner more than 35 years earlier, I gave her a diamond necklace. Anyone think I'm not a romantic?

We lived in apartments for two years before we bought our first house and, on August 2, 1975, Elaine Beth joined us. At least, that's the name we gave her. At age 4, she proudly announced to us that her name was Lani . . . and it's been that way ever since. On July 9, 1979, Amy Michelle made us a family of four.

Harriet spent 37 years as an elementary school teacher—teaching in the same school for all 37 years! This consistency in her professional life explains Harriet—steady as she goes, a real Rock of Gibraltar. While so many administrators and teachers believe that teaching to standardized tests is the way to go, Harriet never believed this. Oh, she taught her children so they would do well on these tests, but she also taught them how to learn. She created a classroom atmosphere conducive to learning and thinking. And she really cared about her kids. At night, at our dinner table, she would wax on and on about this kid or that; what they had accomplished that day; what she was working on with her kids, etc.

She also talked of her frustrations with administrators who wanted to take teaching away from the teachers. She simply didn't believe that kids could be taught by edicts issued by administrators sitting in offices far removed from the classroom. Although frustrated, she remained undaunted and undefeated in her desire and mission to teach.

While so many of her colleagues became frustrated to the point of giving up trying to teach to learn and taught to the tests instead, Harriet never did. The most immediate beneficiaries of Harriet's teaching methods and values are our own two children, who are now passing along those nuggets of learning techniques and her educational value system to their children.

Now, after having taught three generations of kids, she'll occasionally run into some of her "kids" today at malls and shopping centers, some of whom are in their 40s. They'll remember her fondly and show off their children and grandchildren. Harriet always gets a kick out of that. Her dedication was rewarded by receiving her school's Teacher of the Year award multiple times, and being named multiple times in Marquis' Who's Who in America, American Education, and American Women. Not bad for a classroom teacher. I know I'll be accused of prejudice on this, but I wish more teachers were as dedicated and committed to excellence in education as Harriet was, and still is.

Now that we've been married more than 40 years, I'm asked quite often what the secret is to our long and happy marriage. I answer honestly: I wish I knew. But I do know one thing, and without giving away who's most responsible for our longevity, let me just say this: it is impossible to argue with anyone who laughs at someone who's ranting, raving, screaming, etc. If there is one thing that will end any argument, giggling and laughing will do it every time. Now, who's the yeller and who's the laugher? Well, I'm not going to tell you, so there!! What? But Harriet, I don't want to say anymore on this. Aw, come on; do I have to? Oh, ok, well, you see, on rare occasions, I might get a bit upset and since there's no one around to vent my, ah, upsetness, I might raise my voice an octave or two, only to be met not with sympathy and understanding, but with, with . . . ok, Harriet, I'll say it: laughter—a big smile and continuous, infectious laughter. There's nothing that will break tension and anger quicker than laughter. It's impossible to argue with someone who's giggling and laughing at you. Do I get any sympathy from my children? Are you kidding? They're women, too.

It was no different in the understanding and sympathy department during the time our children lived at home with us. While Amy lived home, and after she left for college, our home was occupied by females, and a female dog and two neutered male cats. Knowing the fate of the males in my home, if you think for one second that I was going to argue about anything with anyone, think again. I knew my place, as well as the risk of disobedience.

After more than 40 years of living with the same wonderful woman, and at the risk of overstating my point, I can say with authority that men and women think differently; and if there is no understanding of this, than that relationship is in serious trouble. What I mean is this: women's and men's brains are wired differently. If there is one word that should be removed from a woman's vocabulary, that word is "because." This word allows women to explain in precise detail every nuance or thread of a free-form discussion; usually in one very, very long sentence interspersed with numerous "becauses".

Let me give you an example. Harriet will say "I need to go to the grocery store because we're out of rye bread because you used the last two slices instead of the raisin bread because there were no English muffins for you because you ate the last one and didn't put it on the shopping list because you couldn't find it." See how dangerous this word is? Why couldn't she just tell me she's going to buy rye bread? Nah, that would be too easy. Besides, her wiring makes her incapable of a simple straightforward statement.

I actually had a psychologist tell me that women are more interested in explaining the process and providing information, while men are looking at the bottom line, wondering or asking "What do you want me to do about it?"

Men, how many times has your wife said "You're not listening to me." And how many times have you answered "What?" And how many times have you tried in vain to remember what she said and, in frustration, said something to the effect of "Just tell me what you want me to do."? Come on now, admit it. This is a classic example of a difference in wiring. Please understand that I'm not making a value judgment here; this is not a good or bad thing. It just is what it is.

Harriet will also use a phrase that, while not as bad as the dreaded "because," allows for a running monologue. That phrase is "I wonder . . ." We'll be driving and suddenly Harriet will say something like "I wonder why the people who own that house painted it blue." Now, she's certainly not planning to stop and ask, and I don't really give a rat's rear end why those people whom I've never met and will never meet decided to pain their house blue. But this is yet another example of wiring. I usually get two or three of these "I wonders" for every hour we drive. You can imagine how much fun our trips are to Orlando, Tampa/St. Petersburg, Jacksonville, Pensacola and all points in between. The psychologist says this is really not a matter of wonderment; rather, it's a device used to provide information with no solution. I used to let Harriet's information-providing narratives get to me, but not anymore. And Harriet has become better at saying "You really don't care about that, do you?" Frustration has been replaced by laughter. It's taken a lot of years for this to happen, however. But I still get the inevitable "I wonder . . . ." And when she mixes "I wonder" with "because," well, you get the idea.

Along this line of rampant conversation is the fact that women spend more time on the telephone than men do. At least, it's a fact in my home. When Harriet is on the phone with our daughters, or a female friend for that matter, she'll spend anywhere from 30 minutes or more engaging in what I can only describe as idle chatter or, a word I prefer, palaver. Here's a not-so-hypothetical example. When men are on the phone, they get right down to the bottom line. Jack: "Where do you want to have lunch?" Bill¨ How about Red Lobster?" Jack: "Ok, what time?" Bill: "12:30" Jack: "Ok, see you then." Click. That's it. Women having the same essential discussion will ask what's on the menu, criticize some selections, talk about the color coordination of the place, drive-time traffic, what they're going to wear, what they'd like to do after lunch (probably go shopping), etc., etc., etc. Is all this really necessary? Can't they decide to debate these points after they meet for lunch? If you want to know why men will never understand women, it's because of the wiring.

Because of this wiring differential, men must work extra hard to avoid getting into an argument with a woman. While it's human nature to have disagreements, arguments must be avoided at all costs because women are armed with another set of wires that retain and rapidly produce information with which men can't compete. Here's an example. I'll tell Harriet to please not toss dishtowels in the hamper every time I use one to dry my hands, and to please put the towel on the kitchen counter. She's say something like "Well, do you remember back on November 24, 1998 when you took my bath towel and threw it in the hamper before I even used it? And what about that time on August 26, 2003 when you took my walking shoes and put them next to the bed instead of in the shoe rack where they belong?" Now, I have trouble remembering what I had for dinner two nights ago, but somehow women have these memory cells loaded with incredible recall power that should send a strong signal to any man to avoid at all costs having this kind of discussion. It's a no-win situation, men.

Another thing no man wants to do with his wife is going shopping. I believe that just before a girl is born, she passes through a yet-unknown microscopic passage from womb to world where the baby receives an injection of what can only be called the shopping gene. This gene is coded with such phrases as "I have nothing to wear" and "I need another pair of shoes." Of course, if I'm wrong on this, then it's obvious to me that women are born with an extra link in their DNA that's scientifically called the shopping link. Either way, this unique feature is demonstrated by the number of times a woman will, in a supermarket for example, pick up an item, put it down, pick it up again, stare at it for awhile, put it down, and move on. They will stop their shopping carts in the aisle and, upon looking at a display shelf, develop a catatonic stare at the bombardment of choices and attractive colors. The shopping list itself may have five or ten items, but it will take a woman a long time to go up and down the aisles just looking. This shopping catatonia is also noted in department stores. A man can outfit himself with suits, sport coats, slacks, shirts, underwear, etc., in one hour or so; not so with a woman!

The pattern that emerged during the years our daughters lived with us exists to this very day. They will spend a day shopping and come home with a small bag—if anything—which contains an item or two of clothing or cosmetics. Now, a man could buy the same amount of items in about 15 minutes, but not a woman. When asked why they took so long to buy so little, the stock answer is "I couldn't find anything I liked." Eight hours of shopping and they couldn't find anything they liked? Of course, this is different when it comes to shoes. I own about five or six pair of shoes, including a pair of walking shoes. Harriet owns over 20 pairs of shoes. She has just as many feet as I do, yet she believes she must compete with Imelda Marcos. In my younger years, I used to blame Harriet for all of this; not anymore. I've grown wiser over the years as I see more and more women follow the same pattern. I know now that everything that is shopping is totally genetic. Men, you must never initiate any further discussion on this subject; it will make no sense to you and only wind up upsetting you.

Here's another example of either a genetic insert or a separate gene unique to women. Have you ever gone to a restaurant with friends and notice that when one woman has to go to the ladies room, the others have to go, too? When a man has to go, he gets up, excuses himself and goes. Women make this a group outing. I believe I know why. This gives women time to gossip. Women are great gossipers. Here's a great example. When Harriet takes a walk in our neighborhood during early evening hours, she usually goes with a neighbor. Our neighbor runs a business that puts her in touch with a lot of people in our neighborhood. How do I know this? When Harriet and I take an exercise walk, Harriet will point out house after house and tell me who lives there; whether the owners are ill, retired, separated or divorced; whether the children are doing well or in some type of trouble; whether the house is going on the market, etc. Now, for me, I couldn't care less, but Harriet has to keep me informed. I call her and our neighbor the "Snoop Sisters" and they actually pride themselves on this. But I really don't need to know whether my neighborhood is another Melrose Place or Wisteria Lane. I simply don't care, but Harriet has to keep me informed, or so she believes.

Men never gossip. Of course, they complain ad nauseam on occasion; and they'll argue about relatives or neighbors they can't stand and won't be caught in the same state as them, but you'll never hear them gossip. Only women can gossip about relatives, neighbors, etc. Amazing, isn't it?

Here's another thing that I believe is fairly common among women—an almost panic-driven concern about their hair and their face. I'll ask Harriet if she wants to go out, say, for lunch, and she'll say something like "Give me about a half-hour. My hair's a mess." I don't see anything wrong with her hair; moreover, I don't think anyone will approach her on the street or wherever we go and say "Excuse me, lady, but your hair's a mess." That's not going to happen. Or she'll say "I can't go out now; I have to put on my face." Of course, she doesn't mean this literally; she means she needs to put on makeup. But again, I think I can safely say that no one is going to tell her that all is well with the world, except your face is a mess. In fact, no one is ever going to come up to me and say something like "You're such a nice guy, but what are you doing with someone whose hair and face are a mess?" Guys, you get the point. Ladies, don't worry; be happy.

Finally, something else I notice—and this might involve the aging process—is that women tend to repeat themselves a lot. For example, on Monday, Harriet will inform me that she has a haircut appointment on Thursday at 10. A few hours later, she'll say "I have a haircut appointment on Thursday at 10." A few hours later, or perhaps the next day, I'll casually mention that I'm having lunch with friends on Wednesday. Harriet will say "Well, I have a haircut appointment on Thursday at 10." On Wednesday, I'll be told yet again "I have a haircut appointment tomorrow at 10." I've now heard this several times, including a time or two when I said something totally unrelated. Comes Thursday morning and as Harriet goes out the door, I'll inevitably ask: "Where are you going?" Hmmm, maybe Harriet thinks the problem is my memory cells. Of maybe after being bombarded with the same information, I'm in overload or I've closed my ears to this bit of information. Yeah, it has to be that; I'm certainly not uh, uh, becoming forgetful.

Remember this: women just want to inform and explain; men want to solve. Women want to shop; men want to buy. Simple, but if a man lets it get to him, he's got big trouble. This part of my discussion reminds me of an old joke as to why women live longer than men—because they're not married to women!! Ha, Ha, Ha. Isn't this a funny joke? Not true, of course; right guys? Ladies, it's just a joke!

Let me quickly get off this subject and introduce you to my children and grandchildren. Before meeting them, however, there is something I must say as a word of caution to all parents who have toddlers. If you believe your toddler doesn't understand what you say to your spouse, the chances are quite good that you'll find out the hard way how wrong you are. Here's an example. When I would come home from work and Harriet would ask what kind of day I had, I typically answered "I had a hectic day." I would then proceed to explain why. When Lani was around two, we began taking her to day care. Shortly after she started day care, Harriet asked how her day was. She answered "I had a hectic day." Coming from a two-year-old, Harriet and I thought this was very cute and funny. Just the thought of a toddler saying something that an adult would say has to bring a smile to your face. When Amy came along, she started saying the same thing when she was about two. To this day, whenever I ask how their day went, they would occasionally repeat what they learned from me so many years ago. There are two reasons for this: first, they really had a hectic day; and second, it's their way of remembering a childhood moment during which their father imparted to them so much wisdom and advice.

What I've just said is a cute little story about how children mimic what they hear, but parental reaction is quite different when curse words are involved. Parents, do not use curse words around a toddler. If you do, be prepared. There's nothing quite like being in public when your toddler drops something by accident and yells out "Sit!" I'll leave it at that.

Now, I'll introduce my oldest daughter

Lani

Lani was born on August 2, 1975 in Tallahassee. Almost from the time she first started walking and talking, she danced to her own drumbeat, and Harriet and I raised her to be independent and to stand proud and strong on her own two feet. (Ok, Harriet did the actual raising; I spent most of my time playing games and trying to make her laugh.) As a child, she took acting and dance lessons, which certainly helped to mold her into the fearless, confident, take-charge lady she has become. Being strong-willed, she had issues with a few of her teachers, and Harriet and I were called in by a couple of her teachers and her principal to deal with Lani's attitude. Unfortunately for the school administrators, my wife and I more often than not agreed with Lani's assessment of her teachers. We just had to let her know that, in life, you are going to have to deal with some very good people and some, well, jerks. She fully understands the importance of a strong work ethic and a solid value system. Her word is her bond, and I'm very proud of her.

Just before her 18th birthday, and as she was about to begin taking classes at Tallahassee Community College, she told us she was moving out and renting an apartment. She didn't move out because of us; rather, as I said earlier, we raised her to be independent and she was simply telling us she was able to extend her wings and fly alone. She already had a solid foundation under her.

During this time, she met a wonderful young man who was about to graduate from FSU and move to Alabama where he had family. He wanted Lani to go with him, and she wanted to go. They both asked Harriet's and my blessing. I asked Lani if this is what she wanted to do. When she said yes, I said that if this is what will make you both happy, then you have my blessing. And off they went—Brian Hudgins and Lani—to Wetumpka, Alabama. In June 1998, Lani married Brian in Montgomery, Alabama. She actually did the entire planning for the wedding. I remember Lani running around with a book she prepared that contained everything you needed to know about planning a wedding. She demonstrated the independence and the one-woman corporation mentality and perseverance that have defined her work ethic ever since. They lived in a couple of apartments, and Brian found work at an electronics store while awaiting an opening with the Montgomery Police Department. Lani worked for a health club and resort club.

While living in Alabama, Lani attended and graduated from Auburn University-Montgomery, majoring in marketing, advertising and nutrition, where she served as both a student senator and student body president. After awhile, they found an old home in Wetumpka that they renovated, and lived there until they moved to Seminole, Florida, where Brian's parents lived. They bought a home there and on April 26, 2001, Hailey Elizabeth joined them. When I was asked for fatherly advice, I told Lani that all she had to do was love her daughter 'til she grew up, then love her some more. When, on March 8, 2003, Kelsie Michelle made them a family of four and Lani again asked for advice, I repeated my previous sage wisdom, changing only the name. See how helpful I was?

Brian became a deputy sheriff with the Pinellas County Sheriff's Office and Lani took a few jobs in advertising and marketing, including one with the then-St. Petersburg Times, before she realized that she couldn't work for anyone; dealing with know-it-alls and the frustration over what she viewed as incompetence was too much for her to handle. Lani typically found ways for her employer to become more efficient and productive, and increase the bottom line; employers, however, generally resent any worker offering advice on how to better run their business, and Lani's were no different. Employers tend to believe they know exactly what they're doing and have all the answers to any problem. A few of her ex-employers wound up going out of business. Lani believed that had they listened to her, that might not have happened. I believe she was right in her assessment.

With her marketing and advertising background and skills, Lani started her own company while in her mid-20s, employing several people and relocating in the Pinellas County area as she grew her business. Being young and inexperienced, however, she overextended herself and had to close her business. This led to family tensions and soon she felt the need to start afresh somewhere else. At the same time, Brian had grown tired of, in his words, "playing cops and robbers" as a sheriff's deputy and was looking to move on as well. Finally, after much struggling with business and unhappiness at work while trying to raise two young girls, Lani and Brian decided they would leave Florida.

Lani did her online homework, and found Cary, North Carolina—a thriving community in what is called the Research Triangle with relatively good schools and a dynamic infrastructure located a few miles from Raleigh, the state capital.

So off went the Hudgins family to start their new lives in North Carolina-a place they had never been to before. This meant that Harriet and I wouldn't see our granddaughters as often as we did. What was most important to us, however, was their happiness, and if it took moving to North Carolina to make them happy, then we were all for it. What was best for them was best for us. Simple.

Lani had a job lined up with an advertising company, but that company folded several months after they moved to Cary. Brian found a job with a fireplace and chimney company and, being a quick learner, decided that he could do that kind of work himself. Brian has always impressed me as someone who could look at a car with a broken thigamagig, take it apart, fix it, and put it back together again. Between his handyman skills, good looks and intelligence, and Lani's boundless energy packaged in a perky 4' 11" frame loaded with one-woman corporate conglomerate smarts and ability, they decided to merge their strengths and start their own business selling and installing fireplaces, fixing chimneys, selling and installing gas grills, wood stoves, etc.

As I mentioned previously, my daughter did an search on my family's history. Thanks to my enterprising and persevering Lani, I now know my Waas ancestors several generations back to the 1600s in the Netherlands, as well as both Portugal and Brazil. And she's working on her husband's family.

After just a few years, they now have a successful business, a beautiful home and two great children growing up too quickly for them. Harriet and I couldn't be prouder of our Carolina kids and grandkids—all four of them. We usually get together three or four times a year, particularly at Thanksgiving, which we rotate between their home, ours and my daughter Amy's home in Newberry, Florida. Maybe Amy will convince Lani to do the same ancestry search for her husband. Speaking of Amy, it's time for me to introduce you to

Amy

Amy was born on July 9, 1979 in Tallahassee and was also raised to be independent, confident and strong-minded. She also took acting and dance lessons, which helped develop her sense of confidence, positive approach and determination. I can say precisely the same thing about her as I did about her sister; Amy fully understands the importance of a strong work ethic and a solid value system. Her word is her bond, and I'm very proud of her.

At age 14, she went to work for a veterinarian as a vet technician, and also took horse riding lessons. The owner of the stable had a dog—a Shar-Pei—about to give birth. Now, I grew up in New York City, where my only experience with dogs was the snarling and snapping kind. In other words, I wasn't exactly a dog person, but Amy very much wanted a dog. We had guinea pigs, hamsters, a mouse and a rabbit while the girls lived at home, but they were in cages. Dogs roam free and need lots of attention. They also pee, poop and barf on floors and carpets. I never wanted a dog, but Amy was persistent. To make a long story short, Amy conspired (yeah, that's the right word) with Harriet to appeal to my emotions by convincing me to visit the dog owner and see the dog for myself. Amy also knew that the hardest thing for me was to say NO to her. Her basset-hound eyes and pouty face always melted me. (She also knew how to play the second-born game. Every time Lani would literally go near Amy when they were having their disagreements, Amy would complain that Lani was hitting her. My reaction—as well as Harriet's—was "don't hit the baby." Lani would become frustrated at being blamed for something she said she didn't do, and Amy would smile because she knew that she got the upper hand on her big sister. Of course, we knew the game, and told Lani about it. This served her well when her daughters were little and Kelsie played that game on her sister Hailey.)

When we visited this dog owner, the first thing I noticed was how wrinkled the dog was, but she was friendly—didn't bite or snarl at me, actually licked my face. But I made no commitment. I thought Shar-Peis were so ugly that they were beautiful. As the time drew near for the delivery of the puppies, Amy kept counting the days, telling me that she was given the pick of the litter and that a decision had to be made very soon. What she didn't know was that I already told Harriet that I would let Amy choose her puppy. Somehow, Amy was able to do what both Harriet and Lani gave up on; convincing me to have a dog for a pet. When the day finally came after the birth of the puppies, Amy, who had been previously coached by Harriet to put on a good pouty face and get those basset-hound eyes working overtime, came over and said the time had come to make a decision, that she would make sure the puppy didn't mess the house or destroy the furniture, etc. She pleaded and pleaded. After she finished her rehearsed speech, I just looked at her and said "Ok." She started to repeat her plea, only to stop short and ask what I said. I repeated my response, and Amy went wild with joy. We went to the owner's home and saw the litter of five. Only one of the five was black. Amy picked up the black ball of wrinkled fur that the owner said was a little girl, and out came this tiny pink tongue licking Amy's face. She handed this little ball to me, and it started licking my face. Well, that sealed the deal as far as I was concerned. We took her home and, after introducing her to her bed, food and water dishes, sat down at our kitchen table to come up with a name. On the table were a salt and pepper shaker. The dog was black; pepper is black. Pepper!

But Amy wasn't done. One day a few months later, a sad, lonely cat (Amy's description) was brought to the vet clinic, and Amy, with a heart of gold for "little four-leggeds," told me she needed to bring home a tabby cat just for a short while. Well, Rudy spent his last 16 years with us. Amy still wasn't finished. Yet another tabby cat—one that lived with wolves until the owner died—was brought to the clinic. Amy told me that she needed to bring this one named Jolly home for another short while. So it is that Jolly spent the last 15 years of his life with us. After this, there were no more pouty faces for additional pets.

Amy demonstrated the truth of the saying that the child is indeed the father (or mother) of the man. I learned a lot about myself and how important pets are to one's well-being. They give love, loyalty and faithfulness without expecting anything in return. When they passed, I felt a deep and personal loss. I vowed that once they passed on, I wouldn't have any more animals; not because I didn't love them, but because the pain of losing them was so hard to bear. Harriet and I actually referred to our pets as if they were children, because in a very real sense, pets are childlike. We called Pepper our girl, and Rudy and Jolly were our boys. We thought that once they were gone, we wouldn't have any more pets. I was wrong.

I would like to say that Harriet and I raised Amy the same as we did Lani—to be independent and able to stand on her own two feet; but the truth is the same as for Amy's older (not bigger; Amy at 5'3" is taller than Lani by about four inches) sister; Harriet did the raising, I did the silly, funny stuff.

Amy left home just before her 18th birthday to attend the University of Florida, a second generation Gator. As with Lani, Amy left not because she wanted to get away from Harriet and me, but because she too was independent enough and firmly grounded. During her years as a student, I managed to get to see her quite often, as my business travels frequently took me to Gainesville. We'd do lunch and then she'd take off to class. She got her undergraduate degree in 2001 and her master's in 2003, after which she went to work with the Alachua County Sheriff's Office first as a victim's advocate, then as a crime scene investigator. She now works at the UF as a chemist/ forensic toxicologist.

I don't know for a fact whether Amy ever intended for this to happen, but I certainly believe she's smart enough to have realized that once she left home, Harriet and I would be empty-nesters. I firmly believe that while she wanted pets because she loves animals, she knew she couldn't take them to the university with her; that they'd have to stay with us. This meant, of course, that we wouldn't be empty-nesters; we would have our three pets—which I dubbed our "Three Amigos""—to keep us company. I'll repeat what I said a bit earlier and make it more direct—the child is indeed the mother of the man.

I won't go into all the funny and silly games I played with my girls as they were growing up; I can't possibly remember all of them anyway because so many were spontaneous. I will however describe two, which I hope will give you an idea of my relationship with my daughters. Taking the view that growing old is mandatory, but growing up is an option, the first story I want to tell you involves using my "inner voice" in the many emails I sent, particularly to Amy, while she was a college student. After a short while, Amy started responding to my emails with her "inner voice." Here's a typical example:

> Dear Amy,
>
> Hi, I hope you're having a great day; I certainly am (NO I'M NOT!!! MOM IS DRIVING ME CRAZY, ASKING ME TO TAKE OUT THE GARBAGE, CLEAN OFF THE DINNER TABLE, FOLD MY LAUNDRY, AND OTHER THINGS TOO NASTY TO SAY. I NEED A PLACE TO LIVE. YOU WOULDN'T HAPPEN TO HAVE A SPARE ROOM OR PERHAPS A CHAIR THAT I COULD RENT?) Well, I hope you did well on your tests. We'll talk soon.
>
> Love,
> Dad

By now, you know that my "inner voice" is in capital letters. Now, here's Amy's typical response:

Hi Dad,

Yes, everything is going great here. (SORRY, BUT THERE'S NO ROOM HERE FOR YOU. ALL FOUR SIDES OF EACH ROOM ARE COVERED FROM TOP TO BOTTOM WITH WALLS, AND THE FLOORS ARE CARPETED AND COVERED WITH WOOD. ALSO, THERE IS AIR IN EVERY PART OF EACH ROOM, AND THE COUCH AND CHAIRS ARE COVERED WITH MATERIAL. YOU'LL HAVE TO DO THE BEST YOU CAN WITH MOM. BESIDES, SHE'S NOT THAT DEMANDING AT ALL. ACTUALLY, MOM SPOILS YOU TOO MUCH!!) I did very well on my tests—got all As and Bs. We'll talk soon. Give my love to my three four-leggeds.

Love,
Amy

This is how we carried on for years. Lani would simply roll her eyes at this type of humor, but she has a strong sense of humor herself and certainly knew how much fun I had writing these "inner voice" email.

My second example also involves email. On occasion, I would send Amy an email as if it came from our dog or two cats. I created separate personalities for each pet—Pepper was an "Oh, gosh; gee whiz" type; Rudy was the wise-cracking "rude" cat; Jolly the older, wiser but equally independent cat. Amy would respond by talking directly to whoever was "sending" a particular email, always asking her pet to give Harriet and me—which she called her "two-leggeds"—their love.

Sometime in 1998, Amy suggested that I take this type of writing and write a book. After dismissing such a notion, I sat down at my computer one day on a whim and started writing in a stream-of-conscience manner, using our three pets' personalities I created for my email. In less than three weeks, I had written a 30,000+-word book that I entitled "The World is My Toilet," a dogobiography by Pepper Waas, featuring comments by her feline siblings Rudy and Jolly Waas, and their two-legged parents George and Harriet Waas. I self-published this book, had it copyrighted, had a book-signing at Books-a-Million and sold about 100 copies. In truth, it wouldn't have mattered had I not sold a single one: my daughters had something from me that they treasure to this day. And I had a great time writing it.

Here's another example of our relationship. When both girls were in elementary school, the movie "Close Encounters of the Third Kind" was very popular. Using this title, I dubbed Lani my "Daughter of the First Kind" and Amy was the "Daughter of the Second Kind." Lani outgrew this silliness, but to this day, Amy will occasionally refer to herself in email and in cards and letters as "D2K."

While Amy lived in a Gainesville apartment, a girlfriend who had a Labrador named Sam needed a home for him. Amy's apartment was perfect. Amy was living alone and Sam would be a good companion for her. At the beginning of Amy's senior year, Harriet and I bought a two-bedroom home for her in Gainesville, and she and her large pet moved in. Sam, however, as wonderful a companion as he was, wasn't enough company for Amy. On several occasions, she would call Harriet and me and express her sadness at being lonely and not having a boyfriend. Lani married at 22; Amy was now past 24 and had no prospects, and this was affecting her deeply.

What we—and she—didn't know was that her friends at the sheriff's office were busy trying to fix her up with a nice young man who had recently joined the office as a deputy sheriff. Finally, through her friends' efforts, Amy and Frank met for the first time. During one of Amy's calls to us—she called just about every day and still does—she mentioned Frank, and a couple of months later, when I told her I needed to come to Gainesville on business, she asked if she could bring Frank along for lunch. Absolutely! I took them both to lunch and, after they left to return to work, I called Harriet, who was anxiously awaiting my "assessment." I gave it to her—this looked like the real deal. I told her I was as impressed with Frank as I was when I first met Brian. Frank also is a handyman, capable of fixing just about anything. One day, Frank came to Tallahassee unbeknownst to Amy to show us her engagement ring and promised that he would protect Amy, take care of her and love her. That sealed it for Harriet and me.

Frank planned to take Amy to a restaurant in Cedar Key where they went on their first date a year earlier and, at a designated time, actually propose to her. I told him to bring lots of Kleenex. What Amy didn't know was that Frank's parents, Tom and Beth, and Harriet and I were having dinner at a nearby restaurant and, at a preset time, were to sneak into the restaurant to greet the newly engaged. After dinner, Frank gave Amy a book of poems—except that numerous pages were carved out in the middle to allow for a small box to be placed inside. Inside that box was that beautiful engagement ring. Amy pulled out the box and Frank got on one knee and proposed. Picture-taking was prearranged, and Amy started crying. She put her head on the table and was holding Frank's hand when the four parents approached the table. When Amy lifted up her head and saw us, she put her head back down for a moment, then got up, came over and gave us all a big hug. She was one happy girl.

On November 19, 2005, Frank and Amy became Mr. and Mrs. Frank Kinsey. On June 12, 2009, they were joined by Avery Paige. When asked for fatherly advice, I told her that she should love Avery 'til she grew up, then love her some more. At least, I'm consistent with my pearls of wisdom. When, on August 7, 2012, Connor Brice joined them to form a family of four, I gave Amy the same advice, with one change. Now, I told her, she has to be much quicker when changing diapers. I pride myself on being a great source of wisdom for my kids!!

My grandson's birth made me recall the description of what it feels like to a woman when giving birth. The great comedienne Carol Burnett describe it this way: take your right hand and place in over the back of your head until you reach your top lip. Then, grab your top lip and pull it over your head. I love this description. Several friends of mine discussed their experience with their wives' childbirth. They wanted to be as much help as possible to their wives during this wonderful moment. They accompanied their wives to Lamaze classes and worked diligently in providing both assistance and assurance . . . until that first major contraction. At this point, their stories become one: their wives suddenly turned into Devil-possessed women, like the girl in the movie The Exorcist. The women's eyes bulged, and their voices became growls. "GET YOUR HANDS OFF ME!! IF YOU EVER TOUCH ME AGAIN, I'LL KILL YOU!!! GET OUT OF THIS ROOM." Now, I really have to believe they're exaggerating. I wish I could speak from experience on this; when Harriet was in the room awaiting to be transported to the delivery room, I became queasy and stayed out of the room with the nurses huddled around me for support until Harriet was given an epidural. While I shared the Lamaze experience, I didn't share in Harriet's labor pains leading up to the epidural. I was in the delivery room for the birth of both girls, however. I think the ability to give birth makes a woman handle pain—and I mean PAIN—better than men. When Harriet tells me that I really don't know pain, I really have no way to compare my situation with labor pains. Of course, no man does. But, then again, if Carol Burnett's description is more than just great humor and has a basis in fact, who am I to say otherwise.

If I haven't told you before, I'll tell you now; I have a great relationship with my daughters built on humor and love. I wish every father could have children like mine; bright, beautiful and caring. Great kids, great wives, great mothers.

A word about my sons-in-law. If I had to pick men to marry my daughters, I couldn't have done nearly as good a job as they did on their own. Brian is bright, witty and absolutely loves his three ladies. Frank likewise is bright, witty and absolutely loves his two ladies and young man. In many ways, they are alike. Both men are wonderful to be around; I enjoy them and I hope they don't find me a meddlesome father-in-law. I know they love Harriet. It's been said that a daughter generally marries a man much like her father. This saying doesn't apply in either of my daughter's cases, at least as it pertains to being a Mr. Fixit. When anything broke or stopped working, I used my index finger to repair it—by either dialing or hitting the phone numbers of a plumber, electrician, repairman, etc. In addition, with my sons-in-law's law enforcement backgrounds, they taught my daughters how to care for and use weapons. I've never even fired a gun. Both men do have a great sense of humor, though. Hey, maybe that's where the saying that a daughter marries a man much like her father fits in. I certainly hope so; I could use whatever amount of credit I can get.

As I said earlier, I believe that humor is a big part of raising children. Children tend to remember lessons if they're delivered with a solid sense of humor. I enjoyed playing games and doing funny, silly things with them just to hear them giggle and laugh. When Lani was a toddler, I would call her my "buddy, pal and friend." When Amy arrived, I did the same thing. To this day, we'll exchange this greeting—and now my granddaughters and I have this same greeting. This is just another example of how children remember certain things about their childhood that they pass along to their children. I love it.

Let me tell you about one "game" I play with them now. Even though they're certainly not kids anymore (of course, they'll always be my kids), I still enjoy my version of silly games. Harriet is involved in this latest version. Each time Harriet and I visit them, we tell them we're thinking of buying a home and moving close to them. This way, we say, we can see them anytime we want and generally make ourselves right at home in their neighborhoods. Now, Lani knows that we're not about to sell our home and move to North Carolina. Amy's reaction is another story. You see, she knows we have the financial resources to buy a home in their neighborhood for cash. So Amy gets just a wee bit nervous whenever we bring up this subject. Of course, we would never do that. We've seen firsthand how much pressure adult children are under when parents are too close by. Still, Amy's reaction is always good for a chuckle. At least, I think Amy's chuckling.

Some parents tend to believe that their children—who are busy raising their own kids, working, paying bills, and generally having their own family matters to deal with—owe them primary attention and time whenever they seek it. These parents tend to feel put out when they're not given almost immediate consideration; they expect their children to literally drop what they're doing and attend to their wishes. Neither Harriet nor I buy into this. Our girls have their own families and jobs, and they're under enough stress and pressure as it is; they don't need mom and dad making demands, expecting invitations or dropping by unannounced—you get the picture. Harriet and I are always available to help our two young families whenever they ask. However, we won't impose ourselves on them. That's both selfish and unfair to them. Besides, they are doing just fine without any unilateral intrusion into their lives by meddlesome parents expecting their children to bend to their every wish.

Some parents also believe that there is some obligation to live close to their children and grandchildren. Harriet and I don't buy into this, either. Children have to do what makes them happy. If our children and sons-in-law believe living in another city is necessary for their happiness and peace of mind, that decision should be respected by the parents, and we applaud it and fully support it. It's the children's happiness that is paramount, not the parents' desire to live near them. We live a little over two hours by car from Amy and Frank, and a few hours by air from Lani and Brian. If they need us, we'll be there for them. But we won't move next door or a mile or two away just so we can drop in or lay a guilt trip on them if they don't call as frequently as we might like, or invite us over more often than they do. I've seen the effects of parents living too close to their children and expecting something in return, and we wouldn't ever do that to them. Of course, we would love to see our children and grandchildren every day; that's not an uncommon feeling. It's also a selfish feeling because it puts the grandparents' wishes ahead of their children and their families. What's most important to us are Lani's and Amy's families, not us. In short, it's about them; not us. Parents of adult children who have their own families should never fear asking whether, in their involvement in their children's lives, they're really a pain in the ass—at least sometimes.

The side benefit of this type of approach is that we're asked quite often "When are you coming to see us" or "we're so glad you're here." Believe me, it's far better this way than knowing that they could silently be wishing "When are they ever going to leave us alone?"

Here's another point about parenting that I'm sure you've seen more times than you care to. When I'm in a restaurant or mall—or just about any place where the public gathers—you'll see (and hear) a toddler or very young child crying and perhaps yelling, seeking parental attention of some type. And you'll see the parent react by yelling at the child to stop crying, or even spanking the child for yelling and crying. Now, how in the world do these parents expect a very young child to stop yelling and crying when they're being yelled at or, worse, spanked? Such parental reaction only makes the situation worse. There are many potential reasons why that child is crying or screaming; nap time, illness, etc. What Harriet and I used to do when our girls acted this way—which was very infrequently—are the same things my daughters did (and Amy does) with their children. The first thing that the parent needs to do is do a rapid assessment of the reason for the behavior. Usually, this kind of behavior starts at a low level of crankiness and works its way up the scale to full outburst of loud crying and yelling. The key is to catch the reason early on. With an infant, the first thing to do is get the baby out of the public environment. We used to take the girls outside or Harriet would take them to the ladies' room and go through the mental checklist—hungry, diaper change, diaper rash, nap time, etc. And always talk in a low, soothing voice. I know this can be difficult because the first reaction is to yell louder than the child. Have you ever seen this work effectively? I haven't either.

Patience and positive attention are critically important factors in raising a child. My girls and grandchildren were read to and exposed to words very early in their development, so they were able to verbalize at a very young age. If the child is old enough to verbalize and starts to act out—no matter where this may happen—gently ask him/her to take a deep breath and then ask the child to explain the problem. I know Lani did this when her girls were toddlers, but since Amy is the most recent family member to join the ranks of parenthood, Harriet and I've seen her when Avery acts up, and her and Frank's approach is wonderful.

Amy or Frank will gently move Avery away from wherever she's having a meltdown; get down to her level and tell her to take a deep breath and "use her words" to explain. Avery's reaction is amazing; she'll stop crying or yelling long enough to take that deep breath and tell Amy or Frank exactly what's bothering her. And this has been going on for over a year now before Avery was two. In a restaurant, if she begins to act up, one of her parents will take her outside and, in a few minutes, Avery will be fine. In a public setting like a restaurant or mall, the parent is usually embarrassed and exasperated by the child's behavior, and wants to get things under control as quickly as possible. Yelling at and spanking a child who is yelling and crying only makes matters worse. Using common sense parenting skills in calming down the child and getting him/her to work through the situation is really the only sure way of getting the behavior under control.

I am happy to say that Lani and Brian continue to grow their business; Frank is now Sgt. Frank Kinsey of the Alachua County Sheriff's Office; Amy remains a chemist and forensic toxicologist for the UF. Both families have beautiful homes in Cary, NC and Newberry, Florida, respectively, and are raising their children to be independent, confident and capable of standing on their own two feet. To say I'm proud of my kids—and I include Brian and Frank as well—wouldn't tell the whole story. I burst with pride whenever I talk to, and about, them. If I'm repeating myself on this, then to me it's worth repeating. I wish all parents could experience the happiness and contentment that Harriet and I have for our wonderful young families.

After my daughters were married and became more and more deeply involved in their lives, I found an easy way to find out how they're doing. All it takes is one question—the one I asked of Lani when she and Brian wanted to move to Alabama. That question is: Are you happy? So much flows from the answer to this simple question. When you're happy, even stressful events can't shake optimism and comfort. Raising children, putting a roof over one's head, food on the table, etc., are all stressors. But if the overall assessment is "Yes, I'm very happy," then everything else falls nicely into place. I know my daughters are living active lives, with all of the stresses of raising children and providing for their families and doing things families do. But when they tell me they're happy, the piece of mind I have as a parent could not be more comforting.

There is one thing that I find somewhat troubling about parenting, however. When I compare Harriet's and my childhood and the values instilled in us, with my children's upbringing, and discuss this comparison of both generations with friends, I notice a pattern. Because our parents never attended college for one reason or another (economic depression, war, the Holocaust for Harriet's parents, etc.), they made absolutely certain their children did. Our parents constantly reminded us that education is the key to success. They wanted us to have the kind of life that was denied them. All of their children succeeded; having obtained advanced degrees and important jobs and raising wonderful, intelligent and caring children.

The question is how do Harriet and I do for our children what our parents did for us-give them a better life than we had when we've had everything a parent could want for a child? Harriet and I were not deprived of anything; how can we assure that our children obtain what we've been deprived of, when we've suffered no deprivation? Harriet and I can't wish that our children get the quality college education that we missed out on because we didn't miss out, and neither did our children. We can't wish that our children pursue their dreams that we couldn't because Harriet and I saw ours come true.

Because our children have realized their dreams through their education and their choices of business and profession, in the end, all we can do is wish that our grandchildren and their children have the same opportunities Harriet and I—and our children—had and have. This is a far different situation than the one our grandparents and parents faced, which in turn requires different parenting skills. Now, it's important to impress on our children and grandchildren the value of education both for itself and for a lifetime of personal growth. It's equally important to instill in them the basic core values of human existence that are as old as ordered civilization itself. They consist of three vital components:(1) a strong value system, (2) a commitment to others, and (3) a sense of belonging.

The first promotes a devotion to a higher being; hard work and a strong positive work ethic; respect for and tolerance of others; caring for and sharing with others, etc. The second consists of dependability, honesty, accountability, trustworthiness, etc. The third recognizes that no person is an island and has as its source a sense of being part of something meaningful; something that provides for a sense of accomplishment that results in a sense of happiness. To be happy, we must belong—to a family, community, club, fraternity, etc. These teachings, I believe, will be the great challenge for parents of future generations.

Now, it's time to meet

Our Grandchildren

I've already mentioned my three precious granddaughters, Hailey, Kelsie and Avery, and my precious grandson Connor. After having two daughters, there's nothing like going through the process of watching their children grow as they come to terms with their expanding world. There's a saying that a grandchild is the grandparents' revenge. This is certainly true in my situation, as Lani would call us quite often when her girls were toddlers wondering why they were behaving a certain way. These calls stopped—for the most part—as her girls got older. What we get now are Facebook posts of the latest comments or observations from Hailey and Kelsie. I can't repeat some of them, but I was 30 years old before I knew what they know at their young ages.

We also get these types of calls from Amy, since Avery is a toddler; as well as Facebook posts of Avery's latest opinions. They're always good for a laugh. I've no doubt these calls and posts will continue as Avery grows and Connor moves from infancy; so Harriet and I can continue to expect the "Do you know what she/he did today?" And do you know what "your granddaughter/grandson did last night?" Whenever a child does something good, it's "Do you know what **my** child did." When it's something not-so-hot, it's "Do you know what **your** daughter/son/granddaughter/grandson did?" Like mother, like daughter. Like father, like son. Heh, heh, heh. Whenever our daughters stress with exasperation over something their children said or did, Harriet and I offer this simple, but effective, advice for handling the situation: love them 'til they grow up, then love them some more. I really believe this is the best advice a parent can give. The fact that it's repetitive only shows how well it works.

Whenever I'm with my grand girls, I play the same types of silly games with them that I did with their mothers. Their reactions are identical; the apple doesn't fall far from the tree. And now I can look forward to playing these same silly games with my grandson. My daughters tell me that I get more laughs and have more fun playing with my three granddaughters than they do. I believe my girls are right. I've no doubt it'll be the same as my grandboy grows. My two oldest grand girls tell me that, while their parents act silly sometimes, and grammy acts silly sometimes, I act silly all the time. Out of the mouth of babes . . . .

I believe that what I'm about to say applies to all toddlers; unfortunately, I don't think I appreciated this as much when my daughters were very young, but I certainly do with my granddaughters. Young children simply have no filter when asked a question. Honesty—at least through the eyes of young children—is built into their genetic structure. Dishonesty or deception, as well as other types of less-than-absolute truthful statements, are acquired as children become adults. If I think about this long enough, I'll come up with dozens of examples of the innocence of a child, but let me give you one that happened recently because it's demonstrates childhood innocence, and it's also easier for me to remember.

During a visit to Amy's and Frank's home, three-year-old Avery asked me to play with her as she showed me her new dollhouse. This dollhouse came with three miniature family members—a mother, father and child. Avery told me that—and these are her direct words— "Mommy and me sleep in the big bed in the bedroom." When I asked her where daddy sleeps, she said "Daddy sleeps on the couch." Now, this of course has a certain humorous meaning; but because my son-in-law works a night shift, he spends some time before he goes to work on the couch while watching TV, and might drift off to sleep. Avery's answer therefore is perfectly natural under these circumstances, but for someone who doesn't know the particular situation, the answer could generate lots of laughter.

My older granddaughters have no trouble telling me I act silly all the time even though they understand perfectly what they're saying; Avery has no trouble telling the world where her daddy sleeps in the dollhouse because she has no filter; she hasn't learned the necessity of context, the importance of explanations or the various shades of grey in expressing herself. Amy often tells me that when she asks Avery a question, she really doesn't know what to expect for an answer. I know my daughters had no filter when they were very young; I only wish I could remember some of the things they said that caused me to laugh or hide, depending on what they said. A child's innocent response, no matter how funny or embarrassing, is a thing of joy and beauty because it's so, well, honest.

Lani tells me some of the things that her 11-year-old and nine-year-old say, and they're both funny and embarrassing, but completely honest. My girls never lied to Harriet or me, and my grandchildren never lied to their parents. I think that's a wonderful thing. And now Amy gets to start all over again with her newborn son. Harriet and I love the stories our daughters tell us about their children's comments, observations, answers to questions, etc., and we can't wait to ask Avery a question because, like her parents, we never know what she's going to say. I will tell you this: some of the stories I've been told by my daughters about their children I really can't repeat here. When you think of some of the things your children and, perhaps, grandchildren have said, you understand precisely what I'm referring to.

I could be shamelessly honest and say that my granddaughters are the smartest, funniest, most creative, and simply the greatest kids in the world, and no doubt my grandson will be the same, but why sacrifice my modesty? Want an example? It was Hailey and Kelsie who made the creative decision to call Harriet and me grammy and grampy. We were content with grandma and grandpa. My daughters are raising their children with the same set of values Harriet and I instilled in our girls. My granddaughters have strong personalities; very inquisitive; a solid sense of themselves. The word shy is not in their vocabulary, they're very free in expressing their opinions, and have no hesitation in expressing disagreement with their parents. All they want is an explanation, however. Once their parents take the patience to explain the whys and wherefores, the girls are very accepting—for the most part. I have no doubt Amy will her son the same way. The way Harriet and I feel about our daughters extends to our grandchildren.

I'll stop the gushing and just say that my granddaughters are bright, witty, funny and strong of personality—just like their mothers and, no doubt, just like their fathers—and maternal grandparents, of course. (I'll leave the paternal grandparents to do their own boasting.) I have no reason to expect my grandson to be any different. Having a grandson is, I must admit, a somewhat different experience. My father had two boys; my grandfather had two boys. I knew I was going to break that mold and have girls. I was right. I also believed that my grandchildren would be girls. I was almost right. The birth of my grandson is the first male born in my family in over 50 years. Watching my two daughters and three granddaughters comes to terms with their world was, and remains, a great experience. And now I get to watch this all over again with Connor's arrival.

All of this makes retirement that much more interesting and exciting; two daughters, two sons-in-law and four grandchildren. Life is great. Now, for the last of my immediate family members,

Sandy and Mandy

When you have a pet that you love, he/she is an integral part of your family. With Pepper, Rudy and Jolly—our girl and boys—I learned the value and importance of absolute unrequited love, and the comfort and companionship pets give most generously. Harriet and I had these pets for many years, and when we lost the last one, the specter of a true empty nest was, for me, too much to handle. As is the usual case, I had become used to having these "four-leggeds" around the house. While Rudy was in his last illness and declining rapidly, I mentioned to Harriet that I didn't want any more pets. I didn't feel this way because I didn't want the responsibility; I felt this way because I didn't want to bear the pain of losing a pet again. I never actually admitted this before to Harriet or my girls; I'm doing it now.

I also didn't want to come home to an empty house. So here's this story. After Rudy was put down by our vet, Harriet decided to make a gift to the clinic for the wonderful care our vet and her staff had given to our dog and cats over 16 years. Harriet called the vet and told her we had a gift for her. I decided I should go along, since I wanted to personally thank her and her staff as well.

We arrived at the vet clinic, but while Harriet went to the receptionist's desk, I glanced over to the glassed-enclosed area housing several cats and kittens. I particularly noticed two kittens—a calico and a tabby—huddled together on a mid-level perch. I walked over to the glass and stared at the two of them. Then the sandy-colored calico reached out its paw to me and I placed my hand against the glass where its paw was. You see what's coming? Harriet walked over to me, and I said "Which one do you want?" She said "Both." I said "Ok" and, after the vet tech told me they were female, I immediately gave them the names Sandy (because of her sandy color) and Mandy (because it rhymed perfectly).

The next day, we took them home and quickly learned that female cats are different than male cats. No, not the obvious difference; personality difference. These two, especially Sandy, are extremely independent and want things their way. Sandy will toss couch pillows on the floor, and flip her toys into our bed or the kitchen sink. Both sleep in our bed—precisely where we sleep. Having to move them so we can get into our bed is not as easy as it may sound. Sandy also enjoys digging into the morning newspaper—literally. If I leave the paper on the table after breakfast rather than immediately put it in the recycle bin, the next time I make it to the kitchen, that newspaper will be shredded and on the floor. Sandy likes to root around in the trash basket in our den, and Harriet and I spend a few times just about each day picking up bits and pieces of paper that Sandy shredded after dumping over the trash basket; but we certainly don't mind this. Waking up and finding one or both snuggled up beside us in our bed is worth more than its weight in gold. We refer to them as our girls now.

Harriet and I certainly don't have an empty home anymore. Now, as we put the key in the door when we return home, we have to wonder what we will find in some form of disarray as we search our house. We also have to navigate the minefield that is our family room because of the cat toys that are spread all over the floor. We love every minute of our adventure with them, and the joy and laughter they bring us. Amy was the first to enlighten me that pets are a wonderful way to lessen stress and help with relaxation. She is 100 percent right. I only wish I were ready to accept a dog and cats earlier on; but better late than never.

Barry

This section is the most difficult to write, and the main reason I stress to my daughters—and I'm sure they will do likewise with their children—the importance of remaining close throughout their lives; I had a younger brother who passed away at the all-too-young age of 36.

My brother Barry was born in New York City on October 12, 1947. He also did the same things kids did in the 50s, only we did them together. Even though I was four years older, the age differential never mattered much during the years we spent in New York. He was my baby brother; I was his big brother; that is, until we reached the ages where sibling rivalries kick in. My dad took care of this when he bought us each a pair of boxing gloves were so huge we could barely lift them, we never hurt one another until one day when he "accidentally" kicked me in the knee. I fell over in pain as Barry counted to 10 over me. The next time I put the gloves on a couple of years later, I realized Barry was just as tall as I was. That ended the boxing matches.

Barry was an excellent baseball player; he excelled at the Little League level, and there was some talk among his coaches of a bright future should he wish to pursue the game. He wanted instead to become a doctor to help people. He graduated from Miami Beach High School in 1965, then the University of South Florida, eventually getting his PhD from the University of Maryland, specializing in audiology. He married his childhood sweetheart from high school, Anne Arnold. My daughters remember him because Barry used to call the girls "ankle-biters" and that made them laugh. My brother had a great sense of humor. I remember him as a great kid brother.

Barry developed Hodgkin's disease during his service in the Army, and received a medical discharge. He lived in Maryland and worked for the Veterans Administration there. While the treatment for this form of cancer led to remission, it also prevented him from being able to have children. He had multiple reoccurrences and received several sessions of treatment. Sadly, the chemotherapy over a long period caused him to develop leukemia in 1984. By this time, he had moved to Miami and worked for the VA there. He was told by his doctors that unless he agreed to radical experimental treatment at a cancer institute in Buffalo, New York, he wouldn't survive more than a couple of months. If he went ahead, however, and agreed to this treatment and it didn't work, he wouldn't leave the hospital alive.

Harriet and me.

Kelsie Michelle, Brian, Lani and Hailey Elizabeth Hudgins (l-r)

Amy and Frank Kinsey

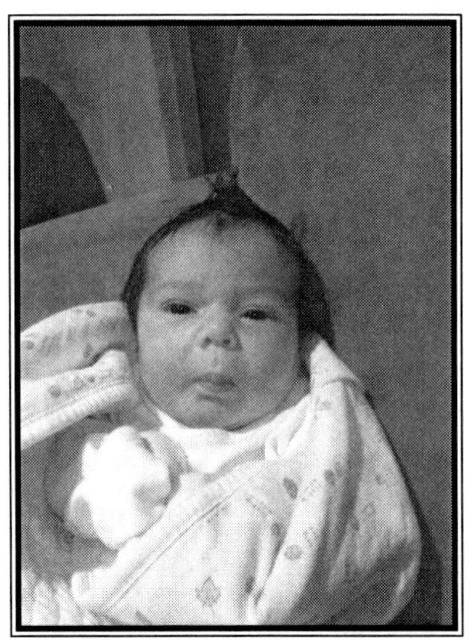

Connor Brice Kinsey

Avery Paige Kinsey

It was a horrific decision that only he alone could make; he never asked for my opinion. (I told him later that I agreed with his decision; it was his only chance, and he had to take it.) He agreed to this treatment and called me one night, asking if I could go to Buffalo with him. Of course I would, and in early May 1984, I flew to south Florida, met brother, and the following day, we took off for Buffalo.

For the three days between his call and our departure to the Roswell Park Institute, I spent time moving my cases around and literally shrinking my private law practice. After arriving in Buffalo, getting my brother set up in the hospital and me in my hotel room, I did as much as I could to keep whatever minimal business that I had left afloat via telephone from my room. While in Buffalo, I called Harriet every night. One night, she told me Lani fell and suffered a slight concussion. You can imagine the feeling of helplessness I had on two fronts: not being there for her, and not being able to do anything for my brother except sit by him every day while he underwent radical experimental chemotherapy.

My brother survived three weeks before passing away, the chemotherapy having changed his appearance drastically during this short period of time. For me, there was nothing harder to bear in my life than watching my kid brother wither away. We both knew the risks; he was fighting two lethal forms of cancer and only an experimental drug offered him any chance. That dreaded day, I received a call from the hospital at about 4 a.m. strongly recommending that I get there as quickly as possible. Since the hotel was about two blocks from the hospital, I dressed and was in my brother's room in less than 30 minutes. He lasted about one more hour.

I had to call my dad and stepmother and tell them Barry was gone. Then, I had to call the funeral home in Fort Lauderdale (my dad had previously called the home because I had told him two days earlier that the prognosis was not good) as well as one in Buffalo; pack his belongings; and make flight arrangements for both my brother's remains and me. I flew to Fort Lauderdale late that afternoon and arrived at night to tell my father and stepmother that there was nothing I could do to help Barry. Although this was an irrational thought, the shock of losing my brother left me with a sense of guilt. My dad, as hurt as he was, assured me that there was nothing more I could have done and that just being with Barry was as much as could be asked for. As hurt and shattered as my dad was, he made sure I didn't have any guilt feelings. This was by far the hardest, saddest, most emotionally draining day of my life and each moment of it remains as vivid today as it was then. I hurt at the loss of my brother and the pain my dad had to endure. I don't believe this is something you ever get over.

For my dad, I can't imagine anything more painful than losing a child. It's so contrary to the natural order of things. A parent who goes through this silently shouts "Why my child? Why not me? I lived a full life; please give my child what I've already had." Of course, there's no answer; it's just God's will. A day after Barry's funeral, the VA hospital had a memorial service for him. My dad and I got to see pictures of Barry attending staff meetings wearing fake eyeglasses, a bulbous nose and handlebar mustache. This was his way of breaking the stress of his staff meetings. We were told that he would greet his patients the same way. Barry never lost his sense of humor, and my dad and I realized that the way his colleagues knew him was the same way we knew him. My dad was too distraught to say anything, so I spoke for the family by saying how much we appreciated their kindness, and pointed out that they knew Barry as we knew him.

I have no doubt Barry's passing led to my father's rapid physical decline; his sense of humor became more strained and he spent more and more time just watching TV. He passed away from cancer less than four years later.

Many years later, I was told by my doctors that if Barry had his condition today, with all of the advances in medicine, he more than likely would be alive and in remission. For him, his illnesses came too early for medicine and science to be of help. My experience with my brother's last three weeks make me frequently remind my daughters that they each have one sister, and that it is vital that they always remain in touch with one another no matter where their lives take them. Both have been faithful to this, for which I couldn't be more grateful or happy. And I know they are passing this important lesson on to their children.

My Life So Far

I've already mentioned that I was born in New York City on July 12, 1943, but it's worth repeating because at my age, I certainly don't want to forget my birthday. My first few years are a blur, most likely because I can't remember a damn thing before my fifth birthday, although I have a vague recollection of living in a white house with a white picket fence in Miami Beach around 1946. I have no memory of how I got there or where I went immediately afterward. I was told by my father, however, that on one hot afternoon there was a family party and those in attendance were complaining about the heat. I found a garden hose and turned the water on to make everyone comfortable. I understand this was not a good thing to do, especially turning the hose on the barbeque pit and all the food. I don't know what my family did to me, but it's obvious that I survived it. Perhaps it's a good thing I have no memory of dousing my family. I do remember, however, my dad repeatedly telling me that as a child, I used to say "Don't do dat." I would repeat this line constantly to family members as well as strangers, the latter of whom would respond by wondering what they shouldn't do. I never asked my dad what made me say this phrase so often, but it's fairly obvious that it was something I heard him say quite often. I guess it's best I don't know why I said this, but considering the dousing I gave my family, I probably wasn't the best behaved child. I suppose that lots of things I did back then I shouldn't have done.

My next recollection of my first few years is listening to a shortwave radio mentioning the name Harry Truman. I certainly know now who he was; back then, it was just a name I heard on a radio.

Nothing of importance that you would be interested in happened to me during those early years. Of course, I would be interested in everything I did back then, if I could only remember everything I did. Preservation of a child's earliest years became much easier by the time my daughters arrived, and I know that this will be even easier with my grandchildren. When the time comes for them to write their books (I can only hope they do so), they'll be able to tell a more complete story. My daughters can come to Tallahassee and see the hospital they were born in and where they lived from birth until they left home to live on their own. I can't go back to the Bronx and visit my early residences because they've either been torn down or firebombed.

With a more improved memory as I got older, I remembered doing the usual things that a kid did living in the Bronx whose parents were separated and then divorced and whose father managed hotels: played stickball, stole a few apples, went to baseball and hockey games with my dad and brother, stayed weekends at my dad's hotel, walked two miles to and from school (yes, this is true), watched a lot of black-and-white TV, and lived in a log cabin (I thought I might try to slip this one past you.)

I do recall that from 1952 to 1958, I lived in a federal housing project in the Bronx because my parents didn't earn enough to avoid subsidized housing. After moving to Miami Beach in early 1958, I went to Miami Beach High School, where I served as homeroom treasurer for three years and took public speaking and was on the debate team during my senior year. Miami Beach High was, in the late 1950s and early 1960s, a very ritzy place. Students dressed to the nines for the junior and senior proms, and the parking lot was full of Thunderbirds and other fancy cars parents bought for their kids. They also lived in large, fancy homes that lined the upper class neighborhoods. A few students, however, didn't attend either prom; get to and from school driving a fancy sports car; or live in large luxurious homes. I was in the latter group; I walked to school from my grandparents' efficiency, and when I moved to an apartment, I took the bus to and from school.

After moving to Miami Beach, I developed asthma. Evidently, mine was a case of traumatic psychological asthma. The relocation from New York to Miami Beach, an unfamiliar environment; my low grades after getting high grades in New York schools; believing I was homesick for New York; and residual stress over my parents' traumatic marital situation appeared to have a greater impact on me as the first-born child. I'm told that the first-born seems to bear the brunt of such stress more than younger siblings. Over six months in 1958, I coughed and wheezed off about 20 pounds. This was a good thing—the weight loss, that is—for I was a rather chubby kid. Both my parents were obese, and I didn't want to be called fatty in high school and beyond. Turns out that this asthmatic condition—which I eventually outgrew, helped me down the road. I'll get to that shortly, but think military and the draft.

I graduated from high school in 1961 and attended Dade County Community College for two years, serving as a student senator and sophomore class vice president, and was also on the debate team (having won a $150 tuition scholarship that covered two semesters; one of the first four students at this community college to ever win such a scholarship. Have times changed, or what? In the interest of full disclosure, this community college was first opened in 1960 and the year I won this scholarship was the first year it was offered). Again, the bus was my only means of transportation. I had to get up 4:30 a.m. to catch the bus a couple of blocks from my apartment so I could timely catch the bus in Miami to the campus. If I missed that 5:30 bus, I'd miss my 7:20 class. Fortunately, during my two years at this college, this never happened. I did develop a good "early to bed, early to rise" habit, however.

While attending Dade County Community College, I worked part-time as a supermarket cashier. Being a cashier then is far different than it is today. There were no machines that told the cashier how much change was owed the customer; all change had to be counted out, and if a cashier gave out more than .50 cents over the register count at the end of the workday, that amount came out of his/her paycheck. Fortunately, this happened to me only once, when I came up $10 short at the end of a 12-hour workday. That $10 just happened to be around the amount of my salary for that day, so I worked 12 hours for almost nothing. I certainly learned the value of a dollar from this experience, however.

It was during this time that I became actively involved in my first political campaign. In 1962, Florida's congressional districts were re-drawn after lengthy litigation in a manner that provided a safe seat for a Dade County (now Miami-Dade County) Democrat. Claude Pepper, who served in the United States Senate during FDR's New Deal, and who had lost the 1950 senate race to George Smathers in one of history's most written-about senate campaigns (for an excellent account of this campaign, see "Red Pepper and Gorgeous George," by James C. Clark [University Press of Florida 2011]), was running for this new congressional seat.

I went to his campaign headquarters in Miami, introduced myself and he asked if I would distribute literature on the community college campus. I said I would be honored to do so. He asked about my family, my career plans, etc. I was impressed that he would spend time with me, a teenager and non-voter. He sent me letters of appreciation which I keep to this day in a scrapbook. Years later, when I visited him in his congressional office, he remembered my name and took me on a tour of his immense congressional office with pictures taking up all the wall space. He took time to explain the history behind many of the photos.

In the late 1980s, just after his autobiography was published, he had a book-signing session in Tallahassee. I brought a few of his letters with me and, although he was nearing 90 and showing the effects of age, he read one or two and again thanked me for my help more than 25 years earlier. I give this brief background to you because after he passed away within a year of the book-signing, The Florida Bar named its highest award that can be given to a government lawyer in his honor, the Claude Pepper Outstanding Government Lawyer Award, which I was both honored and fortunate enough to receive in 2000. I literally went full circle with this distinguished lawyer and legislator, working for his first campaign for the United States House of Representatives and 38 years later receiving an honor that bears his name.

After graduating from community college, I attended the UF in Gainesville. My plan at that time was to teach for awhile and eventually attend law school. However, I received a D in a course, and the college of education wouldn't accept such a low grade for graduation. So, in order to graduate on time, I had to find a program that accepted Ds. I did; the school (now college) of journalism. Over three straight trimesters during my senior year, I took the entire course requirements for a bachelor's degree in journalism, with a specialty in newspaper reporting, graduating in August 1965. Goodbye teaching, hello press. The only person I really knew while at the UF was my friend Raoul, whom I met in high school where we took a band class in the 11th grade. We were the only two students who were assigned to the baritone instrument, which looks like a baby tuba. We had to share one mouthpiece, so when one of us finished our lesson, we'd wash the mouthpiece and hand it to the other. What a great way to meet a friend.

At the UF, we ate lunch and dinner together and, with his first wife, double-dated on a few occasions. He eventually graduated from NYU College of Law and worked as a prosecutor in New York and Atlanta. In Atlanta, he went into private practice with his second wife. When I had a case before the Eleventh Circuit Court of Appeals in Atlanta, I would visit them and their young adopted daughter. My first real friend, Raoul tragically passed away suddenly in 1996 at age 53 from a heart attack, leaving a wife and a five-year-old.

Graduating from college was a watershed moment for me and the Waas family generally. Neither my grandparents (both sides) nor my parents went to college. In fact, my grandparents never completed high school. My dad didn't want my brother and me to have to struggle as he did. As a child of the depression and having served in WW II, he did everything he could to assure that his sons got an education, which for us meant going to college. I was the first generation in my family to graduate from college; my brother followed four years later. Barry went on to earn a Ph. D. and I got a law degree. To say that my dad was proud to attend our graduations would be a gross understatement. My grandfather didn't want my dad to pursue his dream of being in show business; my dad made it absolutely certain that nothing would prevent his sons from living their dreams.

1965 was the year of the great military buildup for the Vietnam War (technically, it wasn't a war because Congress never declared it a war. Tell that to the families of those who never returned or were maimed for life. When a foreign enemy is shooting at you, and you're shooting back, that's a war.) A draft lottery was instituted, and my birth date came up as number 22, I believe. This meant that if I continued to breathe, my odds of being drafted into the Army were astronomically high; say, absolutely certain. So, I decided that upon my return home to Miami Beach after graduation, I would enlist in the Coast Guard., since it didn't appear as if it was sending any of its recruits to Vietnam. I made an appointment and went for my physical. The doctor (at least, I think he was a doctor) examined me and asked whether I had ever had an inguinal hernia. I told him I was born with one and, according to my parents, had it repaired when I was one year old. He said, "Well son, you have another one."

My appointment at the draft board was scheduled for two weeks later, and following instructions from the Army to provide information on my medical history, I got a letter from the doctor who treated me for asthma and, when asked by draft board personnel to present any physician letters, gave him mine. I made no mention of my newly discovered hernia. The Army medical people took my asthma letter and told me to leave. A month later, I received word that I was IV-F, or permanently ineligible for the draft. I guess the Army felt that I might have an asthma attack in the Vietnam jungle and wheeze a secret location. Had I mentioned the hernia and then received my letter, I wouldn't know whether my classification were based on the hernia or asthma history. Since I now knew the precise reason, I promptly called my doctor and two weeks later had my hernia repaired, my putative military career over.

To this day, I wonder what would have happened if the Coast Guard hadn't found the hernia. Kind of like that D I got at the University of Florida—and that D was one point short of a C. One point!! Had I gotten that point, I might have become a teacher and never gone to law school. Without the hernia, I might have gone into the Coast Guard. I would have never met Harriet, etc., etc., etc. Life does indeed take many strange paths, some of which you have absolutely no control over. Frequently, it's these little things that wind up having a big influence on one's life.

As I mentioned earlier, dating was a big problem for me in high school and college because I didn't have a car. When I did get a date, it was a double-date with someone who had a car. I couldn't afford one; my parents couldn't afford to buy me one; and, besides, I didn't know how to drive yet. Why take lessons if you don't have a car to drive? My dad didn't learn how to drive until he was 53. Living and working in New York, with its vast subway system, didn't require a car. It was only after he moved to Miami Beach that he finally learned how to drive.

I remember one dating experience that forced me to do something drastic, but I never felt sorry for doing it. While I was attending community college and working at a supermarket as a cashier, an elderly lady bought her purchases to my register several Saturdays in a row. One day, she said she had a granddaughter who was going to be visiting her and this lady wanted to bring her by the store and introduce her to me. Sure enough, a couple of weeks later, she arrived with her granddaughter, a very attractive 19-year-old. During a break from work, I got her phone number, called her and asked her out to a movie.

Since her grandmother lived about four blocks from where I lived, I walked to the lady's apartment and picked up my date. As we got downstairs, I turned toward the bus stop; she turned toward the parking area. She asked where I was going and I told her that we needed to catch the bus to the movie theater. Her reaction was one of disbelief. For the entire five-minute wait for the bus and 10-minute ride to the theater, she didn't say a single word. In the theater, she told me to get her some popcorn and a large drink, which I did. She sat through the first part of the movie without initiating a single conversation. Every time I tried to engage in conversation, I was met with a one-word response. She was clearly upset with having to take a bus on a date. During the intermission, she said she wanted some candy and another drink. I got up and as I approached the counter, I noticed out of the corner of my eye that the bus that would take me within two blocks of my front door was waiting at the curb. I had two options: I could buy what she wanted and go back and put up with her stuffiness and cold shoulder, or I could take a bus and go home. I took the bus; I never saw the grandmother or her spoiled granddaughter again. It was only after I graduated and returned to Miami Beach in 1965 that I finally learned how to drive and borrowed $600 from my brother—which I eventually paid back—to buy a used car.

After my 1965 graduation, I returned to Miami Beach and spent a few months working for a public relations agency. I applied for and got my first news reporting job with the Palm Beach Post-Times in January 1966. I loaded my possessions in my car and found a small furnished apartment in West Palm Beach across from the newspaper headquarters on U.S. 1. I started with the usual beginner's track for a cub reporter back then: writing obituaries, doing re-writes of previous stories, etc.

Within a couple of months, however, the courthouse reporter called in sick (translation: drunk) and I was tasked with an emergency assignment covering the crime beat—on the very same day that multiple homicides were committed, a major vehicle crash claimed a couple of lives, and the grand jury handed down an indictment of a public official. Thanks to a "sick" reporter, I wrote three front-page stories and wound up getting the crime beat assignment. Because the Post was a morning paper, and the Times an afternoon paper, I worked the Post's hours of 3 to 11. One of my jobs was to "freshen" or update Times stories for the following day's edition of the Post. This "permanent" move to the crime beat, however, lasted only the remaining six months of my tenure with the Post-Times. I was offered a job closer to Miami Beach when the then-Fort Lauderdale News asked me to join the staff as courthouse reporter. I actually had a desk in the Broward County Courthouse, and my salary of $120 a week was $20 more than what the Post-Times paid me. Oh, joy! I loaded up my car and headed for Fort Lauderdale, finding a one-bedroom furnished apartment across from the county courthouse.

Although I still wanted to be a lawyer, it was no more than a pipedream as my finances weren't exactly amenable to my goal. However, shortly after joining the News, I learned that FSU had just recently started a law school. Just to see if I would be accepted, I applied, and received a letter that the assistant dean would be at Florida Atlantic University in Boca Raton interviewing applicants for the freshman class, and that I should schedule an interview with him.

I had the interview and, soon thereafter, was told that a space was mine in the freshman class if I wanted it, and that there was a federal loan program available that would cover my tuition, room and book expenses. Did I want it? I applied for and received the loan, gave up my job, broke the lease on my apartment, sold my car, and took a bus to Tallahassee with all my belongings in one huge suitcase.

During my three years in law school, I worked part-time for the Florida Attorney General's Office; served as editor of the Flambeau, the student newspaper; was student government attorney general; and worked with the FSU debate team under the federal work-study program. Between these paying jobs and my loan money, my financial problems were resolved. When I graduated, all I owed was $3,000, which I paid off over 10 years at $30 per month that included a very low interest rate.

Notice I didn't mention anything about my academic achievements. There's a reason for this: I didn't have any; I was passing all of my courses, and that's all that really mattered. I readily admit, however, that I excelled in extra-curricular activities.

Here are two wonderful stories I love to tell about my choices of involvement in FSU student press and government activities. Before the year I became editor, the Flambeau was a thrice-weekly publication that had no wire service; it was strictly a campus newspaper. The university board of student publications, however, was planning to pick up the Associated Press wire service and publish five days a week, and was looking for someone with news experience. I figured "What a great way to meet people (translation: girls)!" So, I applied, was selected and, the day after my selection, visited the Flambeau offices for the first time. I picked up the key to the editor-in-chief's office and, as I spotted the sign that identified my new office, overheard some voices coming from the newsroom, located directly across from the chief's office. I went into the newsroom where one of the occupants, noticing that I was looking around and appeared to be lost, introduced himself and asked if he could help me. Ok, I was going to have a little fun with this. I told him I was just looking around to familiarize myself with the office layout. This pleasant young man told me he worked for the newspaper as a feature writer and asked if I would be interested in becoming a staff member. I then asked the other two in the office what they did. One was the sports editor, the other handled the news section.

I then asked about the staff, and was told that every staffer was on edge because of the new editor who was coming in. "He's a law student, a former newspaper reporter with a JM (journalism) degree and is supposed to be a real hotshot," one said. The others just uh huhed and nodded their heads. "This guy's never worked here before, and he's coming in here as the editor," he said. More uh huhs and nods. I told them I had to leave and get to work; took out my key and walked slowly out of the newsroom. As the three of them followed me, I walked over to my new office, put in the key, turned it, and as the door opened, I turned to the three of them—mouths open to their knees—and said "Well, I'll see you around." I then closed the door and pictured the three of them standing there absolutely dumbfounded.

After composing myself from a hard-to-stifle laugh, I opened the door, invited them in, formally introduced myself and told them I just had to have a little fun at their expense. I think they appreciated that I wasn't a stuffed shirt. They all remained as staff members in their previous positions. I also instituted something that hadn't been done before. Every member of the staff received some form of remuneration. I felt that I could increase accountability and performance if there were a financial incentive-however small—hanging over the entire staff. This worked out as I had hoped; during my time as editor, I didn't lose a single staff member, and all of them did their work on time.

While I was editor, campus demonstrations were taking place at some major universities throughout the country. A TV station in Boston was doing a series on college campus upheaval, and was flying in student leaders from several universities that had not had any demonstrations—at least, not yet. I received a call from a television news director inviting me to appear, and offered to pay my way. I readily accepted and flew to Boston—in December. When I arrived, it was cold, very cold. My years in Florida must have warmed my blood, as the blustery, well-below-freezing weather was barely tolerable. Nevertheless, I took a cab from the airport to the hotel and was picked up next morning for my interview. I thought I was going to be part of a group interview; I was wrong. I was presented as a student leader of a major southern university that had no problem with radicals on campus causing disturbances. I was interviewed for a full half-hour. I answered the questions as best I could and actually felt very comfortable being interviewed. The TV personnel were very pleased, I was pleased and I got a chauffeur-driven ride back to the airport for my flight home. Turns out this interview was premature in light of what happened at FSU less than three months later.

I did one thing as editor that I came to regret. I promised to write my own editorials for every edition—five editorials per week. I quickly found out that being a law student and being editor writing a daily editorial didn't go hand-in-hand. I had no time to meet, ah, people or for any kind of social life. After eight months, I was burned out, and still had a few months left in my term. Luckily for me, the incoming student body president offered me the position of student government attorney general. I resigned as editor and took the student government job. The pay differential was only $30 a month less (I made $150 as editor, $120 as AG). What an easy way to make $120!!!

Was I wrong on this one!! This was 1969, the Vietnam War was still hot and the university president blocked the publication of an article in a campus magazine. This censorship issue was the tipping point for student demonstrations throughout the campus, including one memorable and frightening night when sheriff's deputies armed with rifles and bayonets came onto campus to quell a potential disturbance. In my capacity as attorney general, I had to address campus legal issues, including those arising out of the demonstrations. The first thing I realized was that I needed a deputy I could trust. Knowing how competitive law students are, I chose the one person I trusted most: Harriet. I took some heat for not appointing a law student, but Harriet as deputy attorney general was of great assistance to me keeping files organized and handling other tasks. It turned out, however, that my student activities involvement would have been less stressful had I completed my term as editor and simply stopped writing an editorial a day.

As a result of the censorship brouhaha, the university president resigned, and was replaced by Dr. J. Stanley Marshall. (The events of this period, including the "night of the long knives" [as dubbed by the students] is compellingly described by former FSU President J. Stanley Marshall in his excellent memoir "The Tumultuous Sixties" (Sentry Press 2006). [In the interest of full disclosure, Dr. Marshall is most generous in his praise of my editorship of the Flambeau. This, however, is not what makes his memoir an excellent recounting of the times; his compelling narrative speaks for itself.].)

My involvement in the "night of the long knives" occurred shortly after I became student government attorney general. When the confrontation reached critical mass, I was on the sidewalk on Tennessee Street, a main roadway in Tallahassee, overlooking the back of the student union. On the grass in front of me were over a dozen sheriff's deputies armed with rifles and bayonets. Other deputies were gathered around the area leading to the steps up to the student union. Students were milling around and a couple of them took turns speaking. The tension was great; at any moment, a spark could ignite a physical confrontation. But fortunately, cooler heads prevailed and what befell so many college campuses in the late 60s and early 70s was averted at FSU. It was, however, touch and go for awhile. Afterwards, the sheriff said the rifles were not loaded; we'll never really know. I do know the bayonets were real.

Following publication of Dr. Marshall's book in 2006, the university sponsored a seminar heralding the book and discussing the circumstances surrounding the events leading up to the fateful night I previously mentioned. The university brought back many student government leaders, as well as the then-87-year-old former sheriff, other government and university officials, "student radicals," and Dr. Marshall. This seminar was broadcast live on FSU TV and replayed frequently over the following few weeks. I was invited to be on the panel, after assisting—along with a few other former student leaders—Dr. Marshall in putting together the outline and protocol for the seminar. I enjoyed visiting with people I hadn't seen in years, and it was quite refreshing to see the path their lives had taken since their days as students, university officials and law enforcement officials. The consensus was that FSU had done what other universities failed to do—prevent violence on campus though dialogue. While the panelists for the most part held to their views of more than 30 years prior, there was a discernible mellowing and at least a tacit understanding of where the others were coming from. That alone made this program worthwhile.

As I mentioned previously, it was during my term as editor of the school newspaper that I met my wife, Harriet. Naturally, being editor made me a "big man on campus" (at least, in my mind), but Harriet wanted to meet the "snobbish, opinionated, self-centered, ego-driven" editor. I suppose that in writing as many editorials as I did, I might have come across as a bit arrogant. Just a wee bit now. Harriet told her friends she just wanted to give this editor a piece of her mind. Well, there was this social gathering, and Harriet saw me talking to another girl, walked over and immediately began talking to me. At this time, she didn't know who I was until I introduced myself. The other girl left, and I was left explaining myself to my future wife. I found out later that she went back to her dorm that night and called her parents to tell them that she had met the boy she was going to marry. She, for some unknown reason, never let me in on this revelation until after we were engaged. Smart girl. Not that it would have mattered by then. I did, however, realize far more than my social goal as editor—I didn't expect to meet my future wife, but I did.

I was wrong in thinking that my days as Flambeau editor were over when I resigned as editor in early 1969. About 10 days before I was to graduate from law school in 1970, I received a call from a university administrator informing me that the entire staff of the Flambeau resigned over an issue that they believed impacted a free press, and would I be willing to take over the editorship for the last five editions. I reasoned that whatever may be the anger level of the staff, the primary consideration was getting the news out to the students. So, knowing I'd be viewed as a traitor by the staff—which included the assistant editor I appointed and who took over as editor when I resigned—I went ahead and, with a staff of three, put out the last five editions. I believed then—and believe to this day—that the responsible thing to do was to make sure the paper got out to the students. The Flambeau published the reasons for the mass resignation, as well as the news the students would have missed had those five editions not seen the light of day. My position was to give the students the facts, and let them draw their own conclusions about the resignations, and provide them with news and other information to which they were entitled and which I believed was important to them.

Following law school and until Harriet and I got married, I lived in a one-bedroom furnished apartment. After we married, we bought furniture that just about filled up this apartment. After a few months, we moved into a two-bedroom apartment and lived there until 1973 when we bought our first house. For the first 30 years of my life, I never lived in a house; only apartments. I never personally owned a piece of furniture until after we bought furniture for our first apartment. Except for her years in college, Harriet always lived in a house. I had adjustments to make, such as not calling an apartment manager when something broke or stopped working. And not hearing neighbors' noises was an entirely new experience for me—a very pleasant one, until I learned that any sounds out of the ordinary meant it was something I had to deal with. Of course, Harriet was well familiar with these matters. We lived in that house off Park Avenue for 11 years until we built the home we now live in—a four-bedroom, two-family-room home with a screened-in porch that features a large hammock. For retirement purposes, of course.

After law school, I did what so many graduates do: spent a few years moving from job to job before finally settling down. I worked for a brief period for the Florida Attorney General's Office under Earl Faircloth; took a job as staff attorney for the Florida League of Cities (an organization that represents the interests of city governments); worked at The Florida Bar as assistant director of its continuing legal education program; joined the state Department of Commerce as assistant to the director of labor for awhile; and became assistant dean of the FSU College of Law, handling alumni affairs and teaching mass communications law and professional ethics—all between 1970 and 1974. The few education courses I took at the UF therefore didn't go for naught as they actually paid off for me when I taught courses in law school.

While employed by the Florida League of Cities, I staffed the Tallahassee office as this organization was about to relocate from Jacksonville to be closer to where the government action is. While working for the league, a next-door neighbor who helped manage the 1970 successful gubernatorial campaign of Reubin Askew, asked if I'd be interested in joining a new political club in Tallahassee modeled after the Tiger Bay Club in the St. Petersburg area. Although I knew nothing about this club except its political nature, I figured that, since dues were only $50 and I was just starting my career and needed to be familiar with political leaders, I said I'd be glad to join. So, in 1972 I joined and became a charter member of the Capital Tiger Bay Club. Each year, the club has a Tiger at Bay night, featuring prominent speakers and, for the past few years, we had the late Steve Bridges appear as George Bush and Barack Obama. He was wonderful and his untimely passing left the club members deeply saddened. Over the years, we've had Jimmy Carter and Ronald Reagan, as well as several governors, senators, and other famous and notorious, such as Rev. Al Sharpton and lobbyist Jack Abramoff. We have had candidate forums for federal, state and local offices over the more than 40 years of the club's existence. Of the original 50 charter members, I am one of only a handful left. I've attended each of the Tiger at Bay annual dinners. I don't know what this says, except that I've attended every one, which allows me to joke that my "streak" of 40 years and counting matches up to Cal Ripken's. This club remains one of the very few to which I still belong.

Because the law school job was impacted by affirmative action, I was informed shortly after I was hired that the school couldn't guarantee that this assistant dean position would be available for a second year. Within a couple of weeks after this good news, I found out that Harriet was pregnant with our first child. I was conflicted; should I complete my year at the law school and hope for the best, or should I look for another job and guarantee income? Guess which one I chose?

I left the law school feeling somewhat betrayed. The dean had to know when he hired me that he would be sending me this affirmative action-impact letter, and could have told me about this before I changed jobs. I felt that, particularly being an alumnus of the school, I should have been treated better. I wasn't expecting special treatment, just plain honesty. My attitude toward affirmative action was and is affected by this. I firmly believe people should be chosen for jobs based on merit; quality performance matters. Handing out jobs solely to achieve some quota or goal is wrongheaded; and that it's patently unfair to punish the innocent for the bad conduct of others many years ago.

A friend told me a position was available at the Department of Transportation (DOT), where she worked. I applied, she went to bat for me, and I got the job. I told the dean of the law school who, although not happy at my premature departure, understood that I couldn't take the risk of being out of work with a baby on the way. So, after just eight months at my alma mater, I left to become a staff attorney at the DOT.

As I began my 2 1/2 years at DOT, I was asked to become familiar with a recently passed piece of legislation that completely revamped state administrative proceedings. Up to this time, disputes involving government agency decisions were not uniformly handled at the administrative level; many wound up in trial court; and the state trial level judiciary, which had undergone its own constitutional reform just a few years earlier, was straining at the bit in large part because of all the government litigation that crowded the dockets.

The 1974 legislature passed this revamped administrative procedures act to allow disputes with government agencies to be handled by hearing officers, with their decisions reviewable in a limited manner by agency heads, and ultimately by the district courts of appeal. I was tasked with becoming an "expert" on these types of proceedings, and handled both administrative hearings and appeals—and began making my name known throughout the practice to boot. I was also involved in Florida Bar activities, becoming chairman of the Administrative Law Section and serving as president of the Florida Government Bar Association.

In 1977, I was offered the job of assistant general counsel for social services with the Department of Health and Rehabilitative Services (HRS)—at that time a superagency that superintended the vast health and social services networks. (To show how large this agency was, when it was reorganized, it was divided into the Department of Health, Department of Children and Families and the Agency for Health Care Administration.) During my 3 1/2 years there, I provided advice and counsel to all of the agency programs, from health, mental health, vocational rehabilitation, licensing, etc.; handled rather complex administrative hearings and appeals; and began to write articles on these subjects. I was also on the lecture circuit for The Florida Bar. All in all, I was enjoying myself and earning a reputation in the fields of administrative law and practice and appellate advocacy. Then came the last few months for me at this agency.

During my six years at DOT and HRS, I received glowing evaluations from my supervisors, the general counsels. However, the last evaluation I received in late 1979 from the HRS general counsel was extremely critical of my performance and conduct. The general counsel at that time was relatively new to her position, and prior to this evaluation, made no comments to me whatever regarding any dissatisfaction with my performance or behavior. In fact, no one ever questioned my performance or demeanor. This extremely negative evaluation came completely out of the blue.

My success rate remained consistently high and I had no reason to believe I wouldn't receive the same type of evaluation as I had in the past. On evaluation day, I was summoned into the office of another supervisor and, with both ladies present, the general counsel handed me my evaluation. I read it and, although shocked, made sure I kept a poker face. I felt that the reason this other supervisor was present was to witness my reaction. I'm sure she and the general counsel were disappointed that I gave no reaction. When asked if I had any comment, I said "Not at this time." I was told to sign the evaluation, which I did, got up and left.

The primary criticism was that I told people "what they wanted to hear" instead of giving sage legal advice. I provided advice and counsel to the agency's top administrators. I viewed my role as doing the best I could to provide them with legal options to accomplish their mission. On occasion, if an administrator wanted to take action that I believed was contrary to law, but could be accomplished another way, this is precisely what my advice was. This criticism made it appear that I was telling them to do whatever they wanted to, regardless of the legal consequences. In short, what I was being accused of amounted to malpractice as well as unethical and unprofessional behavior. This was utter nonsense.

What neither supervisor knew—and probably don't even know today—is that a week later, after my evaluation made its way to my personnel file, I went to the personnel office, had my file retrieved, and wrote a scathing evaluation of my supervisors. I pulled no punches in setting out in detail how unprofessional I thought they were both in the process and method used on me; and that this evaluation made no sense. How could I have gone from a top-performing lawyer to an unethical and unprofessional one in such a short period of time? This question was never answered. Moreover, the evaluation offered no statement of how my "deficiencies" could be remedied. The requirement imposed on supervisors was to not only point out weaknesses, but how they could be strengthened. The supervisors completely failed to comply with this requirement.

OK, I know what you're thinking. Both supervisors are women, so I must have some hang-up on having a female supervisor. This is an easy one to dispel. In my more than 40 years in the practice, I've worked with and been supervised by several very competent leaders who happened to be female, and always got along extremely well with them. In trying to explain to myself what might have been the trigger, at this particular time period, efforts were being made to diversify the public sector, especially as it pertained to women and minorities in the workplace. There was criticism of this effort as being more of a setting of quotas or goals than of rewarding merit. Perhaps these women believed they had to show that the faith placed in them by their respective appointments was justified on the merits rather than to achieve some quota or goal. Or perhaps the general counsel somehow viewed me as a competitor for her job—a job I didn't seek, never applied for, and didn't want.

There may be something to be said for this supposition, however. I continued to write articles for The Florida Bar Journal, and a couple of them were cited as authorities by state appellate courts. While I was justifiably proud of having my writings viewed with such value by the judiciary, I could see how envy or jealousy might creep into the supervisor-employee relationship. Regardless of the motives behind this extremely negative evaluation, however, I made certain that the record was set straight. Since Florida has a very strong public records law, and evaluations are public records, in the immortal words of that great baseball manager and twisted linguist Casey Stengel, you could look it up. (About three months later, I turned in my resignation. Just before I left this agency, the general counsel said she hoped the evaluation wasn't the reason I was leaving. My reaction was to laugh long and loud as she walked out of my office. It wasn't, but I wanted her to think so.)

Perhaps you believe I simply can't take criticism. Believe me, to make it as a newspaper reporter or lawyer, you have to be able to take criticism. What I can't take is a charade, or someone's personal agenda, that serves as the foundation for baseless criticism. And in my opinion, that's precisely what this was.

The fact is that during my last year at HRS, I had several conversations with a close friend, Steve Slepin, who was in private practice. I worked for Steve when he was director of labor. He and I discussed the prospects of joining him in the private sector. Thus, the question arose in my mind: what about private practice? I had never done this before; perhaps now was the time to consider it. Steve had joined with another close friend, Paul Lambert, both of whom had worked in government and had formed a partnership, and I was pleased when asked to join them as an associate. So I joined Slepin, Slepin and Lambert in 1980. Shortly thereafter, the firm became Slepin, Slepin, Lambert and Waas.

Practicing law in the private sector is in some respects far different than the public sector. In the public sector, you know what your salary is, and you get that paycheck either monthly or bi-weekly, plus a benefits package that includes medical coverage and, after a set number of years, a pension. In the private sector, you get what's left after all bills, including overhead and staff salaries, are paid. As for retirement, you're on your own. One month, I might make (called taking a draw) $2,000 and another, $10,000. (I was closer to the former far more often than the latter, unfortunately.) I learned that one of the things some private clients expect is that the lawyer fund their lawsuit. Clients have to be educated that lawyers are not in the banking business; they don't loan clients money to fund representation. Even when a case is taken on a contingency, there are certain up-front expenses that the client must bear. The advantage of private practice is that, at least theoretically, there is no limit on income.

What made my private practice experience so enjoyable is that I got to work with close friends—we never had a written contract, just a handshake—and got to handle some interesting cases. After several years of defending government agencies, I spent the next five years litigating against government, much of which required out-of-town travel. This experience gave me needed business perspective, and paying clients; although on a couple of occasions, collecting my fees required drastic enforcement measures, such as seizing property. I was amazed how quickly non-paying clients who claimed they didn't have the money to pay their bills, could come up with my fees when I undertook collection efforts that involved seizing their property. Once they paid and the check cleared, however, all property was graciously returned. Fortunately, I rarely had to use this nuclear option to collect my fees.

In 1985, the practice of law was changing and business (at least for me) seemed to be drying up. I now had two young daughters and a large mortgage on a new home, and the ups and downs of private practice were getting to me. I was tiring of the late-night and weekend phone calls at home from clients who believed that they owned me 24/7. Also, and most important of all, my oldest daughter stopped asking me if I would attend her school plays and recitals. When I asked her why, she said "You're always traveling and don't come to see me anyway." That was the tipping point.

All of this coalesced into a belief that private practice wasn't for me, and that it was in my best interests to return to the more secure and predictable—although historically less profitable—public sector. My partner Steve helped me get a job with the Department of State division of elections as staff attorney, which I began in January 1986. I had no idea at the time how beneficial this move was going to be for the rest of my career.

As staff attorney (with the title "elections counsel"), I handled the prosecution of election law violations before the Florida Elections Commission, and provided advice to the division director and staff. This job also gave me the opportunity to become familiar with Florida's expansive and convoluted elections laws.

I say expansive and convoluted because so many provisions seemed both inconsistent and ambiguous; but when I realized that the election laws were passed by those having the greatest interest in them—the state legislators and lobbyists—somehow the morass and confusion that is the election code was perfectly understandable. Much of what I did, however, was "desk job" work. I longed to become more than an office practitioner; I wanted to become a courtroom lawyer handling more than just administrative agency cases before hearing officers and executive agencies.

Thanks to a friend in the attorney general's Office, Jerry Curington, I left the division of elections in March 1987 and was assigned to the torts bureau in the general civil litigation division. I quickly found out that just about any lawyer who can find a way to sue government will do so, for one simple reason: state government has a deep—VERY DEEP—pocket. Unfortunately, many of my tort cases involving negligence claims against state agencies required extensive travel, particularly to Miami, Fort Lauderdale, West Palm Beach, Tampa, St. Petersburg and Orlando. I was on the road almost as much as I was in my office. Recall that one of the main reasons I left private practice was to become more involved in my daughters' school activities. Both girls were also taking acting and dance lessons, and I wanted to see all of their plays and recitals, but traveling on business was impacting this as well. So I asked Jerry, who supervised the civil division, if I could transfer to another bureau that required less travel. He graciously accommodated me and in September 1987, I moved to the state programs bureau where I stayed for the next 23+ years before retiring.

My Last Job-State Programs Bureau, Division Of General Civil Litigation

The bureau is called state programs because it was the catchall for cases that didn't fit into any other bureau. During my years there, the civil litigation division was made up of torts, corrections (prisoner litigation not involving civil rights claims—you would be surprised at how ingenious and litigious prisoners are), employment litigation (harassment of all kinds, terminations, etc.), tax litigation, eminent domain and administrative law. If a case didn't find its way into one of these areas, it went to state programs.

Because of my previous experience with the division of elections, I was dubbed the "elections expert" and began getting assigned lawsuits involving challenges to election laws and practices. It's amazing how a lawyer can be perceived as an expert by simply being associated with a particular legal discipline. I always felt that perception is reality when it comes to dubbing someone an expert. Still, if that's how management wanted to treat me, who was I to disagree? During my more than 23 years in this job, I handled dozens of election-related lawsuits. I also handled civil rights claims under the federal civil rights laws. Unlike state tort claims, which have a statutory damages limit, civil rights claims have no such limitation. As a result, civil rights claims can—and more often than one might think—actually do cost the state millions of dollars, which claims are ultimately paid by the state taxpayers.

The greatest exposure to the state treasury is in the area of institutional reform litigation. This type of case involves major programs like Medicaid, where litigants (more specifically, institutional reform lawyers) want to change a state practice because these lawyers claim the challenged practice is in violation of federal law. These cases typically proceed as class actions, whereby legal counsel locate a representative plaintiff and then seek to represent an entire class of people these lawyers claim are adversely impacted in the same way as the representative by the alleged illegal actions of state officials and employees. The state programs section has lawyers who specialize in this type of protracted, expensive and time-consuming cases involving agency meetings and lawyer get-togethers ad nauseam; I handled a few of these during my time, but I found this type of litigation not to my liking; it was too time-consuming, esoteric and quite frankly boring for my rapid-fire work style and extremely low level of patience.

My joy came in handling constitutional challenges to statutes, election cases, legislative and congressional redistricting and reapportionment, non-institutional reform civil rights cases, and generally cases that didn't fit into a particular category even under the catchall state programs banner. Some of my cases were denominated "high profile" cases. I will discuss a few of them, because I am proud that the attorney general had enough faith in me to allow me to handle them, and because I had opportunities that very few lawyers have in either the private or public sectors.

While the general civil litigation division was formally divided into several identifiable disciplines, the state programs bureau was informally divided into specific disciplines. The bureau had its institutional reform "unit" (for lack of a better descriptive word), as well as contracts and prisoner civil rights claims, among a few others. Except for elections cases and suits against judges, prosecutors and high-ranking state officials, what didn't fit neatly into a particular category was quite often assigned to me. This is the type of litigation that allowed me to be as creative as I could possibly be. It also gave me lightning in a bottle early on in my employ by being assigned a case that went all the way to the United States Supreme Court.

Very few lawyers actually get a chance to argue before the highest court in the land. My chance came in January 1990-less than three years after joining the office. Let me give you some background. In 1988-within a year of my arrival at the AG's office (this is how the office is referred to by those who work for or interact with this agency—the office is actually denominated as the Department of Legal Affairs as well as the Office of the Attorney General. You will see one or both of these designations in the statutes and on virtually all office signs.), I arrived at my office one day and found a blue folder (all cases were placed in a blue folder) with a notation from the section chief that the case looks like an easy quickie turnaround case. A quickie case is one that could be finally decided on the law without the necessity of a trial—a single motion to dismiss or motion for summary judgment as a matter of law would suffice.

Not in this case. The case involved a person who appeared before a grand jury and wanted to write a book describing his testimony. Florida had a statute at that time that prohibited any person from revealing in any manner testimony given before a grand jury. Claiming a First Amendment right, the plaintiff argued this statute abridged his freedom of speech. I argued that grand jury secrecy is a well-established principle that protected both the sanctity of grand jury proceedings and the rights and interests of those who are summoned before it or who might be involved in its deliberations. Therefore, the First Amendment didn't trump over grand jury secrecy.

This case presented a classic collision between First Amendment rights and grand jury secrecy. The federal district court ruled in my favor in dismissing the case. The Eleventh Circuit Court of Appeals reversed, holding that First Amendment jurisprudence required the state to prove that the interests of grand jury secrecy substantially outweigh the right to freedom of speech, and the state couldn't meet this burden in this case.

The only way to get this decision to the United States Supreme Court is by filing what is known as a petition for certiorari, which means petitioning the Court to exercise its wholly discretionary authority to hear this case. The petition must demonstrate why the case is of such exceptional importance that the Court should accept jurisdiction and resolve the dispute. I knew when I filed my petition that chances of review were slim. Typically, the Court accepts less than 100 cases each term even though thousands of petitions are filed. However, because this case involved no disputed facts and was purely a clash between presumptive competing constitutional and historical principles, the odds of the Court accepting this case seemed to me to be better. Turns out I was correct, because the Court noted probably jurisdiction in 1989, which meant that I would file my brief on the merits explaining not only the importance of this case, but why it was necessary to resolve competing principles and why the appeals court was wrong, followed by the other side's brief countering mine, and my reply brief countering the other side's argument. The case was set to be argued on January 8, 1990.

What happens when a case is set and notice is sent to the lawyers? Good question. The first thing I did was sweat. I was going to argue a case before the United States Supreme Court! It's every lawyer's dream come true for me. After the euphoria waned, however, reality set it: I must prepare like I've never prepared before, because nine justices armed with a host of the best law school graduates in the nation will analyze and attempt to shred every argument, point, nuance, etc., that was put forth in the various briefs and other filings. I didn't care how the preparation would go for the other side; I was concerned only with my position and how the Court was going to handle it—and me. I was asking the United States Supreme Court to do a very rare thing: overturn or reverse a unanimous decision of a three-judge panel of a federal court of appeals.

The Court sent me a packet of information, including a list of nearby hotels, where to park, when to arrive at the Court, my admission card, where I could have breakfast, what the procedures were once at the Court (including the exact words I had to utter at the beginning of my presentation), that I would have 30 minutes to present my argument that I could divide as I saw fit for my case in chief and rebuttal, what time my case would be heard, etc. The Court sets argument for 10 a.m., 11 a.m., 1 p.m. and 2 p.m. My case was set for the second morning session at 11. I also had to be in the courtroom at precisely 9:50 because I was told that once the doors were closed no one—NO ONE—would be allowed in. Period. I certainly wasn't going to find out whether this was true or not.

I arrived in Washington two days before oral argument. I had several preparatory moot court sessions with lawyers in the AG's office, and one moot court set up by the National Association of Attorneys General (abbreviated NAAG—I am always enamored by that acronym).

I felt as prepared as humanly possible. I visited the Court the day before my argument to get a feel of the courtroom. It is huge, with the lectern very close to the bench. I stood at the lectern and scanned the bench and the large stuffed chairs where the justices would sit. I saw the curtain behind the bench from which the justices would enter. I suddenly felt very small and intimidated. Nevertheless, I vowed to bring all my preparation and forensic skills to bear. After all, I'd argued cases before appellate courts before; I certainly wasn't a novice, but I still felt small and intimidated. The majesty of the Supreme Court building and courtroom will do that to you.

January 8. I got up early (I really didn't get much sleep), got dressed and walked to the Supreme Court building. Somehow, the steps leading to the building were higher, and the outside plaza seemed larger and more foreboding than the day before. I walked through the large doors leading into the rotunda and saw the busts of former chief justices. How did I miss these the day before? After I gave my overcoat to the check-in clerk (checking in overcoats, umbrellas, etc., in restaurants and other places of public accommodation is a northern thing) and proceeded to the clerk's office, where the clerk of court personally led me, as well as other lawyers who were there for the morning session, to the cafeteria below the courtroom itself. I walked into the cafeteria and immediately noticed that one of the justices was having breakfast with several young men and women. No doubt these were the law clerks who tore apart my reasoned legal arguments and were going over the hostile questions I would be asked by this justice.

Now for my breakfast. Breakfast!! Who was I kidding? My stomach was where my heart was; my heart was in my throat. The attorney who I traveled with (the office doesn't let a lawyer about to appear before the high court travel alone) and who had previously argued a case to the Court strongly recommended that I have something to eat; this would avoid the stomach growls which can be quite embarrassing. After a light breakfast, I went up to the courtroom, presented my admission card at 9:40-10 minutes to spare—and with briefcase in hand entered the courtroom.

The courtroom is set up so that there are two rows of tables opposite the bench itself. The first row consists of one large table on each side of the lectern; the second row is directly behind. On the tables before each arguing attorney are two quill pens and a calendar listing the cases to be heard that day. These, along with the admission card, are souvenirs. Directly behind the second row is a bar in front of which is a bench reserved for lawyers who are members of the Supreme Court Bar. Only lawyers who are members of that Bar can argue a case or sit on that bench. The Court requires the lawyers for the morning cases to be at their respective tables and ready to proceed precisely at 10.

At 10 sharp, the clerk announced the opening of the session, the robed justices stepped out from behind the curtain (the chief justice first, then the others in order of seniority), the chief announced the first case and asked the petitioning lawyer by name to proceed. Sitting in the second row, with notes in hand, I really didn't listen to that case, and to this day, have no recollection of what that case was about. I understand this is usually the case for those lawyers awaiting their call to proceed to the front table and the petitioner's arguing lawyer to appear at the lectern. While awaiting for the first case to conclude, I recalled what a lawyer told me about the justices; he said "Remember, they put their pants on the same way you do." Of course, this didn't apply to Justice Sandra Day O'Connor. Still, I wondered why this particular thought came into my mind; I guess I was looking for any way possible to calm my nerves. I really didn't care how human they are. I only knew that in a very few moments, I would appear before them and be at their mercy.

When the first case concluded, the lawyers quickly gathered their material and while exiting from their places, the next group of lawyers—including me—moved quickly to their places in the front row. As the petitioner's arguing lawyer, I stood at the lectern as the chief justice announced my case and said "Ok, Mr. Waas, you may proceed." "Oh God," I thought, "he said my name! The Chief Justice of the United States said my name!!" I took a deep breath, quickly scanned the bench behind which sat the nine members of the Court, glanced at my notes, and began my argument, intoning the required "Mr. Chief Justice, and may it please the Court." After about half-a-minute, I never looked down at another note. There was no time to do this. I was peppered with questions from seven of the justices for the full 25 minutes I set aside for my main presentation.

I saw the faces of Thurgood Marshall, William Brennan, Harry Blackmun, Byron White, William Rehnquist, Sandra Day O'Connor, John Paul Stevens, Antonin Scalia, and Anthony Kennedy staring at me like Mt. Rushmore as seven of them (I learned later that Justices Brennan and Blackmun rarely ask questions) launched their questions. I felt that I was on the receiving end of verbal bombs. At least, they seemed like bombs, although Justice White said he was asking "friendly questions." Sure they were. I wondered why lawyers who appear before the Court bring briefcases or stacks of files with them. There is simply no time for research or examination of files. If you don't know the ins and outs of your case by the time you're standing before the justices, then you are simply out of your element. You can't ask the justices to please allow you time to review your files.

The Court has a lighting device on the lectern that lets the lawyer know how much time he has left. The petitioning lawyer has the option of reserving a portion of his 30 minutes for rebuttal; I reserved five minutes for mine. At the 23-minute mark of my opening presentation, a green light went on; a minute later, an amber light went on that signaled that I had one minute left.

I wrapped up my presentation and sat down as the red light illuminated. After the respondent's counsel completed his 30 minutes, I went back up and completed my five-minute rebuttal—again being peppered with questions—as the green light came on for the final time. After completing my argument, the chief justice intoned "The case has been received" and the justices immediately exited the way they came in. I quickly gathered my belongings and moved out of the courtroom with lightning speed. I was told the clerk locks the courtroom within a few minutes of the completion of the last argument, and anything left behind is permanently left behind. I wasn't going to find out if this were true or not, either.

Once outside the courthouse, I literally collapsed by one of the ornate columns that decorate the plaza; and even though it was a cold January day, realized that I had perspired through my undershirt, my shirt and my suit coat. For the privilege and honor of appearing before the highest court in the land, and being given two quill pens, an appearance card with my name on it, and a copy of the calendar of cases also with my name on it (which my wife put in a box frame that now hangs on my den wall), all I had to do was put up with 30 minutes of grilling by the most prepared jurists in the nation.

One of the techniques I was advised of was to try to frame my answers to questions in a way that allowed me to make my arguments as I originally prepared them. I believe I was faithful to this; I didn't allow the intimidation factor to consume me. I was told some horror stories of lawyers who fainted during their argument, or who admitted not knowing some of the details of their case, or who told justices that their questions were irrelevant.

I was told by more experienced lawyers to follow two simple rules: (1) know your case inside out, and (2) no question is irrelevant. If a lawyer who didn't handle the case in previous courts says he doesn't recall a particular part of the case file, chances are the justices will ask why he's arguing a case he's not intimately familiar with. Because handling appeals requires different forensic skills than trial work, more frequently than one might think, a client will retain a lawyer who had no involvement with the case at the trial or intermediate appellate court, to present the case to the high court. The risk here is that this appellate expert might be asked a question involving an intricate and perhaps to this lawyer an obscure or irrelevant matter that only the trial lawyer would appreciate.

Even though trial and appellate lawyers are linking up more closely, undoubtedly to avoid such a potentially embarrassing situation, the risk nevertheless remains; and I've witnessed firsthand what happens what that unanticipated or "irrelevant" question is asked of a lawyer who is unprepared for it and either has no answer, or, even worse, tries to bluff an answer. Either way, this is one lawyer who will be caught. And when a justice catches a lawyer who has no answer; says he's not familiar with a part of the record; or tries to bluff an answer, that justice will make his/her displeasure known in no uncertain terms.

Shortly after I arrived back in my office in Tallahassee, I learned that each justice had before him/her a brief biographical statement for each lawyer arguing a case. This statement includes the law school attended, employment background, some appellate cases previously argued, etc. Quite a revelation! The homework done by the Court before each oral argument is absolutely meticulous.

A few months later, the Supreme Court ruled that a person who testifies before a grand jury is free to disclose the nature of his testimony, but only after the term of the grand jury is completed. The petitioner had argued for an absolute right once he completed his testimony. As the press intoned, the Court labored mightily, but produced a mouse. To this day, I'm not aware that any book containing the witness's grand jury testimony has been written. Sometimes, all you get for your labors is a split decision.

My next high-profile case involved reapportionment and redistricting of both Florida's congressional seats and the state legislature. This process takes place every 10 years at the next even-numbered year following the decennial census. Since the census was taken in 1990, the process had to be conducted in 1992. Ten years earlier, Congress amended the Voting Rights Act of 1965. These 1982 amendments were the focal point in 1992 for what is ultimately a political process wrapped in legal jargon that can be difficult to navigate.

Several voting rights groups, including the NAACP, the Lawyers Committee for Civil Rights Under Law and the Poverty Law Center, joined forces in claiming that the amended federal voting rights law mandated that where a majority-minority district (translation: majority Black or Hispanic district) could be drawn, the state had a legal duty to draw it regardless of the shape of that district. This was called maximization of majority-minority districts the purpose of which was to "maximize" minority representation by allowing racial and ethnic minorities to elect "candidates of their choice." (Election jurisprudence is filled with such buzz phrases.)

Litigation over the impact of the voting rights law as well as Florida's constitutional requirements for state legislative reapportionment and redistricting was played out in both federal court and in the Florida Supreme Court. Under Florida's constitution, the process for the state legislature is initiated by the legislature itself. Once its plan is passed, the state attorney general is required to petition the state supreme court for a judgment that the plan passes both state and federal requirements. This is where I came into the process. The congressional plan is handled the same as for any item of legislation: by a bill passed by the state legislature and then approved by the governor. The state constitution required districts to be contiguous, compact and respectful of traditional local governmental boundaries. The federal requirements were contained in the amended voting rights act. as well as the federal constitution's "one person, one vote" principle that establishes that one person's vote should count literally as much as any other person's vote, regardless of where the voter resides.

Cutting through the buzzwords, this "maximization" mantra led to the packing of as many traditional Democratic voters into as few districts as possible, thereby bleaching surrounding districts where Democrats might either influence the outcome or actually elect Democrats. The result was that those surrounding districts would now be largely Republican-dominated. A map of the new districts replete with wildly configured shapes showed that gerrymandering, or drawing districts for the purpose of electing particular party candidates to office, was alive and well in the late 20th century. While this process—and the reading of the voting rights law at the time—resulted in more African-Americans and Hispanics being elected to office, it also resulted in the Republican Party gaining control of both houses of the state legislature and the congressional delegation, despite the fact that the number of Democratic voters outstripped the Republicans. Gerrymandering of legislative and congressional districts resulted in very few realistically competitive races for these seats.

Following the 1992 redistricting/reapportionment litigation, I was honored by being asked by the Nova University College of Law to write a law review article on the process and politics involved in this highly partisan enterprise, tracing its history in Florida from the early 1960s to 1992. This article was published in 1994.

I was also involved in the 2002 reapportionment/redistricting cycle, but by then the Republican Party had expanded its majority status in both the state legislature and in the congressional delegation. Today, the Republicans have a strong majority in both legislative houses, and just as wide a majority in the state's congressional delegation. At this writing, however, changes to the process have been made. In 2010, the voters amended the state constitution by requiring the process to be devoid of incumbency protection and political party status. In other words, the constitution now requires the process to be politically neutral. Whether this is a reality or pipedream remains to be seen, and it may well take two or three decennial cycles to get a legitimate answer.

The next high-profile case I handled came on the heels of the1992 redistricting process and focused on the impact of the amended voting rights act on Florida's elected judiciary. The same groups that argued their maximization theory for the realignment of the legislature and congressional delegation maintained that there were not enough minority judges on the trial (county and circuit) courts and that, therefore, minorities were not represented in the state's judiciary in proportion to their population in general. This, they claimed, was a violation of the voting rights law. In Florida, trial judges are elected in non-partisan elections; where there is a vacancy, there is a judicial nominating process that leads to gubernatorial appointment and, if the appointee desires a full term, election as previously described. Those who sought to elect more minorities argued for weighted voting—allowing voters a certain number of votes equal to the total number of judicial candidates or contests, which the voter can in turn cast as he/she sees fit—and other election devices that also were not of a "one person, one vote" nature.

Litigation was brought in federal court where the trial court eventually ruled that because there was no benchmark as to how such a system as proposed by these voting rights groups would actually work legitimately, there was no viable "remedy" under the federal law and where there is no remedy, there can be no violation. The federal appellate court agreed, and the United States Supreme Court rejected plaintiffs' effort to have the decision reviewed. Thus, the Florida judiciary was spared a most radical change in how the voters and citizens of the state elect their trial judges.

My next big case is also the one I'm most proud of, because it actually allowed me to bring a sense of justice to several families that suffered horrific crimes to their loved ones and who had believed the judicial system was unfair to them.

This case arose out of what is known as the "Son of Sam" case that originated in New York. By way of background, David Berkowitz was a serial killer who referred to himself as "Son of Sam." Because of the nature and number of killings, there was rampant speculation in the late 1970s that publishers were offering large sums of money to Berkowitz for his story. Because of the strongly held view that criminals must not be allowed to profit from the notoriety gained from the commission of heinous crimes, New York passed what is known as a "Son of Sam" law that prohibited criminals from profiting from the recounting of their crimes, including selling their stories to publishers. This was done by authorizing the state to seize money earned from movie or book deals, paid interviews, etc. Some of the funds were used to compensate the victims' families.

New York's original version of the law made its way to the United States Supreme Court, where critics of the law argued that the First Amendment prohibited applying the law to a publisher, further maintaining that such a law took away the incentive for many criminals to tell their stories, some of which (noting the Watergate scandal) were of vital interest to the general public. The Court struck down the law, but said a law of this type could be constitutional provided it took into account First Amendment rights.

Florida's Son of Sam law prohibits any felon, or anyone acting on behalf of a convicted felon, from profiting from his/her crimes by placing a lien on any earnings resulting from a recounting of the crimes. My case involved Danny Rolling, convicted of the brutal killing of five students at the UF in Gainesville. During Rolling's incarceration, he befriended a woman who wrote about serial killers. She wrote a book describing in Rolling's own words the murders he committed, and included in that book Rolling's story of how he raped another Florida woman.

As a result of the recounting of Rolling's five murders by this woman who I maintained was "acting on his behalf," I filed suit on behalf of the State of Florida in circuit court in Gainesville, Alachua County, Florida, naming Rolling, his "agent" girlfriend, and brother as defendants. I learned early on that the brother had nothing to do with this and had received no proceeds from any publication.

I also learned, from checking websites, that Rolling and his girlfriend (their words, not mine) had entered into a "cyberspace" marriage whereby they professed their love for one another. Rolling even sang songs to her in the courtroom during the criminal proceedings against him. The girlfriend posted Rolling's artwork, love letters, and other items on her website, and I downloaded and copied each one of them for trial.

Because I was unable to find any record of a Son of Sam case ever having gone to trial, at least on the type of statute Florida had, I had to improvise. My plan was to first seize what money there was (we found $16,000 that was earned through the sale of Rolling's artwork by his girlfriend/agent. We got a court order seizing that money and had it deposited with the clerk of court) and then make sure that the questions I asked of the girlfriend during the trial allowed her to continue talking, believing that the more she talked, the more she would hurt her case and help me make mine. In short, I planned on using her self-confidence and arrogance against her. The third part of my plan was to file the lawsuit under both the Son of Sam law and a separate restitution lien statute that allowed the state to seek a lien on the same earnings as under the Son of Sam law.

My strategic plan worked. Because Rolling's girlfriend believed the First Amendment absolutely protected her from any liability, she allowed me to easily establish a strong agent connection between Rolling and her by her own hand (and mouth), even as she explained that she was no longer "involved" with Rolling in any way. Such an argument rang hollow in light of her own website's postings, including a poorly worded statement that permitted me to show that there was an actual contract between Rolling and his girlfriend. The evidence submitted to the court was overwhelming and totally one-sided. The cumulative effect was that there was no question that she was acting on behalf of Rolling. This is precisely how the judge ruled. In her written decision, the judge also found Florida's Son of Sam law constitutional.

An appeal followed to the state intermediate appellate court, with the girlfriend focusing entirely on the constitutionality of the Son of Sam law. Pointedly, no challenge was made to the restitution lien law's application to the case. The appellate court disposed of the case without ruling on the constitutional claim because of the application of a well-established principle of appellate law that if an appellate court can uphold a trial court's ruling on a ground not challenged in the appeals court, the court is obligated to affirm.

This was the situation here, for the court was free to uphold the trial court's ruling on the independent ground of the restitution lien statute that was not challenged by the girlfriend. Because the appellate court decided the case on purely state statutory grounds, there was no further avenue of appeal for her to pursue, either before the state supreme court or the United States Supreme Court. The case was over, and the $16,000 now belonged to the state.

A while later, I learned that this money was used to help build a memorial in a park in Gainesville. This park has a memorial in one section that is set aside to recognize those students who are homicide victims. In this section there is a plaque that has the names of each of Rolling's five victims. About 75 yards from this memorial is a playground, and as I stood in the memorial area one day, I could hear the squeals and laughter of young children. Needless to say, it is an emotionally moving experience to stand in solemn silence at the memorial while hearing the wonderful sounds of children playing.

During the litigation, I came to know the families of the five students whose lives were tragically taken by this madman. They couldn't bring themselves to understand how anyone could be so heartless as to try to benefit financially from such horrendous, brutal crimes. They well understood the First Amendment, but couldn't understand the lack of humanity in someone who would commit these crimes, or anyone who would presume to profit from them.

This case reached such a level of notoriety that a producer of the television show "Dateline NBC" called me in late 1997 to see if I would agree to be interviewed. I readily and breathlessly agreed, and was then told that the interview would be conducted in my office by Jane Pauley. WHAT? I asked the caller to repeat this, so that I was sure that I had heard correctly. Jane Pauley was coming to Tallahassee to interview me in my office!

Sure enough, several days later, the AG's receptionist called me to tell me that Jane Pauley was in the lobby with some men who had lots of camera equipment and could she let them come up. (No, tell them to go home!) I made my way to the elevator and greeted her and her film crew, sending her crew to our library. I brought her to the state programs suite of offices because she had to make a call (I think she had to call Tom Brokaw). As I escorted her into the suite, and as the other lawyers and secretaries stared and ogled at my "guest," I thought it would be nice to introduce her to the staff. What fun that was for me!! The rubbernecking in the building was intensive, and I preened at escorting her around to the other lawyers and staff on the floor. Eventually, I brought her to our library where the camera crew set up their equipment.

Jane (yes, that's what she asked me to call her) told me that I was the "good guy" and that she would ask me whatever I thought would be helpful. As she asked questions, she would occasionally ask whether a question made sense, telling the cameraman to cut the filming. We also did a walking interview in the hallway where I was told to gesture and talk about anything I wanted to—all of the interviewing was already completed in the library. The interview lasted about 45 minutes, and then the crew packed up and I walked Jane to the elevator, we said our goodbyes and she left.

A couple of months later, in January 1998, I received a call from NBC letting me know that the interview would air on February 17. The entire segment featured the interview with Rolling's rape victim, a brave and strong lady who I found captivating and courageous. The next one interviewed was the girlfriend who came across the same way as she did at my trial—arrogant, pompous, self-assured and condescending. My portion lasted about two minutes, but I was most pleased with the result.

It's amazing how good editors are in splicing film segments. All of the stoppages and pregnant pauses were out, and the interview was crisp and what you are no doubt used to when you view one of these news programs. A couple of weeks later, I received a tape of this segment for my personal file. Recently, I put it on a CD that I will always treasure.

I said earlier that this was my most satisfying case. The reason for this had nothing to do with the TV appearance or the recognition I received for handling this case. For me, the satisfaction came from giving the five families a sense that, ultimately, a grievous wrong was prevented. The money Rolling's girlfriend thought she had made was instead used as startup funds for a memorial; Rolling was eventually executed for his crimes. While nothing can bring back these five young adults, their families can take some small measure of relief in knowing that, in the end, justice prevailed.

The last case on my most memorable list is known as the term limits case. Although I'm not personally persuaded that term limits is always a good thing, it fell to me to defend the constitutionality of term limits, particularly as applied to state legislators. Efforts to apply Florida's provision to United States Representatives and Senators failed because the United States Constitution, which trumps the state constitution, doesn't provide for term limits and any attempt by Florida to limit the terms of congressional representatives or senators would impose an unwarranted additional qualification for those offices.

The application of term limits to state officers, however, was yet to be tested. I didn't believe the issue was a particularly difficult one. I felt that the voters of the state could clearly provide for term limits for state officials, and the Florida Supreme Court agreed. The high-profile nature of this case was driven by the obvious interest of legislators and other state officials—members of the state cabinet and lieutenant governor. The constitutional provision allowed for four two-year terms for House members and two four-year terms for senators. The governor was term-limited (to two four-year terms) by prior constitutional amendment.

There is no doubt in my mind that as a result of these high-profile cases—especially the Son of Sam case—I was honored in 2000 to be the recipient of the Claude Pepper Outstanding Government Lawyer Award presented by The Florida Bar. As I alluded to earlier, this award was established around 1990 in honor of Claude Pepper, who served in both the United States Senate from 1934 to 1950 and in the House of Representatives from 1962 until his death in 1989. His service is of legendary proportions, and The Florida Bar chose to recognize his life and his contributions to the legal profession by naming its highest award that can be given a government lawyer in his honor. That Claude Pepper is the first candidate for public office that I campaigned for makes having this award that much more of an honor for me.

Later that year, I was involved—although only tangentially—in the 2000 presidential election "perfect storm." Unless you hid under a rock—and are still hiding—you know that this election and its aftermath was so bizarre it couldn't have made a plausible work of fiction. At the time, I worked for Attorney General Bob Butterworth, a Democrat who also headed Al Gore's campaign in Florida. The Secretary of State, Republican Katherine Harris, was the head of George Bush's Florida campaign. The governor, Jeb Bush, was (and still is) George Bush's brother.

Ordinarily, when a lawsuit involving the secretary of state is served on this officer, it's sent to the attorney general for representation. Not this time. Once again, because of my perceived election law expertise and experience, I was tasked with participating in this litigation. Only this time, I spent my time cloistered away in the AG's offices below the main office, at times watching the news reporters interview one election expert after another through the main office windows while simultaneously watching these interviews on TV monitors. The contrasting sight of live and TV interviews was surreal. My job was to research various election and constitutional issues pertaining to recounts, election contests and protests, and the like. I also assisted in drafting legal documents, and appeared as counsel of record in one case that made it to the Florida Supreme Court.

Originally, I was assigned to handle the oral argument in the Florida Supreme Court, but Attorney General Butterworth, recognizing that

I was a career government lawyer and that this case could well be a career-ender, assigned it to another high-ranking lawyer who was a political appointee and would leave his job at the end of Butterworth's term anyway. He also didn't want me to be the public face of his team of lawyers working on the case. This is why he had me cloistered out of the media's eye. Although I certainly wouldn't have minded a more public role at the time, I thank General Butterworth for thinking of my career. I'm told that over 300 lawyers were involved in some manner with the 2000 presidential election litigation. I can tell my children and grandchildren—if they ever ask—that I was one of them.

Up to 2002, I was an assistant attorney general. That year, the front office managers created the position of senior assistant attorney general, and my designation was changed to this new position. (I assume this change had nothing to do with age.) I had this designation for two years. The office also had a designation of special counsel and, while I didn't know what this designation meant, it was obvious that, because there were so few with this title, there must be something really special about it; so in 2004, I casually asked my supervisors how one became a special counsel.

A few weeks later, while sitting at my desk, my two immediate supervisors, including Jerry Curington, came into my office and congratulated me on becoming a special counsel. The next day, I received a call from then-Attorney General Charlie Crist congratulating me on this appointment. I received a large certificate from him designating me as special counsel, and this certificate now hangs on my den wall. I was very proud to receive this appointment, and honored that then-Attorney General—and now former Governor—Crist would personally call me to confirm the appointment and offer his congratulations. No, there was no salary increase with this "promotion." And not a single thing changed regarding my work assignments. What I did as an assistant attorney general and senior assistant attorney general was no different when I became special counsel.

I continued to handle the same type of cases during my last few years with the AG's office, but never again did I have the good fortune to be assigned the type of high-profile cases that I've described previously. Oh, I had more than my share of victories in important cases—those that meant something to those responsible for managing or operating a particular governmental program or function, including cases that saved the taxpayers hundreds of millions of dollars—but nothing of the magnitude that generated broad publicity and attention.

During my time with the AG's office, I received glowing annual evaluations from my supervisors, who were the head of the general civil litigation office and the chief of the state programs bureau. However, in 2007, with a new attorney general and director of the general civil litigation section on board, a new bi-annual evaluation system was put in place. This new system replaced the prior annual evaluation system and had a lengthy form that was far more detailed and required more work in completing than had been the case previously. At the same time this new evaluation system was instituted, office policy made it abundantly clear that (1) the lawyers representing agencies had to get explicit approval from the agency client before any document of significant importance was filed with the courts; (2) civil litigation lawyers were expected to work at least 1,800 billable hours each year or face consequences; (3) another office that was designated as specializing in appeals was given the authority to take cases from trial lawyers; and (4) lawyers could no longer talk to the press about their cases unless cleared through the communications director. I suspect that what I'm writing next had to do with my opposition to these policies; while I voiced my opposition privately to my supervisors and colleagues when the subjects came up, I never voiced my opinions publicly until now.

In late 2007, I was working on a case involving the governor's office and was required to file a request (or motion) for permission to extend the deadline for filing a significant document. I did this rather routine filing without having this one-page item reviewed by the governor's lawyer assigned to monitor the case. At this time, filings with the local federal court had recently switched to electronically filings, and because of a misunderstanding on my part regarding efiling, I had to file multiple versions of this one-pager. Evidently, the governor's lawyer—who had previously worked in the AG's office—checked the court's docket sheet and, noting this routine filing, telephoned my supervisor to complain that he didn't have occasion to review this insignificant one-page document, and he must have been put out over this.

I was sitting in my office one Friday afternoon when my two supervisors walked in and told me I needed to accompany them to the front office located in the Capitol (most of the AG's staff was located in the Collins building about two blocks from the Capitol) to discuss the case. Since the case involved the governor's office, I thought nothing of this. After all, I had handled numerous cases involving the governors, and had been in the Capitol numerous times to brief managers on the status of cases. The three of us walked into the AG's conference room where we met up with a third supervisor. I immediately sensed this was going to be different kind of session. And it certainly was.

While the front office supervisor remained silent, the other two proceeded to ream me out over my handling of the case—I failed to have the governor's lawyer review my perfunctory filing; I was not following policy; etc., etc., etc. This was not a session to discuss case strategy; it was a "woodshed" session. After about an hour of pretending that I took this seriously, the meeting ended with a strong admonition to follow policy of, in effect, allowing the agency lawyers to dictate the contents of my filings with the courts. After this meeting, I went back to my office, dropped off my papers, shut down my computer, and immediately left for home.

To say I was angry would be a mischaracterization; I was livid. My initial plan after this confrontation was to walk in Monday morning, drop off my resignation letter, tell them to take this job and shove it, gather my personal property and walk out. Over the weekend, I called a close friend whose opinion I highly regard and explained my situation. He rightfully said that I needed to calm down; that I had only two and a half years left before retirement; that the state was depositing a few thousand dollars each month into a retirement account separate from my already earned pension; and that the job market was not very promising. He was right on all counts, so I swallowed my pride and went to work as if nothing had happened. What I found so humorous is that the division director came over Monday morning and said he was glad that I returned to work. What I wanted to tell him I won't say here because a child or lady might read it.

Performance Evaluations

It was shortly after this woodshed session that I received the "evaluation from hell" from both supervisors, critical of just about everything about me. According to them, I was slowing down, getting old, appeared out of touch, didn't communicate properly or well, was over-the-hill, washed up, etc., etc., etc., ad nauseam. I am not prone to anger; but I had never been as angry in my entire professional life as I was when I was blindsided by this evaluation. Not a single word came from my supervisors that I was going to get a low evaluation. My caseload continued to be among the highest—if not the highest—in the state programs office; my success rate remained consistently high; not once had any judge, agency official or employee uttered a single negative word about me; in fact, one Florida Supreme Court justice asked when I would be appearing before the court again because several lawyers from the office who had appeared were not well prepared, and that I had always come before the court well prepared. In addition, I had been named in several Who's Who publications, including Who's Who in America, the latter at approximately the same time as I received this evaluation. Since I concluded that this evaluation couldn't have been performance-based, it was obvious to me that its purpose was to send a message that I needed to conform and that, unless I did, I was no longer appreciated or wanted. Of course, I also wondered how someone could go from being a top-level trusted lawyer with my documented credentials to being washed up in six months. It didn't make sense to me then, and doesn't to this day. Perhaps its purpose wasn't to make sense. When a person's self-worth is attacked as mine was here, I believe the reaction is usually predictable: first there's anger, then resentment, followed by reflection and finally, change. I went through three of these stages; I saw no need to change. I reasoned that I didn't make it this far by being characterized as I was by these supervisors.

Because evaluations of professionals are, for the most part, subjective, I did check with one objective measurement that used to be of importance when the state gave merit pay increases. Each lawyer was required to maintain reading files. The files consisted of each month's filings with the courts, and correspondence. Over the years, the volume of paperwork served as a measure of work production and caseload volume. I can say that, for the vast majority of the time, my reading files were the most, or nearly the most, voluminous of all lawyers in the state programs bureau. This high volume of production didn't change during the period of my evaluation from hell. While the Internet and email caused a drop in correspondence over the years, the drafting and filing of court documents remained consistently high for me. So, checking this objective measurement only confirmed what I already believed: there was no legitimate work-related basis for this low evaluation.

I understand the importance of evaluations. A valid evaluation system serves the purpose of accurately measuring performance and of gauging whether expectations are being met. Evaluations accomplish this by pointing out strengths so an employee can expand and capitalize on them, and also showing areas for improvement along with how improvement can be achieved. However, when used as a battering ram or to intimidate, blindside or sandbag employees, evaluations are nothing more than a disingenuous euphemism that serve no useful purpose in building morale and improving performance. I understand that in 2007 supervisors were told to include more "areas of improvement" in evaluations because they were becoming too positive. If that were the case, than it's up to management to take the high road and come up with a system that truly evaluates performance, not condemns by using meaningless buzz words or useless oversimplifications devoid of specific, defined perceived aberrant conduct and specific ways to improve. This evaluation system was instituted at a time when state employees stopped getting annual pay raises, so on top of receiving no additional compensation as the cost of living increased, employees were getting more and more critical evaluations. What a great way to boost morale!!!

Expressions such as "The employee did not meet required expectations" without factually explaining this failure with specific examples render the evaluation worthless. As a personal example, one of the evaluation areas concerns courtroom performance; I was graded down on this in 2007 even though not a single supervisor ever attended a court session with me during the evaluation period. When it comes to expectations, for a lawyer, this means that it is expected that the lawyer will conform to the Code of Professional Responsibility and handle his/her cases in a timely, professional and ethical manner. Not once did a supervisor point out where I was deficient with regard to these expectations. I considered my evaluation from hell to be a sham because it violated every principle of an effective performance-measuring system.

I believe that for an evaluation system to work effectively, there should be a method in place whereby managers can be evaluated by the managed or supervised. I've never personally seen a situation in which subordinates evaluated supervisors, but I understand it's been done, and I see no downside to this. I presume the prevailing attitude that focuses exclusively on top-down evaluations is born of the notion that "inferior" workers aren't competent enough to evaluate the "superior" supervisors. This is hogwash. Workers are smart enough to judge the effectiveness of a supervisor. Unfortunately, managers are judged only by managers with absolutely no input from the managed or supervised. In short, in the evaluation process, the opinions of the workers don't count. This makes the process more one of potential intimidation of an employee rather than a legitimate assessment of actual performance. Any bottom-up evaluation component of a global evaluation system would, of necessity, have to be anonymous to avoid retaliation of any kind, however subtle. If one or two evaluations of a supervisor are low, but the rest are high, this would signal to upper management that these evaluations are more of a vendetta than an honest appraisal. If, however, the evaluations of a manager demonstrate a clear pattern of low performance, then the problem lies with that particular supervisor and must be addressed by upper management.

Lawyers are not trinket-makers or assembly line operators; they are professionals schooled and trained in exercising reasoned judgment. Using a widget-based system to evaluate lawyers is nonsense. Moreover, any evaluation system that is more directed to undercutting professionalism is a failed system—and that's precisely what this evaluation system was. I say this even though my last couple of evaluations were, for the most part, extremely positive and glowing, with the exception of work ethic based on the 1,800 hours of billable time policy, which I'll get to shortly. If a lawyer files his papers on time, has a good track record, schedules and attends meetings and hearings on time, is well regarded by the judiciary and peers, there is no need for any time-consuming evaluation system. If there are deficiencies, by all means point them out with specific examples and suggest ways to improve. If there is no improvement, show him/her the door. Evaluations are really that simple when they pertain to lawyers. The best measure of a lawyer's performance is results. This criterion was relegated to the back seat in this new evaluation system.

As I considered this evaluation from hell, I recalled a psychology course I took in college in which I learned that there are basically two types of people: other-directed and inner-directed. Those who are other-directed need to be constantly prodded to get to work and stay on task. They are the procrastinators. I understand that most people are other-directed. The inner-directed need no such prodding or guidance; all they need is to be given an assignment. Once given, you can bank on it being timely and properly performed. They are better time managers; more organized and more efficient. I won't say I'm inner-directed; I believe my results and recognition for my work speak for themselves. I certainly don't need to be prodded to do any task. I do not procrastinate and have no difficulty making decisions. Against this backdrop, to effectively be told otherwise cut deep. I simply refused to accept it, and I moved on, doing what I had been doing for the previous 35 years. Some may call this arrogance; if it is, I proudly plead guilty.

As I said about the evaluation I received 28 years earlier when I worked at HRS, I have no trouble accepting criticism when it's constructively directed and serves a useful purpose. I had been on the receiving end of criticism during some of my hearings and appellate arguments, and I took them at face value because in the vast majority of instances, the criticism was both constructive and instructive. It was never mean-spirited. The evaluation from hell was not constructive, served no useful purpose, was mean-spirited, and I firmly believe was the result of some agenda or motive that was never shared with me. To put it more directly, I don't like it when people use their authority to take a cheap shot at someone simply because they can. And I believe to this day that this is precisely what happened to me.

There is also a psychological description called Type A and Type B personalities. At the risk of oversimplification, Type B folks are laid back and are generally inclined to let the world go by. Type A folks are generally on task and "get-it-done-now" types; they are the screamers and door-slammers. I would characterize myself as a benevolent Type

A. I don't scream, yell, look for scapegoats, pull hair or slam doors. I just like to get things done quickly and efficiently; I have no patience for unexcused delays. Once I'm done with a project, it's up to others to move things along. I believe that by completing a task early rather than putting it off to a later date, I allow for time to deal with the unexpected event. If a person puts off doing something, and does this with increasing frequency, when that unexpected event occurs, he/she doesn't have time to handle it properly and complete the matters on which he/she procrastinated. A person's reputation is all-too-often sullied because of the one time he/she promised to deliver but, because of procrastination, failed to timely do so. Letting people down on a promise or commitment is not good for one's reputation; people are more inclined to remember the one failure than the many successes.

I used to take a good ribbing from my colleagues because my office and desk were so neat. Papers were placed in orderly fashion on my desk; there were no piles of books or papers on the floor. Except when I was actually working on a project that required use of several books, my desk usually had a notepad in the middle, the day's mail in one corner, drafts of documents awaiting final reading and filing in another, and the item currently being worked on next to my notepad. That was it. Once the document was completed, the books were returned to the library and my desk returned to its former state.

During my 40 years of practice, I was constantly amazed at how a lawyer's office arrangement manifested that lawyer's personality and actions. Some offices were so cluttered with paper, it looked as if a tornado had gone through it. Others had dozens of stacks of paper all over the desk, credenza, the floor, on window sills, etc. These lawyers would scurry around with furrowed brow, looking busy or distracted, doing the White Rabbit's "I'm late, I'm late. For a very important date. No time to say goodbye hello, I'm late, I'm late, I'm late" routine from Alice in Wonderland. Their conduct more often than not matched the state of their offices.

A few offices were neat and organized, as were the lawyers. I couldn't work in a cluttered, disorganized environment. However, as the saying goes, different strokes for different folks. I am proud, though, that in all of my years of practice, never once did I have to ask a court for a postponement or continuance resulting from anything I did or failed to do. I wonder how many lawyers can make this same statement.

In attempting to be as honest with myself as possible regarding my evaluations, and recognizing that emotions can color logic, I also wondered how I could get such a poor evaluation considering how many times I volunteered to take cases others didn't want and refused to take. Or how other lawyers in the office who were disorganized as their offices indicated managed to receive high evaluations. As I surmised earlier, perhaps the reason for this was to shock me into following agency policies and not complain about them to my colleagues. If this were the purpose, however, the evaluation from hell failed miserably. I discuss these policies and my view of them under the heading "Dysfunctional management."

Another failing I have, in addition to being too impatient, is that I have a long memory when I believe someone has wronged me. I have never forgotten the 1979 set-up evaluation, or the woodshed session and evaluation from hell in 2007. While I chose not to have them affect my performance, they remain part of the public record of my more than 32 years as a state government employee. While I certainly agree that no one is perfect, I also believe my record speaks for itself in a manner that renders these evaluations suspect. I believe they are more a statement of the supervisors than they are of me. If they believe otherwise, let them tell their version in their books.

What hurt more than anything else is that, between the 2006 election and the inauguration date of the new attorney general, I was called by a transition team member for Bill McCollum and asked about the person who at that time was a colleague in the same bureau, as to his fitness to become civil litigation director, an assistant deputy attorney general. I recommended him for this job. Over several years that we worked together, I thought of him as a friend as well as a colleague, and would visit with him frequently in his office and we'd have lunch together quite often. After this evaluation, that feeling of friendship on my part came to an abrupt end. Whether right or wrong, I nevertheless felt a sense of betrayal. While I remained civil and cordial, I didn't seek him out or visit him in his office unless absolutely necessary. This evaluation was a relationship changer—never again did I have any feeling for either supervisor other than the usual employer-employee relationship. They were management; I was labor. That was it.

Throughout my career in government, I considered myself a team player, the proof of which is that quite often, I volunteered to take cases others didn't want; offering advice to those who sought it from me—in short, doing whatever I could to assist in the operation of the agency. No more. After this evaluation, I became a free agent. While I still helped others who sought advice, and visited with my colleagues to discuss cases, never again did I volunteer to take cases. Never again did I approach my supervisors unless absolutely necessary. I stayed as far away from their offices as I could. For the very first time, I gave more than a passing thought to retirement. I really wanted to get out, but I had 2 1/2 years to go. I vowed to make the best of it, but lower my profile in doing so. While my relationship with my co-workers remained the same, I did whatever it took to avoid contact with my immediate supervisors.

I put up a good front and played the bureaucratic game, but it was all smoke-and-mirrors on my part; inside, I was seething. I never again felt the comfort or sense of trust that I previously had for either supervisor. Time supposedly heals all wounds, but this one cut too deep because the things they wrote are a permanent part of my personnel file and are a public record. Even though I eventually received glowing evaluations from them toward the end of my employment, and they even spearheaded a wonderful retirement party for me, the truth is I changed nothing with regard to my work habits or methods from that evaluation forward; but I believe they thought I did. None of these low evaluations affected my employment or the awards and honors I received. In fact, they didn't affect anything related to my employment status. Since my employment time was short, there were no more promotions to be had, and no pay raises would be given during the rest of my tenure. What they did by their evaluation was to affect me and my record; and that was more than enough to make me angry and to engage in supervisor avoidance techniques for the remainder of my time with the office.

Dysfunctional management

Despite my supervisors' admonition, I refused to follow their policy of effectively giving agency lawyers the final say over my work product before filing my papers with the courts. One of the things I learned in my years of practice was how to work the system; I put this knowledge to work in avoiding this ludicrous policy that, in my view, conflicted with my duties and obligations of independence of judgment set out in the Florida Supreme Court-adopted Code of Professional Responsibility. If an agency lawyer made alterations to my draft documents that didn't affect the issues I was arguing, I'd let them go under the "no harm, no foul" rule. However, on the few occasions where changes were made that were consequential and that I couldn't live with, I simply filed my version, and sent a hard copy or a separate email containing the agency lawyer's edited version to him/her. Only once did an agency lawyer call me on this, and I white-lied it by explained that my filing with the court was an oversight and that I would correct it. Fortunately, the next day the court issued a ruling in my favor. The agency lawyer never followed up further, and neither did I. One other point—in every situation where I filed my version instead of the agency lawyer's edited one, I prevailed before the court.

I took then—and continue to take seriously today—the lawyers' Code of Professional Responsibility, especially the parts that provide that a lawyer shall exercise independent judgment in all his dealings, and will not make any argument that is frivolous or dishonest. The Claude Pepper Outstanding Government Lawyer plaque says in the engraved lettering that it is given in recognition of the "highest ideals of dedication, professionalism and ethics in serving the public as a government lawyer." On more occasions than I care to note, I have had to literally save the agency client from itself, and under no circumstances was I going to compromise my integrity, "dedication, professionalism and ethics" to the whim of an agency lawyer, many of whom were recent admittees to The Florida Bar and had little trial or advocacy experience.

I reasoned that if the AG's office wanted to have agency lawyers dictate the handling of a case, then by all means, let them handle the cases from start to finish. The attorney general's lawyers are not needed if all they are going to do is submit drafts to agency lawyers who control the contents of the final product. Can you imagine any private practitioner submitting his work product to a client for approval? Can you imagine any client dictating to his lawyer what must be included in or removed from that lawyer's written papers? That client would become a former client and sent packing in a nanosecond! I wasn't going to be part of this charade; if I was going to be assigned a case and become attorney of record with my reputation on the line with the judges as well as my peers on the other side, I was going to fully abide by the lawyer's professional and ethical standards, policy to the contrary be damned.

Here's a minuscule practice that was instituted in 2007 that didn't make sense: the civil division assistant deputy invited all special counsel to attend his bureau and section managers meeting. I was familiar with managers meetings; although not a supervisor or manager, I used to attend them at the DOT and HRS during my time at these agencies because I handled cases that impacted policy. Usually, they were presided over by the secretary, deputy secretary or division director. A lot of what happens at these meetings is posturing by lower-level managers who are more interested in looking good in the eyes of the boss than actually contributing to any decision-making or management execution. I saw the same pattern at the AG managers meeting. Often, I'd find myself sitting at this huge rectangular table wondering what the hell I was doing there; I was not a manager and had no management information to impart.

Typically, the presiding manager would make some comments about meetings he attended with the top managers from other parts of the agency, proceed to go to the other civil division offices located in other cities (hooked up by internal TV or via conference call), then go around the room seeking comments. The "look-at-me" posturing that went on was a great source of entertainment for me. Occasionally, just for fun, I'd do my own posturing by mentioning a case I was handling, or make a comment that generated discussion on matters of questionable importance. The only benefit to me in being there is that these meetings allowed me to find out what was going on in the department that other staff lawyers in the office were not be privy to. It was a good way for me to gain information; perhaps I learned too much.

The next evaluation in early 2008 was much more positive, but not like the ones I received during my first 20 years with the agency. To show how unproductive this new evaluation system was, toward the end of my employment, the immediate supervisor instituted a procedure whereby the lawyers themselves prepared their own evaluations, to be submitted to the managers for their review and final action. In doing the drafting, however, the lawyers were admonished to be honest. Sure! Of course, this took the drafting burden from the supervisors and put it on the staff lawyers; perhaps the supervisors viewed this evaluation effort as a waste of their time. If so, I certainly concurred with that. However, if this was the system that they were going to rely on, I certainly wasn't going to draft anything of a negative nature. Why should I do the supervisors' work? The evaluation form required several pages of drafting narratives for what were called KPIs, or Key Performance Indicators. For my last few evaluations, I put all my writing skills to work in drafting glowing narratives praising my performance, my contributions to the office, extolling my virtues, etc. I deliberately laid it on real thick. And what did I get back? Almost verbatim of what I submitted. What a great system for evaluating employees, eh?

Toward the latter part of my years with the AG's office, another policy was instituted that I found personally objectionable and another real morale buster. In 2001, the office hired a solicitor general whose duty it was to set up an office similar to the United States Solicitor General's Office wherein appeals would be handled. This meant that this new office had the authority to take an important case from the trial lawyer when that case was appealed. This office focused primarily on cases that were taken on appeal to or review by the United State Supreme Court, the Florida Supreme Court, or the federal Eleventh Circuit Court of Appeal. I worked with many of the lawyers in this new office, and had a good working relationship with them—until 2007.

In the latter part of 2006, I headed up a team of lawyers who successfully handled an election law case involving the propriety of the use of touch screen voting equipment in a non-jury bench trial (judge only) in federal district court. When that case was appealed, it was transferred to the solicitor general's office without any input from me. At the time, I was a 35-year member of The Florida Bar; a 20-year employee with the

AG's office; received numerous honors and glowing evaluations. I had argued cases before both the United States and Florida supreme courts and every federal and state appellate court in the state's jurisdiction. Despite this, the case was inexplicably assigned to a relatively new lawyer who was to have his first appellate oral argument. While this lawyer had an exemplary academic record (I didn't) and had clerked for a federal appellate judge, I nevertheless felt that I should have been consulted and either given the option of handling this case on appeal or at least be assigned as co-counsel.

Taking a case away from a lawyer who handled the matter at the trial level was a new experience for me; and quite frankly, I was put out by this cavalier treatment. No thought was given to my feelings or sense of pride I have in handling my own cases; nor was consideration given to the fact that I knew the trial record inside out. After the case was over at the appellate level (an easy win for the handling lawyer, since the trial record was carefully and fully made and the legal memos drafted for the trial court set out the legal arguments used on appeal), I inquired why this transfer was done. It was explained that appeals are within the domain of the Solicitor General's Office, this office was created specifically for this purpose, and I was not to question staff's judgment. My reaction to this explanation is an epithet I don't need to spell out.

There are two theories of the practice of law that are involved here. The first is the creation of a special office skilled at handling appeals. The other is the "hired gun" approach whereby a client will retain a high-profile lawyer to handle the appeal. The reason for this approach is that the judges will be impressed with the "hired gun," which in turn will lead to a favorable ruling, or so the theory goes. I have never seen this approach work effectively.

I understand the reasoning behind hiring a skilled appellate lawyer to handle difficult appeals; but I don't agree that simply because a specialized office exists, it should have the unfettered authority to take a case away from an experienced lawyer. Moreover, I don't buy into the "hired gun" mentality upon which this policy is essentially founded. I've personally argued cases against "hired guns"—former legislators, former supreme court justices, former judges—and felt embarrassed for them when they were asked a question for which they were totally unprepared. For the most part, these lawyers don't always make great advocates. Just like great baseball players don't make great managers, so it is with judges, legislators and other public officials who are hired to be advocates in a judicial forum. Judges tend to look at all sides of an issue; legislators are thinking of how things will play out for constituencies; executive directors and secretaries of agencies are focusing on policy considerations. Legal advocacy requires a different set of skills finely honed over years of experience. At the risk of overstating my point, you can't make a silk purse out of a sow's ear.

Another litigation strategy I've seen used is the retaining of prominent lawyers to simply sit at counsel table. This is what a friend of mine calls the "potted plant" approach and is done to persuade the court to rule in that party's favor. Having a former judge, legislator, governor, agency secretary, etc., sitting at counsel table might give a client a sense of comfort. In my experience, however, this form of gamesmanship is also rarely—if at all—effective. When these types of games are played, everyone knows it.

When a case is reassigned simply because it can be done by those in an office created especially for this purpose, the policy is not conducive to effective staffing unless the trial lawyer is permitted to be involved in some meaningful manner as counsel of record; if for no other reason than that it's a morale buster for the trial lawyer.

Lawyers generally work for government for two reasons, money and pride. Since government lawyers who work in the trenches rather than simply push paper as administrators don't make that much money, all that's left is pride; when that's unceremoniously stripped away, the result is low morale. And during the last few years with the AG's office, morale was low; very low. Some of it was due to the lack of pay increases; a lot of it was a result of bad policies dumped on staff lawyers who were overworked and felt unappreciated. Here's a funny one. In an effort to build morale among the entire staff, the managers held ice cream socials periodically, at which the managers would personally serve ice cream. Publicly, everyone voiced happiness; privately, quite a number told me they thought this was a joke. We got a good laugh out of this wonderful effort at boosting morale. Staffers need to pay their bills and what do they get? An ice cream social!

Here's the second most graphic example of a bad policy dumped on staff lawyers. During the period beginning in 2007, the AG's office began rigidly enforcing the requirement that each lawyer doing work for another agency under contract bill or record a minimum of 1,800 hours per year. "Billable hours" means those hours for which a lawyer can reasonably be expected to bill a client; both rule of court and our jurisprudence define what is and is not proper to be billed to a client. Recall that this is on top of the absence of any pay raise and the requirement for agency review of a lawyer's work product before filing with the court. The agency managers reasoned that this is what most—if not all—lawyers in the private sector bill. Evidently, no one involved in the formation of this policy bothered to read The Florida Bar reports on lawyers' billable hours. Had they done that, they would have found that most lawyers bill in the 1,400-1,600-hour range.

The office managers equated 1,800 hours with work ethic. I usually averaged about 1,500-1,600 billable hours or so each year, so when I failed to meet this required standard, I was evaluated as deficient in my work ethic. In light of The Florida Bar's standard for billable hours, and my recognition by the Bar for, among other things, my dedication to the practice on behalf of the public—including ethics—this method of evaluation is not only faulty, but downright ludicrous as it was applied to me. What these managers failed to understand is that it's not the number of hours recorded as having worked that's really important; it's the amount of actual work done in those hours that's critical. Holding all lawyers to the same billable hours standard, particularly in the public sector, fails to take into account different levels of performance. It's obvious some lawyers work faster than others, are better organized than others, and are more efficient in time management than others. Why should speed and efficiency be punished at the expense of inefficiency and slowness; particularly when the recording of billable hours is based entirely on the honor system? There is no way for a supervisor to know whether a lawyer reporting having "worked" 1,800 actually did so.

I was always a fast worker—no doubt a direct result of my news reporting days when I had to constantly meet fixed deadlines. I could read a lawsuit and quickly focus on how to properly deal with it. I didn't waste time gnashing my teeth or thrashing about trying to come up with a case strategy; both strategic planning and legal research came naturally fast to me.

The rules of The Florida Bar expressly prohibit padding of billable hours, the practice whereby lawyers add hours to their bills to clients for which they performed no work. The reason for this flat prohibition is obvious: no client must ever pay for nonperformance, and no lawyer must ever effectively defraud a client. A private lawyer's hourly rate is supposed to take into account his background, knowledge, expertise and efficiency. In the AG's office, the respective agencies that retain the office are billed for the staff lawyers' work, and the so-called rate range for an assistant attorney general, senior AAG or special counsel is not that great—perhaps $10-$20 per hour billed directly to the requesting agency that has funds budgeted for litigation purposes. The question I frequently asked myself is why should a lawyer who works fast and is very efficient be treated the same way as a lawyer who doesn't work as fast as or isn't as focused? For example, if it takes lawyer A two hours to perform a certain task, and lawyer B can do the same task in one hour, why should lawyer B be penalized for working harder and faster by billing one hour while the other lawyer can bill for two hours? Since the relative level of compensation for government lawyers is not comparable to the private sector, a government lawyer can't bill for his expertise and proficiency as can his private counterpart. Besides, payment to the AG's office for a lawyer's time was coming from the taxpayers anyway, rather than a private client's pocket.

Taking all these factors into account, I can certainly see how lawyer B could conclude that if he were going to be treated like those other lawyers who worked at a slower pace, he wasn't going to cheat himself by paying a price for his efficiency. Therefore, in order for lawyer B to be treated fairly, he could easily add additional time to, or pad, his actual hours worked to reflect what it would take other less efficient, less organized and less focused lawyers to perform essentially the same tasks.

I felt that the billable hours system rewarded the inefficient; to me, this was a silly rule that made no sense in the public sector except perhaps for the administrative number crunchers. I believed then, and believe now, that this was yet another situation where, if a government lawyer is performing well as demonstrated by results, there is no need for this type of requirement; if he or she is performing poorly, then it's up to competent supervisors to take care of this problem.

In the private sector, a lawyer's primary means of compensation is based on the number of billable hours of work performed multiplied by his/her hourly rate. That rate is usually in the hundreds of dollars per hour range, in significant part because the lawyer must pay all overhead from that income. Taking the income levels for lawyers billing 1,800 hours and factor in what the AG's office didn't-the average hourly rate of pay-and the result is a significant income well over what a government lawyer makes. For example, a lawyer who bills at $250 an hour for 1,800 hours will bring in $450,000 a year. If his/her overhead is even half of that, his/her personal gross income is $225,000 a year. And this is only at the rate of $250 per hour! More experienced lawyers are permitted to charge substantially higher hourly rates than $250.

The AG's effort to treat the 1,800 billable hours in the private sector as the standard for measuring the staff lawyer's work ethic, in addition to being faulty for failing to take into account individual work habits, is also faulty because of the vast difference in income level between the private and public sectors. In the public sector, a lawyer is paid a salary; regardless of the outcome of the case, he/she still gets that same salary—a salary that must be provided for in the government's budget. Only the AG's attorneys that represent state agencies or state officials are placed under a billable hours system. This, however, is not done for the purpose of compensating the lawyer, but to provide an objective measure of the lawyer's performance. For purely management purposes, the AG's office breaks down a lawyer's salary to an hourly rate—frequently far less than $100 per hour and more around the $55-$75 range per hour. This hourly rate is in line with what is used when billing an agency for a lawyer's time. For example, if a special counsel's assigned hourly rate is $75 and he works 10 hours on a case, the agency will be billed $750. What's important here is that this is not what the lawyer will be paid. If the lawyer is paid $90,000 a year as salary, and he bills 1,800 hours, his hourly rate would be $50. No lawyer in the private sector bills at such a low rate. The AG's method simply allows the agency to know how much to pay the AG's office from the agency budget. That's it. I hope you readily see that the number of billable hours reported by AG lawyers has no bearing on the lawyer's salary or the taxpayers who fund the agency budgets through legislative appropriations. In short, there would be no loss to any taxpayer by lawyer B's reporting of billable hours.

For the first 20 years I was with the AG's office, there was no need for lawyers to bill 1,800 hours a year. During this time, there was no criticism of the quality of work done by the lawyers in the state programs bureau of which I'm aware. In fact, several lawyers were recognized for their outstanding contributions to the profession. How this rigid adherence to billable hours enhanced the quality of work or heightened the morale of the lawyers escapes me. In fact, except for a change in budgeting, I don't recall any explanation for this change from a quality assurance perspective, except that it was going to be done this way from now on.

Unfortunately, some government supervisors tend to look for easy, objective measurements of a lawyer's performance, and billable hours is certainly at first blush an easy standard to employ. The more hours billed, the more productive and efficient the lawyer is, so the reasoning goes. This is absolute nonsense. A far better way to judge performance are, in addition to results obtained, opinions of the judges and agency clients; recognition by peers; and sharp supervisors who know good lawyering when they see it. This approach, however, takes more effort than simply looking at billable hours. Far too often, well-meaning people take the path of least resistance rather than the more difficult path that will produce better results. That was certainly the situation here.

In my state government experience, I found that all-too-often supervisors, instead of evaluating an employee on the full one-year or six-month period between evaluations, will pick a single, isolated event and have that govern the entirety of the evaluation period. If an employee is to be given a negative evaluation, generally he/she will be blindsided by it. There won't be any prior counseling or forewarning of this permanent record in one's employment file. To me, this sandbagging demonstrates poor management. If a supervisor is truly going to manage properly, it is his/her duty to counsel an employee before dropping the axe on the unsuspected. I believe this lazy method of supervision is far more pervasive than one might think. The reason: again, it's the path of least resistance for the supervisor.

I believe one of the driving forces behind the biannual evaluations, my evaluation from hell, and the rigid adherence to these policies is that the deputy involved in their enforcement had a strong military background and evidently believed that good management meant superimposing this military management style on lawyers who are schooled and trained to be independent thinkers responsible for the exercise of sound judgment. Mixing the two in the public employment sector simply won't fit, unless the goal is to decrease morale. With AG lawyers not getting a pay raise for several years, office morale wasn't very high to begin with; but adding this fuel onto the low morale fire only further lowered morale. I don't think this was ever understood. If it was and not addressed, well, this says more about management than about the staff lawyers. End of sermon on evaluations.

Well, not exactly. Florida Trend magazine performs an annual survey among lawyers throughout the state and publishes an edition on Florida's best lawyers, which the magazine dubs its "Legal Elite." I was chosen as one of 62 government lawyers throughout the state for this designation in 2008, and for a second time in 2009-after the woodshed session and evaluation from hell. Only my announced retirement prevented consideration for future editions. Over-the-hill and washed up? Indeed!!!

The discussion of my last couple of years with the office raises an issue that has perplexed me during the entirety of my career. There is a perception that placing a lawyer in a management position converts him/her into a leader. There is a vast difference, however, between occupying a management position and demonstrating effective leadership skills. Anyone can be a manager simply by being put in a management position; it takes a special kind of person, however, to be an effective leader that accomplishes clearly defined tasks and produces positive results. I have seen dozens of men and women appointed to management positions who were not effective leaders; conversely, I've seen lawyers who, although not in management positions, were nevertheless sought out for advice and counsel that they couldn't obtain from their managers. The reason for this is because these non-managers possessed effective leadership skills.

In the government sector, where a manager literally holds the employee's career in his/her hands (through promotion, evaluations, pay increases, etc.), the all-too-typical management style is that of intimidation. This is the "do this or else" approach which may get the intended results in the short term, but usually at the price of low morale and an overall reduction in the quality of work because of the undue pressure and stress such a method places on the employee. I have also seen managers who exerted leadership through the time-tested method of inspiring others by honest and ethical conduct, humility, sensitivity and loyalty, clarity of communications and good listening skills, preparation and organization, confidence and positivity, instilling motivation, demonstrating wisdom and generally leading by example rather than by edict or threat. In my experience, however, this has been the exception, not the rule. In my view, too many managers use the intimidation method because it's easier and driven by ego and power.

The bottom line here is that employees will gravitate to those who demonstrate the qualities of leadership if those who are put in charge fail to do so. Lawyers are, by dint of Supreme Court rule and tradition, trained to use analytical mental processing. They don't make widgets or operate on an assembly line. The traditional employer-employee relationship, when imposed on lawyers, creates a unique situation that requires skills not ordinarily found in that traditional relationship where measurement can be made by relying on objective production numbers. Relying on objective standards to judge those whose function is subjective in nature is a slippery evaluation slope. It behooves government managers—especially those who supervise lawyers—to realize this and work to truly equate management with effective leadership and adopt an evaluation system that takes the judgmental nature of the profession into account and eliminates the widget-counting approach.

My reason for devoting so much attention to evaluations is that employees will be subject to evaluation, regardless of the nature of employment. Therefore, it is vital that whatever system is in place must be a fair one. Each employee who works for a supervisor—particularly in the government setting—is going to be evaluated in some form or another. More often than not, what is learned by others about an employee will be what's contained in those evaluations. Any employer looking for employees will want to look at employee evaluations. Therefore, they must be both accurate and honest in the totality of their appraisal. The problem is that it takes more time to perfect a fair system tailored to the type of work involved and overall mission of the office; human nature, however, dictates that the path of least resistance be taken. Simplicity must be avoided if the employee evaluation system is to function properly. A good manager will seek full input from others in crafting a fair plan; beware of the plan that is thrust upon employees without their input.

By this rather lengthy narrative on evaluations and management, I'm certainly not suggesting that the entire AG's office was run this way. In fact, during my time there, the agency had some outstanding managers/supervisors with whom I got along with extremely well. I am just reflecting on what it was like for me—as well as for my close colleagues—during my last few years with the office in the State Programs office. Had the managers not imposed on the civil litigation section the silly policies I've discussed above and stuck to the previous management style, I think the agency would have been far better off. The morale is don't tinker with success; it can only make matters worse.

The high-profile cases that I discussed previously all took place during the almost 16 years that Bob Butterworth served as attorney general. I also served under three other attorneys general: Richard Doran (who was appointed by the governor to serve the last couple of months of Butterworth's fourth term when he resigned to run for the Florida Senate), Charlie Crist (2003-2007) and Bill McCollum (2007-2011). Government lawyers have long been considered by the private bar as second-class lawyers. Whether true or not, when Butterworth became attorney general, he promised to raise the stature and enhance the image of those who chose to make government service their legal careers. He was faithful to his promise. He was instrumental in increasing salaries;

providing for an awards incentive program; and getting The Florida Bar to create a government lawyer section and provide input to the Bar's Board of Governors; among other innovations, all designed to elevate the government lawyer in the minds of his/her peers in the private sector, and the public generally.

During Butterworth's years, I had full authority to talk to the press when contacted about a case I was handling. I believe other lawyers had similar authority. I didn't have to deflect such calls to a communications director or press aide; being a former news reporter myself, I know how to talk their language and not make misstatements that could come back to haunt. All that was necessary was to let the managers know of a press contact so as to avoid being blindsided should a member of the press contact the attorney general directly about a particular case.

In the last few years of my service, and after Butterworth left, the changes that he initiated had to a large extent faded away. Beginning in 2007, when lawyers were contacted by the press about their cases, they had to inform the media they were not permitted to talk to the press; all media contacts had to go through a press aide. I can understand letting the managers know of a contact, but having the press shuffled off to a non-lawyer press aide to discuss the intricacies of a case simply didn't—and doesn't—make sense. All too often, all the press aide can do is offer a "no comment," "the case is under review" or some other trite and curt brush-off that is unresponsive to the inquiry. Not only doesn't this satisfy the reporter, it has the potential of raising a red flag to the press that the attorney general (or any agency official) is trying to hide something. I can see the wisdom of this policy if the inquiry is about whether a case is going to be appealed, or perhaps any other question that implicates a policy decision. But it makes no sense where the press inquiry—like most of them in my experience—is simply to find out what a decision means, or what a point made in a legal document filed by the lawyer means. I know I was embarrassed when I had to tell a reporter that I couldn't make any comment on my cases, even if the inquiry concerned a matter I wrote about or mentioned during a hearing, trial or oral argument. I don't believe it's in the best interests of the office to effectively centralize and control media access to lawyers by imposing a press aide or media director between reporter and lawyer.

By way of summarizing my last few years with the state, the almost maniacal 1,800 annual billable hours requirement; the requirement to get the agency lawyer's approval before filing a document; the unfettered authority to take cases from a trial lawyer when that case is on appeal; and prohibiting a lawyer familiar with a case to talk to the press about the case, individually and together undermined morale, adversely impacted professionalism and stunted the efforts to heighten the standing and stature of government lawyers. If the so-called management style of the last two or so years of my employment taught me anything, it's that leadership by threats, intimidation, whip-cracking, or any similar method, is not leadership that will lead to positive, productive results. To me, this is simply bad management.

Under the management scheme in effect during the last few years of my time, there is no way that I would have had the opportunities to handle such high-profile cases as I did during Butterworth's years. With the establishment of the solicitor general's office and the ensuing ability to take cases from the trial-level lawyers, I certainly wouldn't have been permitted to argue a case before the United States Supreme Court.

It is with some sadness that I write these words because there remain many excellent, highly competent lawyers with whom I worked who will never get the opportunities I had simply because they won't be given the chance. Butterworth was proud to say he would pit his lawyers against any lawyer in the country; I never heard this type of expression in my last several years with the agency. Having said all of this about these policies and practices, I don't know whether any of them remain in place today; I can only hope that the light has dawned on current management and that these ineffective policies in the AG's office are no more. I have no doubt, however, that some of these policies exist somewhere in state government in one form or another. And that's sad.

My Last Few Months On The Public Payroll

As 2010 unfolded, the number of cases assigned to me began to dwindle, which I certainly expected. Those that were newly assigned were quickie turnarounds—usually a disgruntled litigant who sues a judge because he didn't like the judge's decision, or one who sues a prosecuting attorney for bringing charges against him and taking his case to court. These suits against judges and prosecutors usually end with a single filing based on well-established legal doctrines of absolute immunity from such lawsuits against these constitutional officers for simply doing what their jobs call for.

I also spent a lot of time transferring cases to other lawyers in the office. As my workload dwindled, more and more friends and colleagues were giving me friendly advice, usually in the form of "With your experience and institutional knowledge, your phone will be ringing off the hook with great offers and opportunities." Very well-meaning atta boys and pats on the back. As of this writing, however, I have yet to receive that first phone call. As I absorbed these compliments, I was under no illusion. I knew that, if I were to work again, one of two things had to happen: either a government agency or a private law firm would have to hire me. With a pension and Social Security as my income and safety net, and not wanting to risk my wife's and my life savings, I couldn't risk hanging up a shingle and going into practice for myself. The financial risks were too great for me. So, my options for working again were—and remain—limited. Very limited.

State agencies are in the process of cutting the number of employees, so what chance did I have as a senior citizen to find work with a state agency? Private firms—at least those that are hiring—are more inclined to hire young recent law school graduates; those who could bring in a book of business; that is, paying clients, to the firm; or those who are former judges, legislators, agency heads—called rainmakers—who could attract clients and parlay their reputations into both a greater volume of business and courtroom success.

After almost a quarter century strictly in the public sector, I had no clientele to bring with me; all I had was a wealth of government experience—and in Tallahassee, government experience is literally in the "dime a dozen" category. If there is one reality I faced as retirement drew closer, it was the very real probability that once I left the state, I would never work again. So far, this has proven to be the case, and I'm perfectly ok with that.

The last few months also gave me time to reflect on those law-related activities I undertook away from the practice itself. During my career, I was quite active in The Florida Bar and the local Florida Government Bar Association. I was chair of the Administrative Law Section of The Bar, and served as both chair and member of several committees. I also served as an officer for the Florida Government Bar Association, including its president. However, the service I'm most proud of was my four years as a member of the inaugural State and Federal Government and Administrative Practice Certification Committee (SFGAP).

Several years ago, The Florida Bar initiated a certification program whereby, by dint of experience, continuing legal education pursuits, and passing a test, a lawyer will be certified as an expert in one or more particular legal disciplines. The responsibility for developing certification criteria and exam questions fell to certification committees the members of which were appointed by The Florida Bar president with the tacit approval of The state supreme court.

The SFGAP committee consists of nine members. Because the first appointees couldn't demonstrate experience or knowledge via an exam to any committee (there was no committee set up for either purpose), these inaugural appointees had to be chosen based upon their respective reputations. I was fortunate to be selected because of my background both as an administrative law practitioner from 1975-1987 and as a civil litigator in both state and federal court from 1987. Most of the original committee members knew each other, and we worked diligently as a team in devising policies and preparing the certification exam. Most of the members were primarily involved in administrative proceedings; only two of us were predominantly practicing in state and federal court. Because of this, I was tasked with drafting most of the multiple-choice questions and one of the two essay questions. I found this to be a labor of love, and I know the other members felt the same way in putting together the exam, as well as drafting policies. We checked our egos at the door and simply got to work on our assignments. I will treasure my service on this important committee. My term ended at same time I left my employment.

As the months dwindled to days and the days dwindled down toward my retirement date, I became more apprehensive, but accepting of my anticipated new status. Just before the R day arrived, the lawyers and support staff with whom I worked—including my two supervisors who 2 1/2 years earlier reamed me out—gave me a nice sendoff. They had a luncheon for me at a nice local restaurant at which I was given a few gag gifts—straw hat, corncob pipe, a clock with the hours scattered across the face—those types of things. A few co-workers offered pleasant albeit roast-type comments. I got the last word in and thanked them all for their friendship and support.

Then, on my last official day in the office, they gave me a reception replete with all types of snacks and finger food. I was given a large poster with my name, the office logo and a big "Thank You!" printed across it. This was signed by over 100 lawyers and staff. It's now on my den wall. I was given four bound volumes containing all of my cases reported by West Publishing Company (the company responsible for publishing appellate and federal district court decisions) which are in my bookcase; an acrylic trophy showing my term of employment—March 9, 1987 to June 30, 2010-which is on my desk at home; and the most prized gift of all, a Resolution of Appreciation from the Governor and Cabinet which also adorns my den wall. That resolution says that I am "a living legend in the realm of State Government Law . . . ." This is very heady stuff. I suppose there are legitimate reasons why Harriet calls the den my "ego room." I have to remind her that the quoted words are not mine. Then, she tells me I have to take out the garbage. She's very good at bringing me back to earth.

At my retirement reception, a few colleagues with whom I worked for many years made some pleasant remarks, and I got a chance to thank them all. I completed my goodbye comments by quoting that great philosopher Yogi Berra in thanking everyone "for making this day necessary." All in all, it was a wonderful gesture by my colleagues and co-workers. I gathered up all my goodies and walked out the door as an employee for the last time, and I've not looked back.

I also reflected on the tokens given out by the AG's office for 5, 10, 15, 20 and 25 years of service. I received a paperweight for five years; a shall we say rather inexpensive battery operated clock (which gives me the correct time twice each day) for 10 years; an acrylic picture frame for 15 years and an acrylic pen set for 20 years of service. The office gives a small but not inexpensive grandfather's clock for 25 years. I'm glad I wasn't eligible for that one; something about giving a person a clock after working 25 years at the same agency sends a peculiar message. I think it's a statement that your time is up. I certainly didn't want that, although my time was indeed up.

There is a myth that needs to be dispelled regarding government lawyers' income level. Lawyers generally are perceived as being wealthy, and certainly their income level is well above the average. Not all lawyers, however, can truly say they're wealthy by any stretch of the imagination. While there are lawyers who are multimillionaires, they are very few and far between in the public sector, and usually only after a very successful career in the private sector. Unless a lawyer is also a manager/supervisor or a high-ranking non-supervisor, chances are that government lawyer's salary is below $100,000 annually. I'm not saying this is a low salary; it certainly isn't. For lawyers, however, it isn't the stuff of accumulation of wealth. The designation of special counsel, which is given to very few in the AG's office, usually carries with it a higher salary; and several of them earn more than $100,000 a year.

When I left the state, there were a few senior assistant attorneys general who were earning over $90,000. I won't say what my highest salary was, but I was not among the highest paid special counsel. In short, I didn't accumulate financial wealth during my years of practice, and my pension certainly isn't in the range of these supervisors/high-ranking special counsel. I have enough income, however, to live a reasonably comfortable life providing I don't go on a spending spree for boats, cars and world travel. I had opportunities to handle cases that I most likely wouldn't have had in the private sector—cases that made a difference to the people government lawyers are hired to serve.

If I entered the legal profession with an eye to wealth accumulation, I wouldn't have taken the government employment route and would have, of necessity focused on aspects of business and property law—areas that I found boring in law school. But I have been fortunate enough to live the American Dream—a wonderful wife, wonderful children and grandchildren, professional satisfaction, honors and awards, professional and fraternal activities, etc. I don't know whether it would have been different had I chosen another path in my legal career, but that doesn't matter. I had a wonderful career of which I'm most proud, and money alone can't buy personal and professional satisfaction.

Something else I noticed also gave me pause. During my career, I had the opportunity to work with some brilliant lawyers, some of whom were left-handed. As I began to reflect on the many people I was privileged to work with, I noticed that many of them were left-handed. So, I logically concluded that left-handed people are more brilliant, intelligent, articulate and creative than their right-handed counterparts. In fact, tests conducted by St. Lawrence University in New York found that there were more left-handed people with IQs over 140 than right-handed people. Left-handed intellectuals include Albert Einstein, Isaac Newton, Charles Darwin and Benjamin Franklin. One of every four Apollo Astronauts were left-handers. Now I know what you're thinking, and being left-handed myself has nothing whatever to do with this unbiased analysis.

I must, however, not gloat over what I've set out above and point out the distinctive downside to being left-handed. I can say with all honesty that those of us who are left-handed suffer (ok, so I'm using an overly dramatic word here) from the most subtle form of discrimination known to humankind. Just try using a pair of scissors or check the serrated edge of a knife. Also, check some firearms, and try using certain power tools or saws or power saws as a lefty. You'll see what it's like. Some scholars note that left-handers may be one of the last unorganized minorities in society because we have no collective power and no real sense of identity. Here's a better way of seeing what lefthanders have to deal with. For one day, use your left hand, except to write. Notice what happens when you open doors, and continue observing as you use only your left hand. It won't take very long to get the message. Although studies show that left-handedness runs in families (for example, Queen Elizabeth II, her mother, her son Prince Charles and his son Prince William are all lefties), I can't recall a single member of my family that was left-handed. My paternal grandparents weren't, my parents weren't, and my children and grandchildren aren't. I guess I'm just the lucky one.

Left-handers suffer the slings and arrows of being different. For example, a "left-handed compliment" is actually an insult. The Oxford English Dictionary defines left-handed as being crippled, defective, awkward, clumsy, inept and characterized by underhanded dealings, doubtful, etc. Research indicates that left-handers are more likely to stutter, become alcoholics, delinquent, dyslexic and autistic. Many sources claim that lefties may die as many as nine years earlier than righties. I believe the overriding reason for this is the scissors, knives and other tools that are made for righties that we lefties must struggle with. Also, studies also show that more than 20% of all schizophrenics are left-handed. No they're not. Yes they are. No they're not. Yes they are.

To make matters even worse, the right hand is mentioned positively 100 times in the Bible; the left hand is mentioned only 25 times, all negatively. For me, the problem with being left-handed first affected me in elementary school, where teachers would take the pencil out of my left hand and make me write with my right hand. While about one in 10 are left-handed, about one in every 10 left-handers are dominant left-handers who have little use of their right hand. That's me. I had to sit at a desk that had an arm rest on the right side, but none on the left. Thus, I had a double whammy—I couldn't use my left hand to write with, and I couldn't grasp the use of the right-side-only arm rest. Fortunately, my dad went to the school and told the principal and teachers that I was left-handed and that I should be left alone to write without being "corrected" by the school system. Writing left-handed was as natural for me as it is for a right-hander using his right hand.

Famous lefties include Paul McCartney (Yeah! Yeah! Yeah!), Julia Roberts, Alexander the Great, Thomas Jefferson, Leonardo DaVinci, Michelangelo, Madame Curie, Gandhi and Babe Ruth. Infamous southpaws include John Dillinger, the Boston Strangler, Jack the Ripper and Osama Bin Laden.

(You can check out these and other fascinating facts about left-handers by going to any search engine and typing in "56 Interesting Facts About ... Left-Handedness & Left-Handed People.")

Some of the greatest baseball players were lefties. If I could only throw or hit a curve ball ....

PERSONAL OBSERVATIONS

This section contains some of my thoughts, observations and opinions formed from my life experiences. I don't believe there is anything novel about that; we all form our value system from our own experiences. Some of my basic beliefs which drive this section are that a man's word is his bond; a dollar's worth of work for a dollar's worth of pay; and that the more complex an issue, the greater the shades of gray that must be addressed. In short, no one has a monopoly on the so-called "right" answer.

Some of my observations and thoughts are admittedly controversial; I don't expect readers who disagree to change their views. I do hope, however, that these comments make readers think, and engage in dialogue with family, friends, neighbors, etc. Where there are disagreements, I hope that people at least agree not to be disagreeable. Considering the current state of our federal government and Florida state government, this hope may be overly idealistic. In any event, if you find some of my comments to much to handle, skip this chapter and go to the next one. See how easy I am to please?

Technology

I begin this personal observation on technological progress with another confession. And since this book is about my life, warts included, I must admit that when it comes to technology, I'm old-school. It took me quite a while to come to grips with document creation and email usage. When I started my legal career in the late 1960s, the mimeograph machine and carbon copying were the way to go. While co-workers were using first-generation computers, I was still getting by with dictating belts and hand-held tape recorders. I used this old-school technology for as long as I could; that is, until my bosses at the AG's office told me I needed to get with it, particularly since in the late 1980s, the office had purchased a computer for each lawyer. My first reaction at being told I had to come to terms with this new technology is how I managed to miss what was going on in our country.

Did I sleep through this advancing technology, or did I simply ignore it, believing it was for others, and not me? Well, this no longer really mattered; to keep my job, I had to join the modern world of exploding technology. So I learned what I needed to survive: document drafting, saving, printing; and using the developing Internet for legal research. The more "advanced" stuff I left to my secretary. One secretary per lawyer, however, was becoming a thing of the past; lawyers were expected to do what secretaries used to do: draft documents, correspondence, etc. (Now, it's one secretary for every two or three lawyers, with the secretaries doing mostly filing and recordkeeping.) Just as I was "mastering" one type of computer system, another more advanced system was instituted, forcing me to literally forget what I just learned and learn a new system.

I thought Windows were the things you open to let air in, and wash when they got dirty. I was doing well with this pdf thing when Word came along. Although the jargon reminds me of the great Abbott and Costello "Who's on First" routine (you could look this up), I nevertheless learned what I needed to survive; and what I couldn't do, my secretary was there ready to bail me out; and she did this on more than one occasion—much more than one. To this day, I still can't deal with many of the page layout options, the inserts, the references, etc.; but since I only have my home computer to deal with, I do only what I must for my own purposes, such as create documents (like the drafts for this book), use the Internet for searches and email, and just this year I learned how to use a flash drive. In short, I can get by to my satisfaction, and when I have a problem, Harriet is there to bail me out. Ok, so I can't compete with my wife and daughters, and even my granddaughters are becoming proficient in using computers. But I don't feel like a dinosaur any more . . . until the next wave of technology hits, which usually strikes on an annual basis.

Recently, I bought a Nook and learned how to download books; only shortly after I bought it, a newer version came out. I guess it's possible to teach an old dog a few new tricks every so often, eh? I'm somewhat reluctant to discard my seven-year-old cell phone because the ones today are so different. All I need a cell phone for is to make and take calls; but sooner rather than later, I'll need a newer one that has all the apps and gizmos already built in. Then I'll have to learn how to use it, only to discard that one down the road when a newer version hits the market. Just another part of our disposable society; things don't get fixed much anymore. When something becomes obsolete, we just toss it and buy the latest version. Try to get a toaster or iron or even a rear-projection TV fixed—if you can. It's cheaper to buy a new one.

I believe computers should play a role in assisting us in our daily lives; I don't believe they should be the be-all and end-all that they've become for so many. When I was in school, I had to go to the library and actually read books and articles in order to properly write essays, book reports, etc. Today, there is no need to go to a library in order to do research; just go to a search engine, type in the subject, find what you need, and copy and paste. Over the past couple of years, I have been asked to judge science and history fairs at both elementary and middle schools. The participating students were required to supply a bibliography along with their project. I was amazed at the number of students who listed Wikipedia as a primary source, and the number who listed websites rather than books and other original writings. And these are the bright, motivated students who take the time to put together a project and enter the fairs!! Having discussed this with educators not only where I live but elsewhere—including other states—this reliance on shortcut research seems to be a fairly fixed pattern. I wonder what the other, less motivated students are learning about research and writing; I have my deep concerns.

Too much reliance on computers and technology generally affects one's ability to engage in critical analytical thinking. Andy Rooney, the late commentator/curmudgeon for CBS's "60 Minutes," made the statement that while we have greater abilities to communicate with one another and gather information, he couldn't say that technology made us a better people. I fully agree with his assessment. When we rely on machines to give us answers, we lose the ability to arrive at the answers through logical reasoning or critical thinking. Judgment is sacrificed at the altar of the computer. Plus, if a student doesn't know "their" from "there" or "they're" and doesn't know the difference between "lose" and "loose," a computer won't solve his/her problems. Reliance on computers to do one's thinking isn't of any benefit to society. Students must be taught to think; otherwise, fewer and fewer will do the thinking and the number of blind followers will grow. The logical extension of this should be quite obvious and most ominous.

Here's a scary thought on the subject of computers and privacy. Have you ever wondered, when you sit in front of your computer and stare at the screen, whether there is someone sitting on the other side watching your every move and gathering information about you? Have you ever given any thought to the possibility of someone who can view from his/her computer everything that's on yours? Someone who can view all of your files, check all of the websites you visit, etc.? When you post on Facebook or any other social network, are you absolutely certain that your post can't possibly be viewed by anyone without a computer? Many news media and organizations conduct online polls, which are said to be anonymous. Are you absolutely sure no one can tie your response to you on your computer? Does this paragraph make you feel even the slightest bit uncomfortable?

Let me give you this example of this putative anonymity. Harriet orders products both online and from department stores. When she plays an online game, like Scrabble for example, advertisements pop up promoting either the same or similar products that she recently purchased. I have no doubt that others who do this face the same scenario. This leads to my questions in the previous paragraph. With so much social networking, and communications technology advancing literally on a less-than-annual basis, how is our right of privacy truly protected? This question is particularly pertinent because government itself has so many means of accessing information about us—some of which we don't even know about—that seeking privacy protection from government is iffy at best insofar as legitimately protecting our right to be let alone and free from intrusion. I raise this not to try to offer a solution, because I don't know if there is one; I mention this for the sole purpose of starting a dialogue on the subject. George Orwell wrote "1984" with this subject—Big Brother—in mind. Was his work truly one of science fiction, or was he being prophetic?

With the continuing rapid expansion of technology and concomitant advances in social network, privacy becomes an issue of greater and greater concern. I don't believe any of us really want our lives to be completely open books. But has our security-mindedness led to the very problem we're trying to deal with? I'm referring to User IDs and passwords. To access the Internet and just about any online activity—from banking and finance to eBay and other businesses too numerous to mention—each person must have a User ID and password. However, each company or entity imposing such requirements has its own personal conditions for selecting an ID and password. The ID and password formula used by a particular company may include a minimum number of letters and numbers; letters only; numbers only; etc., etc., etc. Some even require answering a question that only the user knows the answer to. This means that each of us must have or develop a great memory for recalling which combination applies to which online site, or storing them in your personal computer or on a flash drive, or by way of a hard copy stored at home for easy access. And if a question is involved, what answer might be remembered at one moment may be forgotten later, so this information must also be stored in some manner. Presumably, the purpose of IDs and passwords is to prevent hacking into our computers and obtaining personal information. Having to store numerous IDs and passwords on our computer defeats the very purpose of this supposedly secure information. Having to put this information on a flash drive or create a hard copy also defeats the purpose of security in the event of a burglary or fire.

With all the technology we have, we should be quite capable of creating a universal ID and password similar to a Social Security number. If such a number is good enough to last a lifetime, why couldn't each of us create a universal ID number and password? I'll call them the UNIVID and UNIPASS. Each one could be nine digits in length—the same number as the Social Security Number—and consist of four letters, three numbers and two symbols (like @,#,$,%,^,&,★,(,)—pretty much all of the symbols on a computer keyboard. Each person could use the arrangement for the UNIVID and construct the UNIPASS. For example, let's go with 1234ABC#$ for the ID. The pass could then be 1324CAB$#. But this arrangement would be up to the user; he/she could choose an entirely different set for each one. This would mean having to memorize only two series to access anything from your computer.

Many of us have our Social Security committed to memory; why not just two additional sequences for security protection for all online access? Who would be responsible for assigning these IDs and passwords? Well, the user would, in the same manner as he/she does now when registering online. Just use the same combination all the time. Each company, of course, would have to make sure its system is compatible, but I would think that the costs and effort of compatibility would be offset by making protection of personal privacy as easy as possible for the user/consumer.

Considering how many times we learn about companies losing hundreds of thousands of IDs and passwords, or computer geeks and whizzes hacking into a company's computer and stealing personal information that puts our privacy at dangerous risk, personal privacy should be given paramount consideration. I believe we have the technology to accomplish this; the question is that, considering the cost and time involved, do businesses have the motivation and will to do something like this? Or will it take a national crisis of privacy invasion costing us billions of dollars to get this type of action?

The early 60s to the early 70s

There is a tendency to describe at least some of the decades of the 20th century by catchy phrases. For example, the 1920s is often referred to as the Roaring 20s. For me, however, the period between November 22, 1963 and April 22, 1975 is the "cultural upheaval decade," although it's not neatly packaged in an absolute 10-year period beginning with 0 and ending in 9. This 11-plus years of domestic turbulence was wracked by one shock after another. Look at the cataclysmic events that jolted our nation during this period: the assassination of President John Kennedy; the escalation of the Vietnam War and the draft; the racial tensions impacted by the passage of the Civil Rights Act of 1964 and the Voting Rights Act of 1965; the assassinations of Robert Kennedy and Dr. Martin Luther King, Jr., in 1968; the violent Democratic National Convention that same year; the Kent State shootings in 1970; the resignation of a corrupt sitting vice president in 1973; the Watergate scandal that captivated the nation from 1972 through Richard Nixon's resignation in 1974; the last of the airlifts from Vietnam on April 22, 1975 and the fall of Saigon a few days later.

The feel-good era of the 50s following World War II was over; our culture underwent dynamic change during these tumultuous years. Campus demonstrations captivated our nation. The Pentagon Papers were published despite the government's frenetic efforts to prevent disclosure. With good reason: the papers revealed that the government repeatedly lied about Vietnam. We had draft card and flag burnings. No longer were our young listening primarily to American music; the British Invasion groups—especially the Beatles—were singing about peace ("All we are saying is give peace chance") and love ("All you need is love."). Over here, songs were calling for an end to war ("war . . . what is it good for. Absolutely nothing."). And that the answer "was blowin' in the wind." These weren't just songs; collectively they became an anthem of the time.

I came into adulthood in the 60s and 70s, going from ages 16 to 32. What students are learning today about this tumultuous period (at least, I hope they're learning about it) I lived through, and the events of that decade undoubtedly helped shaped my life. Living through the 60s and 70s, having worked around government as a newspaper reporter and beginning my career in government as a lawyer during this period, allowed me to form more precise observations and opinions on how our government is supposed to function, and how it does in reality. These opinions were confirmed as I grew older and passed through the various stages of life.

The 1960s began with so much hope; the tranquil or feel-good 50s and the 1960 election of a young, charismatic president filled so many of us younger Americans with dreams of a bright future. Then came November 22, 1963. I was sitting in my American History class at the UF when a student assistant rushed in and said "President Kennedy has been shot." Classes were dismissed throughout the campus and I walked back to my dorm room, turned on my radio, and listened for the fateful announcement of his death. I then went downstairs and joined dozens of students sitting on the sidewalk, saying nothing, watching others walk by, crying, stupefied. I sat there for hours. I was numb. The entire campus was numb.

I was 19 then. John Kennedy was "our" president; he talked to us and listened to us. Now, he was gone, and in his place was "their" president, a man of the older generation who turned Vietnam into a full-fledged war that almost tore the country apart. Then a president was elected on a promise to end the war and return honesty to government and civility to our nation. Only, turns out he gave us a corrupt vice president and Watergate. So many older Americans were perplexed at how our nation's youth were acting out and not conforming to their standards; I don't think they ever really understood what trauma—both mentally and physically—the young of the early 60s and early 70s were going through, particularly with the draft hanging over their heads. Government deceit during both the LBJ and Nixon Administrations caused so many to ask what our troops were fighting and dying for. So many of our youth wondered whether they would have a chance at a productive live. So many of those of the "Greatest Generation" believed that the war they fought was no different from Vietnam. But there were great differences. First, WWII was a war of nations against nations seeking world domination. Vietnam was based on the ill-conceived notion that if that nation fell to the communists, others would fall like dominoes. I know that I carried the memories of these turbulent years with me as I moved further and further into adulthood.

Social, political, economic and behavioral observations

Casting our eyes around the world, our planet is seemingly more at war than at peace. Violence and turbulence; poverty amidst wealth; greed, avarice, and selfishness appear to predominate our globe. And for what purpose? Power? Wealth? At home, we continue to see corruption and greed at the highest levels, as well as poverty and neglect in this the wealthiest nation in the world, and the grave consequences of not adequately addressing these concerns in economic and infrastructure deterioration and in falling behind other countries educationally. And it seems that just about every day we read or hear about another famous athlete, entertainer, movie star or political figure abusing drugs or alcohol, committing crimes or in one way or another is awash in scandal. These wealthy megastars and political figures are fawned over, praised, pampered and literally have everything one could ever hope for. And because of this, they believe that the laws and moral code that apply to us don't apply to them. Because, after all, they are special, or so they are led to believe. Recall these famous words: "What shall it profit a man to gain the whole world and lose his soul?" And this stark warning: those who fail to learn the lessons of history are condemned to repeat them.

My social and political philosophies are products of the teachings of my paternal grandfather and father; my understanding of American history; having lived in a federal housing project in New York because my parents' income wasn't enough to avoid government subsidized housing; having lived in an efficiency apartment surrounded by much older people and watching them struggle to make ends meet while dealing with medical issues associated with old age; having lived through the turmoil of the 1960s and 1970s; and working in and around government for more than 40 years. My grandfather was born a few years after the Civil War ended, during the Gilded Age and the Industrial Revolution. He saw firsthand the excesses of the "laissez-faire" (or leave alone) attitude of government toward Big Business. He became a man during the age of the Robber Barons, the corporate trusts, the sweat shops, child and women labor abuses, and the neglect of those in the labor force when they were no longer of any value to the Robber Barons and their ilk. My dad was a young man when he saw his father lose so much of what he worked for during the Great Depression. Both my dad and grandpa knew which political party was responsible for instituting much-needed relief through Social Security, child labor laws, and the job-driven alphabet agencies created in the aftermath of the Great Depression. My dad certainly knew which party provided for Medicare and Medicaid, and the Voting Rights Act and other voter reforms that eliminated so many obstacles to casting a free ballot. My dad and grandpa, the two most influential men in my life, made sure I knew the difference in philosophy between Republicans and Democrats, and that for government to succeed, there had to be dialogue, negotiation and compromise.

For the past few years, we've had stalemate instead of governance. Both parties claim to want what everyone wants—lower taxes, business growth, job growth, economic growth, efficient government, better education, etc. To accomplish each of these, however, legislation must be passed. So, if both parties want the same thing, why can't they get it done? Because of the strings attached by special interests, predominantly on the right.

There is a purge taking place within the Republican Party whereby the evangelical right, or true believers, require Republicans to take a litmus test on conservative "purity" to curry their favor, the failure of which means being jettisoned from the party. Moderate Republicans are being forced to adopt the far right wing line on religious and social issues or risk becoming pariahs within their own party and ousted from office. The Republican Party has become the "true conservative evangelical right wing" party, with no room for moderates or for anyone who doesn't fully support the right wing agenda. Today, there is no need to campaign as a "conservative Republican" because there is simply no other kind. These folks—whether called evangelicals, true believers, Tea Party members, or social conservatives—label anyone who's a Democrat a liberal, as if this word were an epithet. To them, it is; and they use it as an explanation for all the nation's ills. They believe that if all their opponents disappeared or accepted the "true conservative" line, all would be well. It certainly would be—for them. For the rest of the country, well, it's live it their way or it's too bad for you. To them, all Democrats are liberal; there is no moderation or shades of grey; everything is either black or white. Theirs is a politics of belief; belief is fact; belief is everything. To the right wing, unless you're a true believer or at least accept the wisdom of the far right agenda, you're a leftist, etc. Of course, everyone who disagrees with the right wing is leftist because it's impossible to be any further on the right (unless it's the Attila the Hun).

Since one of their "epithets" is to label opponents as "progressives" who want to design the country into the form of a socialist society, blaming the nation's ills today on the likes of FDR, Truman, Kennedy, Johnson, Carter and Clinton (notice no progressive is a Republican), I will call these right wingers regressives, since they want to revert or regress to another time. They not only deny—but will not hear of—the historical reality that only when both major parties work hand-in-hand is there any prospect of compromise and, concomitantly, any chance for real progress. Those who call themselves Republicans but don't share all of the right wing ideology or agenda are cast aside as "too liberal" by those whose agenda or platform is driven by a rigid moral code born at least in significant part of a doctrinaire religious foundation. Engaging in a fact-based debate with them is virtually impossible because debating a hardcore belief system is impossible, no matter how illogical or devoid of fact these beliefs may be. When faced with facts, these people will dismiss the source with a word or phrase that, for them, is tantamount to an epithet. The more ultra right wingers have as one of their goals to compel people to live as they do or face eternal damnation. The right wing stands for stalemate or inaction unless the opposition caves in and accepts the right wing political agenda of benefits for the wealthy and an occasional bone or two for everyone else. Government, however, can't properly function by demands that "nonbelievers" live their lives according to the right wing doctrine or face stalemate. These groups profess individual liberty and don't want to be told how to live their lives; yet, they have no problem telling others how to live their lives. These right-wing regressives are zealous in their claims of individualism, yet they speak only for individualism that accepts wholeheartedly the right wing religious and social agenda while ignoring the critical importance of community. The interests of the individual must be balanced with the needs of the community for government to properly function. This is a fatal flaw in the right wing's approach.

These regressives have been very successful in demonizing those who disagree with their mission. Their appeal is successful because it embraces two key elements: fear and the ability to generate fear by simple words and phrases. You can bet the mortgage that, in responding to any challenge to their mindset, you'll hear the usual one-word dismissals of "socialism" and "liberal," plus the "destroying our freedoms" and "redistributing the wealth" chants. They believe that they possess all the right answers to the problems of the world and have clothed themselves in such self-righteousness that the word "compromise" is not in their vocabulary—unless it means that those who disagree with them see the error of their ways and blindly accept their agenda. Using simple words to convey simple messages, they blame society's ills on liberals, Democrats, unions, university intellectuals, progressives, the media, etc. The simpler the message, the easier it is to garner support. The right wing simply doesn't believe the people are smart enough to critically analyze and question the sound bites and snippets. Unfortunately, judging from the decline in our standards of education and performance levels, there is legitimacy to this view. The problem the right wing has is that there are enough who can think through their socio-religious agenda and not be sold by it.

This form of vilification by labeling is certainly not new; we saw this most glaringly during Nixon's presidency with his enemies list. We also know the outcome of his corrupt administration. Is this the direction we want our nation to take? Do we want to go back to a time when overt secrecy and criminality ruled the highest level of our national government? If it hadn't been for an aggressive media, Nixon would have gotten away with his vengeful attacks on those whose names appeared on his enemies list and the crimes that we now call Watergate. Astonishingly, some still blame the press for his downfall; for them, the lessons of history mean nothing. They remain satisfied with their beliefs, ignorance of the facts notwithstanding.

For the regressives, the solution for all our ills is first dismissing and silencing the dissenters; then protecting the wealthy from tax increases and allow them to retain their tax breaks, loopholes and havens; then cutting spending on social programs designed to help the middle and lower classes. At the same time, they want to reduce or eliminate government involvement in overseeing and regulating business and provide for more individual freedom for corporations and certain religions, but not for women and those who choose alternative lifestyles. They also want the government to endorse their view on social issues such as abortion, contraception, gay rights, gun and assault weapons regulations, etc. If you simply take their mantra of "cutting spending, less government, less taxes and more individual freedom" the sound bites will fool you. They sound good, but the devil's in their details. They want tax cuts across-the-board, which will permit greater wealth to accumulate at the top of the economic food chain, reduce federal revenue, thereby forcing deep cuts in social programs. They blame progressives for being societal designers, wanting only to push a government regulated socialistic system on the country. They make such a claim even as so many of them collect their Social Security checks and receive Medicare benefits. Perhaps they don't include these in their definition of socialism. For them, socialism in the form of checks in the mail is perfectly acceptable.

The so-called "red state" leaders and their ilk rail at the federal government for involving itself into matters of state affairs, asserting states' rights as their polestar .... until a catastrophe strikes, such as a hurricane or massive tornado. Suddenly, the enemy "federal government" becomes a friend as states' rights claims take a back seat to pleas for the federal government's assistance. These people rail at the federal government until they need it. They do the same thing with the media; they'll rail at the media until they need them to make them look good or tell their story. You recall how many GOP states railed at the federal bailouts first approved by President Bush, then President Obama, until the time came for money to be sent out. The right wing doesn't appear to remember how many conservative corporate executives quietly took the bailout money. So much for rejecting federal government handouts. While hypocrisy is certainly not limited to one political party or group of people, the regressives carry out theirs with far greater hubris and arrogance. It's the old "If you don't like it, too bad" or "Love it or leave it" that we first heard ad nauseam during the Vietnam era.

Let's take the redistribution of wealth claim. This is the one made most often when the issue is increasing taxes on the wealthy. A federal income tax has been around for over 100 years, and was finally included as an amendment to the United States Constitution in 1913. This tax is a progressive tax because those with greater income pay more. The proposal with which the right wing takes issue is any increase in the amount the wealthy must pay via a tax increase. This is a classic redistribution of wealth, and has been around for quite some time. The point here is that redistribution of the wealth is nothing new or a novel idea, but the GOP certainly wants you to think it is. Would the right wing repeal this system in favor of another? Today, the wealthy are the sole beneficiaries of huge tax breaks, exceptions, exemptions, etc.; and other legislation that favors their interests. They rail at government largesse that takes money from the rich and gives it to the poor. But how did the rich become rich? I believe we can agree that government tax breaks and other benefits play some role in the accumulation of wealth. Otherwise, why have these breaks in the first place?

I assume they want to keep these breaks and benefits while securing more tax cuts (and breaks, etc.) that the GOP undoubtedly will try to provide for them. This would be human nature to keep what one has while trying to get even more benefits. But the wealthy join the rest of the right wing in clamoring for individual rights and responsibilities, so let's take them at their word. Let's consider a trade-off; keep the current progressive tax system, but eliminate all breaks for the wealthy. If they want a fair system, what's wrong with treating everyone equally? No tax breaks or economic advantages for anyone. What could be fairer than that? Individual responsibility prevails over handouts in the form of tax advantages and favorable legislation.

Some will undoubtedly say that businesses must be given incentives, since these incentives spur economic growth. My response is why? I thought business growth is a result of individual initiative, hard work, commitment, etc. If these people need incentives to grow, why is it that they get these incentives and no own else does? After all, according to the right wing, it's all about fairness, a level playing field so all of us can achieve success. What's good for the wealthy goose should be equally good for the middle—and low-class gander: if the wealthy don't want to be taxed, then reduce or eliminate tax breaks and other legislative benefits. As sub-proposal: use a sliding scale approach; reduce breaks for the wealthy to the same degree that taxes are not increased. Do you think the GOP would accept any of this? I don't either. They'll take handouts, but won't hear of it for the middle and lower classes. Hmmmmmmmmm.

The bottom line on taxing the wealthy is this: if the accumulation of wealth is attributable in any way to the tax breaks and other governmental benefits they enjoy, why shouldn't they pay more in taxes? After all, while they rail at Democrats in government for even thinking of raising taxes on the wealthy, they have no problem accepting these breaks courtesy of the Republicans in government, and even contribute mightily to candidates and incumbents of their choice to secure even more and greater breaks. Perhaps when the blast the Democrats, they forget that they owe at least some measure of their wealth to government benefits not available to others. So, if the wealthy are not going to pay more in taxes, why not eliminate or reduce their breaks proportionately? It seems unfair that they can get their breaks without having to pay taxes on the income earned at least in part from those breaks.

On the subject of taxes and the wealthy, it appears that, on one hand, the wealthy believe they earned their money legally and they shouldn't be singled out for having to pay higher taxes just so their money can be given to those who haven't earned it. On the other hand, those who might be the recipients of tax revenues from the wealthy claim that the rich earned their money through tax breaks and other benefits, and if they are going to be singled out for the breaks, they should be singled out for paying a greater share of taxes on revenue generated from those benefits that are only available to the rich. This view is born of the notion that great wealth is generally accumulated by inheritance or investment, or both. The tax rate for income through capital gains is less than the rates for salaried employees. Therefore, it is expected that the wealthier a person is, the more he/she will earn by way of investments, thereby increasing one's wealth, which will also be taxed at a lower rate. In short, this cyclical investment/lower tax rate results in more real income for the wealthy. This poses several questions that appear logical to the "have-nots": why can't investment income be taxed at the same rate as for other sources of income? In short, why does this "break" exist in the first place, since it favors the investor who's more apt to be wealthy? And how is it that those who become super-wealthy by investments seem to know what to invest in? Is it too much to believe that some have access to solid information not available to others?

The visceral debate over tax increases for the wealthy is a result of several realities: first, the growing concentration of wealth in the hands of fewer people; the decline of small businesses in favor of larger businesses; the shrinking middle class; and the increase in numbers of those who require some form of government aid to survive. It's a matter of more people chasing fewer dollars. To make more dollars available through the myriad of aid programs, the government has essentially two choices: raise taxes or cut spending.

The only place where taxes can be raised is on the wealthy simply because they have more and will miss the taxed amount less. Obviously, taxes can't be raised on those who can't afford to pay their bills, much less additional taxes. Then there's the spending cuts side of the ledger. The wealthy aren't worried about spending cuts because they're not receiving any form of government financial aid like the middle and, more profoundly, the lower class poor. Therefore, the spending that the right wing wants to cut are those that currently fund programs that provide some form of a safety net for those in need. Cutting spending places the entire burden on the middle and lower classes; it's a classic case of the rich getting richer and the poor getting poorer.

Interestingly, Rep. Paul Ryan, Gov. Mitt Romney's choice for vice president, has gone on record as supporting a reduction of tax breaks for the wealthy as part of an overhaul of the nation's tax code. "We should ask: Who should get them?" Ryan said in an August interview with Bloomberg in New York. "We should circumscribe these tax benefits to middle-income and low-income people, and not to higher-income people." The devil's in the details, however, and Ryan declined to identify which benefits ought to be cut to finance his proposed tax overhaul. Previously, the House of Representatives approved his budget plan that calls for consolidating the current six individual tax brackets into two, with rates set at 25 percent and 10 percent. The top rate now is 35 percent. His plan would make cuts in food stamps, Medicaid, Pell college tuition grants and other programs for the poor. (I said the devil's in the details.) Ryan's plan calls for financing the reductions by cutting individual tax preferences; however, once again, he didn't identify which ones. Ryan has said the tax-writing GOP-controlled House of Representatives will sort that out later. It would need to come up with about $4.6 trillion in revenue over the next decade to pay for the lower tax rates, according to the nonpartisan Tax Policy Center in Washington. Lots of promises; no details. Now, where do you think the GOP will look to come up with this revenue? Why, making deep cuts in social and education programs—programs that the majority of the country are dependent upon in varying degrees. And if Ryan's plan doesn't become law, well, the current tax breaks for the wealthy will remain in place.

What needs to be done is to identify those programs that are wasteful or fraud-riddled, and actually cut only government fat, while leaving the meat, muscle and bone intact; and provide the strongest possible disincentives to reduce and, hopefully, eliminate fraud. Earlier, I said the wealthy aren't worried about spending cuts. What they are worried about is any tax increase, even though whatever amount they must pay is of minimal significance at best when weighed against their level of wealth. Another thing that they're worried about—rightfully so—are reductions to or elimination of tax breaks and favoritism legislation. If the right wing pushes too hard against tax increases for the wealthy, you can bet there will be an opposite push for an in-depth examination of the myriad of breaks, etc., enjoyed by the wealthy through years of legislative grants and gifts. I'll talk a bit more about quid pro quo a little later.

These regressives also want business to take over traditional government services. This means that profits will replace service as the primary function. They seriously believe that businesses, if left to their own devices, will somehow become predominantly consumer-oriented and sacrifice accumulation of profits for the greater public good by creating jobs and acting in the public interest. Human nature doesn't work that way. For business, the bottom line is money; for government, it's service (or it certainly should be). Individual freedom is a disingenuous euphemism for freedom for those who follow the right-wing agenda, but not for those who think otherwise. Does anyone really believe the right wing favors freedom for a woman to choose; or for gays and lesbians to be free to marry; or for people of all religions to freely choose which prayers are to be said in places where the public congregates? Putting the stamp of government approval on the supremacy of one group's belief system over another's is not what our nation is about. Here is a critical difference between the far left and the far right: too many on the right want to force others to live as they do; I don't hear voices on the left clamoring for others to live as they do.

If the regressives don't get its way, they threaten to hold hostage the functioning of government by gridlock. With increasing regularity, the GOP is using the filibuster to prevent passage of needed legislation unless tax increases for Big Business and the super-rich are taken off the table, and other parts of its agenda are allowed to become law. Where is the consensus and compromise necessary for government to function when one party threatens inaction? One of the biggest mistakes a leader can make is to try to negotiate with those who absolutely refuse to do so. Of course, the filibuster is nothing new; the difference is that our problems are becoming more profound, affecting more people; yet, government seems less and less able to even address the problems, much less attempt to solve them.

The right wing believes we must return to the days of "traditional family values." According to the 2004 GOP platform, this phrase means promotion of traditional marriage and opposition to sex outside of marriage; support for a traditional role for women in the family; opposition to same-sex marriage; support for particularized roles for men and women in society; opposition to legalized abortion; support for abstinence education; and support for policies that are said to protect children from obscenity and exploitation. Social and religious conservatives often use the term "family values" to promote conservative ideology that supports traditional Christian values.

This phrase is not owned by the GOP alone, however. Liberals define this term as a living wage, universal health care, the acceptance of adoption by gays, the acceptance of the non-traditional family (single parent households, same-sex marriages); social programs and financial aid for families. This phrase has also been used to support such values as family planning, affordable child care, and maternity leave.

"Traditional American values" doesn't appear to be susceptible to a fixed definition, but it is noted that former Sen. Rick Santorum ran for the GOP presidential nomination on a platform of restoring such values, as did former candidate Herman Cain (although as will be seen, Cain didn't live by what he preached). Therefore, I'll use these two terms interchangeably.

There is an obvious disagreement between the major political parties over what these phrases mean. However, as is the case when words and phrases are cavalierly tossed about, the devil's in the details. They harp on any "value" that they believe smacks of socialism; but let's look more closely at their value system. Would they repeal Social Security? Medicare? Medicaid? Aid to Families With Dependent Children? Food stamps? Programs for women, infants and children? Workers' Compensation? Unemployment compensation? (Oh, excuse me. The Florida Legislature changed this to reemployment assistance. This should make the unemployed feel so much better.) Are these programs not in keeping with "traditional American (or family) values?" What specific programs passed by Congress over the past 75+ years and signed by presidents—Republican and Democrat alike—are socialistic or contrary to American and family values, and must be repealed?

Isn't one of our main traditional values to extend a helping hand to those who, through no fault of their own, are less fortunate? Isn't another of our traditional values to provide some measure of a dignified life for those who are no longer able to work after spending years in the workforce? Isn't yet another of our values to help the elderly who are physically and mentally incapable of providing for themselves and have no other means of assistance? Isn't another of our values helping those who've lost their jobs through no fault of their own? How about those who can't afford or can't get health care coverage through no fault of their own? Don't we value lending a helping hand to the less fortunate; are we to sacrifice these several noted values in the name of that tired, worn-out hollow claim of socialism? In the name of "traditional American (or family) values," must we harden our hearts to any segment of society that legitimately needs a helping hand? My suggestion is the next time you hear a politician or candidate for office claim he/she is for traditional American or family values, ask what he/she means by this, including the value points I've made in the form of questions in the last two paragraphs. I don't think those who really believe in what they claim to believe in can be selective in their choice of values. To do otherwise is the height of hypocrisy and disingenuousness.

What I find particularly galling is the blatant hypocrisy of those purists who rail against the Democrats for not adhering to the right-wing's self-serving version of traditional family values, only to find that those who rail the loudest don't practice what they preach. From a cursory Google search, here is a representative, yet incomplete, list of 10 congressmen who campaigned on a platform of "traditional family values" but got caught up in sex scandals. This list also includes House members who railed at President Clinton's infidelity while having their own affairs: Christopher Lee (R-NY), Mark Souder (R-In.), Vito Fosella (R-NY), Mark Foley (R-Fla.), Larry Craig (R-Id.-Sen.), Ed Schock (R-Va.), Newt Gingrich (R.-Ga.), Robert Livingston (R-La.), Bob Barr (R-Ga.) and Dan Burton (R-In.). What amazes me is that Gingrich received a significant number of evangelical votes in the 2012 primary season even though the voters had to know of Gingrich's moral failings. Are we to conclude from this either a short memory span by these voters; or perhaps that it's perfectly ok for these voters to give a pass to a right-wing candidate who fails to practice what he preaches? Herman Cain also received a sizable number of votes—at least until his campaign crashed when it was revealed that he had a sex scandal, including claims of sexual harassment, in his closet. This is a classic example of the hypocrisy of the right wing's righteous indignation. The moral (pun intended) of this paragraph is beware of those on the right wing who preach the most about family values and who scream and yell the loudest at the immorality of the Democrats. Remember, anyone who points a finger at others has three pointing back at himself.

Of course, those who are desirous of countering the failings noted above are quick to point out similar failings of Democrats. It's the difference between the two parties, however, that's critical here. Remember, it's the Republicans who claim the moral high ground by holding themselves out as the epitome of moral rectitude. The Democrats exercise no such hubris. These ultra-moralists claim they have God on their side and He is striking back at the immorality of the Democrats and their proposals. I wonder if they are concerned about what God thinks when these self-righteous hypocrites are caught—figuratively—with their hands in the cookie jar.

It seems that so many want to go back to a time when business was given a free hand; sort of a modern-day revival of the days of the Industrial Revolution and the Gilded Age. Do you remember how government's laissez-faire approach to Big Business ended almost a century ago? I'll give you a hint: 1929. Stock market crash. Great Depression. Unemployment lines. Food lines. Remember the party that was in power during the 1920s? The GOP. Harding, Coolidge and Hoover. Do we really want go back to a time when we had Robber Barons feathering their own nests and no protections for our workers, and wind up with conditions even reminiscent of what our nation lived through during the late 19th and early 20th centuries? You remember the sweat shops, child labor practices, etc., of the early 20th century? Is this what we want from conservative leaders? I certainly hope this reactionary form of governance is not what we're about. At least the Robber Barons weren't of a mind to control government; the big difference between then and now is that Big Business is exercising tremendous influence on government decision-making, and wants to exert even more.

Want proof? The GOP rails at the president for not creating jobs. How can a president order a private company to hire anyone? He can't. No president can wave a magic wand and create jobs, unless Congress is willing to do what it did when FDR took office and create new alphabet agencies. So, the GOP must, of necessity, refine its finger-pointing by accusing the president of not creating a "climate" for private companies to create jobs. How can he create that climate? By letting business grow with minimal oversight; cutting spending on social programs; not increasing taxes on the wealthy; cutting regulations on business; and repealing Obamacare. Sound familiar? Isn't this so-called "climate change" right out of the right-wing playbook? Right down the line. The truth is the GOP-run House won't pass a single bill that encourages business growth unless it meets the above conditions. And businesses won't hire until they get a better deal from a GOP White House. This is a primary reason we have stalemate as far as jobs and economic growth are concerned. The GOP simply doesn't want to see a Democratic president succeed.

As government becomes more and more beholden to the wealthy, the majority of Americans in the shrinking middle class and the lower class are becoming further and further alienated from their own government. I believe that this growing distance between the vast majority of our citizens and the government that is supposed to serve them is the greatest risk to our democracy. I am reminded what then-Soviet Union leader Nikita Khrushchev said during the Cold War of the 50s and 60s: that no nation would have to defeat us, that we would bury ourselves; we would wither from within.

Thomas Mann and Norman Ornstein have been studying Washington politics since the late 60s, and have been critical of both political parties during this time. This is what they say in the April 27, 2012 edition of The Washington Post: "We have been studying Washington politics and Congress for more than 40 years, and never have we seen them this dysfunctional. In our past writings, we have criticized both parties when we believed it was warranted. Today, however, we have no choice but to acknowledge that the core of the problem lies with the Republican Party. The GOP has become an insurgent outlier in American politics. It is ideologically extreme; scornful of compromise; unmoved by conventional understanding of facts, evidence and science; and dismissive of the legitimacy of its political opposition. When one party moves this far from the mainstream, it makes it nearly impossible for the political system to deal constructively with the country's challenges."

Compare this statement with recent statements by elected conservative officials. When Rep. Allen West, a Florida Republican, says that "78 to 81" Democratic congressmen are communists, and the GOP remains silent rather than condemn such McCarthy-like tactics, the Republican Party should face public indignation. When Rep. West was asked by the press to present evidence to support his claim, he did what is typical when an accuser has no evidence: he railed at the media for not "investigating" what the Democrats' real motives are, imploring them to get the facts straight. Of course, he never mentioned his lack of any facts to support his outrageous claim, and never answered the question.

When the Republican candidate who ousted Sen. Richard Lugar of Indiana has as his message that there's too much bipartisanship in Washington; and when he says bipartisanship, it should mean Democrats coming to the Republican point of view, there is a serious problem with our government. When Rep. Michelle Bachmann and four of her right-wing cohorts in Congress, with support from Newt Gingrich, accuse members of the Muslim Brotherhood of infiltrating the highest levels of our Government without any credible evidence to back up this claim, and then try to backtrack from their allegations when faced with challenges to their claims, where is the outrage at such blatant McCarthy-like tactics? Is this what they mean by "traditional American (or family) values? These people should be ashamed of their conduct.

Yet, they continue to instill fear for the sole purpose of energizing their base. This is not what we're about; this isn't an example of the tolerance our forefathers fought and died for. There is entirely too much of this nonsense going on, and we're all paying the price of this intransigence.

The ability to make unsubstantiated claims impugning the reputation of anyone in unfettered fashion is precisely what McCarthyism was about. Could this be what the regressives mean when they want to go back to "traditional American values?" McCarthy was eventually shown to be a fraud; I have no reason to believe our 21st century McCarthyites won't suffer the same fate.

Recently, the Republican Party of Texas considered a plank in the party platform that said it opposed "the teaching of Higher Order Thinking Skills (HOTS) critical thinking skills and similar programs that are simply a relabeling of Outcome-Based Education (OBE) which focus on behavior modification and have the purpose of challenging the student's fixed beliefs and undermining parental authority." Let this sentence sink in: the Texas GOP opposes teaching children how to think critically. Is this another example of "traditional values?" Under this line of thinking, if a student believes his/her teacher is the Anti-Christ or the governor is the Devil, it's ok to take action to remove this evildoer because the student's fixed beliefs must not be corrected! This is the kind of nonsense that is dangerous and should be called out and condemned. Yet, there is no outrage. Perhaps the message here is that the Texas GOP believes it's necessary to dumb down the educational level of the voters so that they're not capable of asking pointed questions of the many holes in the right wing's agenda.

History's teachings are unwavering in showing that for government to function properly, there must be balance, moderation and compromise—conditions that are alien to the right wing. The only way to end stalemate government is to use the ballot box to remove the intransigence and elect representatives—moderate Democrats and Republicans—dedicated to doing the people's work and who agree to be held strictly accountability for failure to perform in the public interest, and who agree to end the ideological demagoguery that grips our government today.

Karl Marx said "religion is the opiate of the masses." My research of articles on what he, and others who have used this phrase over time, meant by this phrase was that religion, being a set of rules to follow in order to guarantee an afterlife, is used by the people in power to control the people who are not in power (the masses). It convinces them to accept and endure the suffering and injustices in this life because heaven awaits them. It prevents the masses from questioning and ultimately changing the controlling doctrine so the people who are in power can stay in power. There are those who believe organized religion is Big Business; and that if these groups are going to act like a business in raising funds and building huge, well-staffed lavish facilities run by those who've become quite wealthy, then they ought to be treated as a business, at least to some degree. They say there's a difference between teaching religious doctrine and holding religious services on one hand, and blatant fund-raising to promote a social agenda and fund political activities on the other. If not having wealth or huge buildings was good enough for Jesus, Muhammad, Abraham and Moses, then it certainly should be good enough for today's religious leaders.

Against the backdrop of our nation's historic support for the separation between church and state, we see religion-based government—theocracies—throughout the world, especially in the Middle East, and how those who are subjected to theocratic government live in fear for daring to speak out on individual freedoms. Yet, look at how much influence religion is having on our own government!! In 2005, I read author Kevin Phillips' book "American Theocracy: The Peril and Politics of Radical Religion, Oil and Borrowed Money in the 21st Century." As I prepared to write this portion of my book, I recalled Phillips' work, re-examined the book and did an online search of reviews that succinctly described his effort.

Briefly stated, Phillips is critical of the Republican party coalition. He accuses the GOP of ideological extremism, catastrophic fiscal irresponsibility, rampant greed, and dangerous shortsightedness. Phillips points to three unifying themes holding this coalition together. First, its tie to oil and the role oil plays in American and world events. The Bush presidencies is a perfect example of this tie. Second, the growing influence of social conservatives, evangelicals and Pentecostals. There is no question that the religious beliefs of these groups are at the forefront of the Republican Party. Finally, the "debt culture" of this coalition, and to a coming "debt bubble" related to the debt of the U.S. Government and U.S. consumers. He argues that similar issues have been prevalent in the past, when other world powers, such as the Roman Empire and the British Empire, declined from their peaks and fell into disarray. In Phillips's words, these groups would seek to establish an American theocracy in which religion would serve as the basis for government policy. He believes the historical wall of separation between church and state is crumbling piece by piece. Phillips maintains that religion, which ultimately is a private matter between the individual and God, is becoming more and more a major participant in government policy making. Phillips' book was written three years before the great economic meltdown of 2008 and the aftermath of significant job loss, foreclosures and bailouts.

A bedrock principle of our country is religious freedom; that is, freedom to worship as one pleases free from persecution for daring to believe differently from others. This principle flows from the view that no single religion has the one true pipeline to God. There is, however, a disconnect between the exercise of this principle and the practice of some Big Religion groups.

For the Christian conservatives, their belief system defines their political agenda. To disagree with their belief system is to engage in Christian bashing. Their world view has successfully seized the initiative in fear-mongering and simple word or phrase demonization. Because of this, the Democrats have the harder task of asking voters to consider issues that require explanation and critical thinking. For example, how do the Democrats succinctly inform of what the country was like when business ruled supreme? How do the Democrats (and the moderate Republicans who are forced to remain silent in the face of the social conservative onslaught) convince the vast majority of voters that governing according to religious doctrine is what our forefathers fought against? I don't accept or condone bashing any religion; what I object to is forcing government to adopt as national policy the views of one religion over others. Further, I don't agree with any religious doctrine that demands blind obedience or face severe consequences. The history of the inquisitions should provide sufficient cause to blindly accept any form of obedience.

The Judeo-Christian bedrock of our nation teaches, among those principles set out in the Declaration of Independence, tolerance of those who are different, whether that difference is racial, religious or ethnic. Historically, America has prided itself as the "Great Melting Pot." Over the past generation, more and more have "come out" with regard to their sexual preferences. What I see, however, is that while there are pockets of tolerance in our country, as a general matter, a significant number of Americans are demonstrating less and less tolerance of those who are different from them. Instead of celebrating our status as the world's great Melting Pot, we see more and more examples of intolerance.

Here's a relatively recent situation that deserves consideration. It seems that one of the family members who own Chick-Fil-A publicly expressed his belief that marriage is between a man and a woman. The owners are Catholic and this view espoused by Catholics is certainly nothing new. However, this comment has been interpreted as being anti-gay, and certainly the Catholic Church believes homosexual acts are immoral. While most of the franchises are near or south of the Bible belt, some northern officials, notably Chicago Mayor Rahm Emanuel, have criticized the Chick-Fil-A owners as being insensitive and not possessing values of inclusion, and are asking people to boycott this company or not offering licenses for the business. My first reaction upon learning of this is that I go to Chick-Fil-A to eat a chicken sandwich, fries or salad, and a drink. What do I care what a business owner's personal religious or political beliefs are, so long as he/she doesn't discriminate against anyone and serves food that I choose to eat. I'm not aware that Chick-Fil-A refuses to serve anyone. Federal law would prohibit that anyway.

I understand that according to the Catholic Church, homosexual behavior is not approved, but the orientation is begrudgingly accepted. Unfortunately, disapproval of the former often leads to condemnation of the latter. Homosexual acts are deemed to be against natural law, and those who are gay suffer from a disorder, according to the church. The Catholic Church is locked into this difficulty because any changes regarding homosexuality would affect the position on issues like abortion and birth control. I don't think that it would surprise Catholics to know that there are Catholics who are gay, priests who are gay, and a cursory Google search discloses articles pointing out that even a few of the 265 popes were gay. I remember reading in high school about ancient Rome and the number of bathhouses frequented by the leaders of the Roman Empire. Does anyone seriously believe that there is no such thing as a gay Catholic? The fact is, homosexuality is not a modern phenomenon; and no religion is free of gay membership.

An important figure in the Catholic Church was quoted in 2012 as condemning the arrogance of those who presume to know what the word of God is on the subject of homosexuality, averring that homosexual acts are absolutely forbidden, and the Bible is clear on that. This person's initial problem is that the words "homosexual" and "homosexuality" don't appear in the Bible. These words first appeared sometime in either the 19th or 20th century. Therefore, it was an interpretation of what the writers believed was in the original Bible that led to their inclusion in later versions. This leads to this commentator's second problem: since the subject involves interpretation, why is it an act of arrogance for those to question the view that homosexual acts are absolutely forbidden, but not arrogant for those who believe to the contrary? In short, why is one view arrogant, while the other isn't? Does the Bible differentiate between acts of abuse—such as rape, incest—and acts of love, regardless of sex? And if the original Bible is the word of God, isn't He a loving God toward all humankind? And if the Bible is the true word of God, then wouldn't He have to know what homosexuality is in order to be able to write about it as this commentator says is the case? And if God knew about it, why did he not include these words in His writings? Perhaps these weighty questions are why more and more appear to be taking the "live and let live" view on this issue—which is probably the best policy. We have enough problems as it is without adding this one to our list.

The Chick-Fil-A brouhaha, however, forced me to think about the issue in different contexts. Assuming there is no discrimination regarding providing service to anyone, let's move the fact situation further down the line. Suppose that instead of gays being the issue, the owners said "We think the Jews are the cause of all the problems in the Middle East?" Any different reaction? I certainly believe the various Jewish organizations would react. How about the owners saying "I think African-Americans are an inferior race?" Do you think Black leaders would lead a national boycott of the company? How about a non-Catholic owner targeting Catholics? Suppose a business owner declared that Catholicism is based on a false premise, that Jesus Christ was not resurrected, etc.? Do you think the Christians would stage a nationwide protest against this owner? In a heartbeat. See what happens when the fact situation is changed? Even the slightest change can alter one's opinion. To be sure, no government can prevent the exercise of such First Amendment rights as exercised by the chain restaurant owner, but the offended group also has the right to protest such a comment in the exercise of its First Amendment rights. This time, it was the gays who were offended; could the Jews, Blacks or Christians be next?

It seems to be all about the dollar. Gays evidently don't make up a large percentage of the consuming population, especially in the south, to matter much to the Chick-Fil-A owners' bottom line. However, I don't believe any business owner would be stupid enough to express opposition to any large and influential group. Still, this is a subject that should bother our consciences because the gays in this situation could be the Jews, African-Americans, etc., in another setting. In short, it could be a group in which you are personally involved. And that would be disturbing to each one who's personally involved, to say the least. Of course, what we have in the Chick-Fil-A situation is a government official calling for a boycott, rather than the group leaders themselves calling for one. That's the part that, quite frankly, bothers me, because if there's one thing that may well grow out of this experience, it's the prospect of more support rallies and boycotts. And with this, more and more government leaders will be called on to voice their opinions. Business economics will merge with religion and politics to produce a boiling cauldron. Certainly, a public official can offer his/her comment, praise, or criticism, but using his/her office to call for a boycott of a legitimate business solely based on the personal beliefs of the owner is troubling. Still, if another group were the target, wouldn't its leadership ask for a response from government leaders? That seems to be the way these scenarios will now play out. For me, there's entirely too much hate in both words and deeds. Now, we even have a separate category now of hate crimes. This is a strange oxymoron, but the times are such that this phrase is now part of our culture. Very sad, isn't it?

I draw the line when people of a particular faith profess that their religion is superior to others, and that those who don't follow their beliefs are to be condemned unless they convert. The Islamic fundamentalists condemn non-believers as infidels who, in the name of Allah, must be destroyed. This type of twisted, tortured view of religion and religious persecution of non-believers are precisely what the oppressed fled from when they arrived at our shores and began to colonize our country 400 years ago. You would think that the horrific history of religious persecution would prevent this kind of bigotry in the 21st century. Sadly, yet again, those who fail to learn history's lessons are condemned to repeat them. I can't put this any simpler: I will never presume to tell anyone how to live his/her life, and I don't expect anyone to tell me how I must live mine.

I strenuously object to being labeled a liberal simply because I'm a registered Democrat. While I certainly don't mind being called a liberal if it pleases one's need for the simplicity of labeling, I don't like the underlying arrogance and superiority of the right wing when it uses this word to dismiss any challenge to their world view. I have voted for Republicans—moderate Republicans—although the vast majority of my votes are for Democrats. As a former news reporter, I well understand that a simple label or slogan resonates more easily than a more complicated message, and simply applying a label as a means of brushing off someone's views is far easier than engaging in debate. I believe labeling is a simple way for groups and individuals to dismiss what goes against their grain; name-calling and labeling do nothing to solve serious societal problems, however. In fact, such simplicity says more about the sloganeers than it does those who are branded by them. Instead of labeling into two categories, liberal and conservative, let's move to pragmatist, realist, moderate, common sense and logical. Wouldn't striving for these labels make more sense?

I get a kick when the right wing calls President Obama the most liberal president we've ever had, as if this alone is a criminal offense. This shows both nearsightedness and a lack of understanding of American history. Although historically wrong, this statement has as much value as saying a particular president is the most conservative we've ever had. In short, it adds nothing to the problem-solving purpose of government. Those who make such a statement aren't bothered by what historians say, but for the record, historians rank Franklin Roosevelt and Woodrow Wilson as the most liberal presidents. Of course, the "true believers" simply lump historians with the campus intellectuals who can't be trusted. How dare these people use facts and their education and intelligence to try to upset the right wing's hardcore belief system!!

Those who castigate Obama this way typically add the "he's going to take us down the road to socialism" link. The same thing was said about FDR. For them, I suppose there are different categories of socialism; one that is acceptable, another that isn't. I suppose that Social Security, Medicare, Medicaid, Aid to Families with Dependent Children, food stamps, etc., passed and amended by members of both parties over the years since the New Deal of the mid-1930s are part of the acceptable level. Funny, they never identify those programs that are in the unacceptable category. For the millions and millions getting Social Security checks, Medicare or Medicaid coverage who stick the word "socialism" on virtually any plan offered by the Democrats, you need to check your history books. I haven't seen one conservative currently receiving a government pension, Social Security, Medicare, etc., offer to return a single penny to our "socialist" government. Perhaps they limit their claim to entitlement programs like food stamps, aid to families with dependent children, Medicaid, etc. Again, these programs have been passed and amended by both parties over the years. When did they suddenly become evil to right wing conservatives? Does a return to traditional values mean eliminating these programs for the legitimate needy?

I have to laugh when my middle-class GOP friends rail at President Obama for doing nothing, believing with all their heart that the right wing will provide all the necessary programs and relief the middle and lower class need and seek. Here's a simple test. Name a single piece of legislation passed by a GOP Congress and signed by a GOP president in the last 20 years that benefitted the middle and lower classes without providing a single added benefit for the wealthy upper class, Big Business, Big Oil, etc. I can't think one; but if you do, please write a letter to your newspaper and point out this act of generosity and sensitivity toward those not in the upper class on the part of the GOP.

The regressives blast the Democrats for passing a national health care plan, and blame the Democrats for not having a viable immigration policy. Let's check the facts. In 1995, the GOP took over the House of Representatives, with then-Speaker Newt Gingrich proudly brandishing his Contract for America. In 2001, George H. W. Bush took over the White House. For six of Bush's eight years in office, the GOP had total control of the House of Representatives and White House. Where was their national health plan? Where was their immigration reform plan? The right wing claims that Obama's health care plan has been driving up the costs of health care. Where have these people been for the past 10-15 years? Do they expect us to believe that health care costs were low before Obama took office and that the skyrocketing costs of health care are directly and solely attributable to the Democrats when they passed a health care plan? The fact is health care costs for all Americans have been skyrocketing upward long before Obama took office. Immigration has been a problem long before Obama took office. The GOP rails at Obama's every move; begging him to take action; complaining of his inability to address problems from energy, immigration, health care, infrastructure relief, banking, securities, etc. Yet, the fact remains that the GOP has blocked virtually every effort by the Democrats to get legislation through Congress. The GOP's line is that it will pass only what the right wing wants, and will prevent passage of anything they disagree with. Does the right wing expect the Democrats to become social conservatives? Well, maybe they do; they're certainly rabid enough in their efforts. What they shouldn't be allowed to get away with is blaming the Democrats for inaction while at the same time thwarting their efforts. Nevertheless, they do so because their simple mantra is working in influencing so many of the masses to blindly accept it.

The GOP takes to the airwaves to complain about the Democrats' failure, but where is their legislation to deal with across-the-board problems? They curry favor with the media to get their message out, only to demonize them when they take the GOP to task. The right wing believes voters have a short—very short—memory, and they fervently believe that you can fool all of the people some of the time, and some of the people all the time. Promises, however, mean nothing. The GOP wastes time and our money by trying to repeal the health care act more than 30 times, knowing that this was only posturing—serving no useful purpose except to foolishly waste time and spend taxpayers' money. The GOP is very adept at beating back programs designed to help the majority of Americans; the party is very good at securing benefits for the very wealthy; it's woefully inept at introducing, much less passing, plans for helping the middle and lower classes. The GOP now has a majority in the House of Representatives; where is their proposed legislation to address our economic problems? Again, where is there a single piece of legislation that passed the House that doesn't provide some benefit to the wealthy? The GOP blames the Democrats and president for inaction, yet when they propose action, the GOP blocks it. It seems all the right wing really wants is to repeal, repeal, repeal and block, block, block.

Where were Nixon's, Ford's, Reagan's and the Bushes' health care and immigration reform plans? What years were they filed and debated; when were the votes taken and what were the results? Truman wanted a health care plan; so did Clinton—both vehemently opposed by a GOP Congress claiming rampant socialism. It's the same tired complaint you hear today. You won't see a health care plan or immigration reform plan from the GOP, unless there are huge HUGE benefits built in for Big Business and the wealthy. If you want a health care plan from the GOP, please don't hold your breath. One reason all Republicans voted against the health care plan is because the bill didn't provide for so-called tort reform and other types of relief for the wealthy special interests. They're not thinking about the victim or victims of shoddy and negligent business or professional practices; they're thinking of ways to insulate business and certain professions from accountability and liability for their negligence and malpractice.

The GOP claims to be the party of individual responsibility. Where is this responsibility for those individuals who engage in bad business and/or professional practices? Why are these entities seeking the right wing's assistance in order to avoid individual accountability and responsibility for negligent or reckless acts that harm the public? Beware whenever you hear the word "reform" bandied about by politicians. When words such as reform or relief are used, they're usually euphemisms for providing benefits to certain special interests. Tort reform in connection with the medical field generally means effectively immunizing medical providers from acts of negligence or malpractice by drastically limiting the amount a patient/victim may recover, and limiting the amount of attorney's fees that can be recovered as well. In short, they want to put as many obstacles in the path of securing financial relief from professional negligence and malpractice and shore up immunity for the incompetent or reckless, all designed to give Big Business big breaks.

The biggest fear on the part of those businesses or professionals who cry for tort reform is the class action lawsuit. In such a case, one or more representatives of a group injured or harmed in the same or sufficiently similar manner serve as the representative(s) of the harmed class and sue a company that caused the injury or harm to a large enough population so as to justify a single lawsuit in one venue rather than multiple lawsuits throughout the state or nation. Frequently, these lawsuits seek relief for negligent manufacturing of a product and/or failure to inform of risk associated with its use, which use then causes harm to hundreds or even thousands of people. Damages for such actions can be well into the multimillions of dollars; and attorney's fees are usually a third of the total amount recovered. When a company that has to pay out this kind of money for its negligence screams for tort reform, what it really wants is to be able to engage in business as usual, with damages and attorney's fees limited by a dollar cap, regardless of the degree and scope of the harm caused.

Reform and relief therefore generally mean providing special benefits for providers, pharmaceutical companies, and other manufacturers or organizations involved in product development and health care so their bottom lines aren't damaged. Those who must pay large malpractice insurance premiums complain that this cost is far too high. But what makes these premiums high in the first place? Are we to believe that juries are punishing innocent businesses and professions? Any damages awarded are done so through a jury or a judge sitting as the trier of fact, and only after hearing evidence and testimony. While I believe jury awards can be excessive, I also believe a jury can best assess the degree and extent of injury caused by negligence or malpractice—and if a jury's award is excessive, the courts can, and often do, reduce the amount of recovery. As for attorney's fees, the several states' codes of ethics or professional responsibility adopted by or under the auspices of the state supreme courts set limits on what attorneys can recover. What the GOP wants is to take negligence and malpractice claims, as well as attorney's fees, from the judicial process and replace it with special interest legislation. Undermining the judiciary is not a solution; right wing legislation is a virtual escape hatch for the incompetent or reckless providers. The competent and conscientious have no need to worry, regardless of the circumstances.

In the health care field, we see ads on TV just about every day about companies that developed a vaccine, medication or device that they market as providing miracle relief; only it turns out that this product is linked to horrific side effects about which the companies failed to inform the public. We also learn of vehicle manufacturers that knew of a dangerous situation that could have been remedied, but decided that the cost of the remedy exceeded the risk to the public. Do you really want these companies to effectively experiment on us or a loved one, and if found negligent, have damages limited to an amount that provides very little true compensation for your loss, while effectively insulating that company from true accountability by having to pay for its aberrant conduct and the cost of adjusting its method of operation? If, for example, a company knew that the extent of its liability was, say, $10 million for a defective product, regardless of the number harmed, with attorney's fees capped at 10% of the amount awarded; but the company was making $100 million on that same product, what incentive would there be to remediate the problem? And what incentive would there be for a law firm to devote the extraordinary amount of time to investigate and try such a case? Again, it's all about the bottom line. I wonder if those who clamor for tort reform in Congress have a change in tune when they become the victim of shoddy practices and defective products.

On the subject of health care, no issue received more attention from 2010 to 2012 than the debate over the Affordable Care Act, derisively called Obamacare by the right wing. I loved watching the town hall meetings where people would stand up and, with veins bulging and faces as red as beets, demand the federal government to get its "hands off my health care," or "keep your hands of my Social Security" (or Medicare), adding that familiar refrain "Obama will lead us down the road to socialism." These folks were stirred up most successfully by right wing government officials and wing candidates scaring the hell out of them not by facts, but by raw appeal to emotion via buzz words or emotive phrases, or outright lies offered as fact, leading to planned demonstrations of anger, hatred, etc. We've seen this type of scenario before. Think about history. Recent world history-the Middle East. Recent American history-McCarthyism. Fear is a great motivator; the more fear instilled in people, the more rabid and thoughtless the reaction.

What made these town hall meetings so humorous is that many of these irate folks are recipients of Medicare and Medicaid; receive health care coverage through government-regulated HMOs or government-regulated insurance companies; and most likely receive a pension of some type. I think it's safe to say that some of them might even have received social service benefits like food stamps or aid to families with dependent children, and unemployment compensation and workers' compensation at some time in their lives. I guess to them what they've received or are receiving doesn't count as socialism. These town hall meetings represented the height of disingenuousness and hypocrisy. I don't fault the well-meaning folks who've been whipped up into a frenzy by their right wing gurus; it's the gurus who should know better. Perhaps these citizens don't recall or believe that health care costs have been skyrocketing for many years now. Certainly the right wing isn't going to inform its base of this. The notion that costs will go up solely because of Obamacare is, in light of recent history, ludicrous on its face. So long as insurance companies can set rates at whatever level is permissible to assure a guaranteed rate of return, with no checks and balances on the system that's concerned with the bottom line, you can bet that costs will continue to increase, Obamacare notwithstanding.

Parenthetically, the United States Supreme Court's decision upholding the Affordable Health Act turned on whether the individual mandate to purchase insurance or pay a fine was a tax that the majority found permissible under the U.S. constitution. I never thought the Commerce Clause argument would go anywhere; there was no "activity" that was at issue. Rather, it was a non-activity that triggered the mandate. I believe the Court stretched on the tax issue; for me, the case was an easy one based on two constitutional provisions; the first empowers Congress to enact laws that provide for the general welfare, which includes the nation's general health; the second is the "necessary and proper" clause which allows Congress to enact all laws "necessary and proper" to fulfill its authority to enact laws in the other delegated categories. Combining "general welfare" with "necessary and proper" was all that was necessary to authorize Congress to pass the health care act.

I must digress a moment since I'm discussing health, one of the fundamental issues of our time. People are living longer, but quality of life issues are impacting health and welfare considerations. It seems to me that, generally speaking, a person's concern with the overriding issues of our time is dependent upon the closeness that person is to the issue. For example, I doubt 20-or 30-somethings are concerned very much about Social Security or Medicare. People who live in Iowa or North Dakota probably are not as concerned about immigration as the folks in Texas or New Mexico. As a retiree, I'm not that concerned personally about a job, and my children have either a solid business or good, steady employment. While I have a concern for my grandchildren, they're bright, extroverted and will do well because of the work ethic that is being instilled in them. Having said this, I am concerned about Social Security and Medicare. I am concerned about my government pension. For a very good reason. My monthly income now consists of two checks: my pension and Social Security—which together don't equal what I earned when I was a state employee. Harriet is in the same situation as I am. Together, these four checks make up the totality of our spendable income

If these two sources are reduced or compromised in any way, Harriet and I face serious financial problems because I can no longer work and there isn't much of a market for those in their 60s and 70s anyway. Medicare and my supplemental insurance plan take care of our medical bills, but if I can't pay the supplement, we're one or two health crises away from blowing our savings—and my particular medical situation makes this possibility more than a mere afterthought. As it is, our "nest egg" will see us through for a few years, but then what? I don't want our nest egg to become scrambled by changes in pension, Social Security and Medicare that we can't recoup. This is why I fervently believe that whatever changes are made—and sooner or later they will be made—must not impact current retirees for one very solid reason: for the vast majority of us, we're simply not capable of recuperating losses, either in the job or stock market. This is also why I oppose privatization and indeed any system that purports to remove government from its responsibility to provide for health, safety and welfare of its people. If government wants to get out of the pension and social services business and turn these over to the private sector, then the government must provide a fail-safe mechanism to protect the recipients in the event the business goes belly up, or the market tanks, or both, causing irreplaceable losses. If this is being selfish, well, then so be it. I paid into both Social Security and Medicare, and I took a government job at a lower income level than the private sector in return for a guaranteed monthly pension. If there are those who still think I'm selfish, I can assure that as that as they get closer to my age, their opinion will change dramatically. Believe me, self-preservation is a very strong motivator. In addition, there are millions who are far worse off than I am, and if those in my situation suffer adverse consequences, what about the others? Think they're going to sit around and take it?

With all the clamor over revamping Social Security and Medicare, and perhaps Medicaid and social services programs generally, the question that I pose is would elimination or substantial reduction of these programs be valid under the United States Constitution. We can agree that providing for the general welfare of the people is a basic goal of government. The preamble to the Constitution cites promotion of the general welfare as a primary reason for the creation of the Constitution. But because the preamble itself is not a source of power, the scope of providing for the general welfare has sparked controversy only as a result of its inclusion in the body of the Constitution.

The first clause of Article I, Section 8, reads, "The Congress shall have Power to lay and collect Taxes, Duties, Imposts and Excises, to pay the Debts and provide for the common Defence and general Welfare of the United States." In 1936, the United States Supreme Court, in United States v. Butler, interpreted the general welfare clause as giving Congress broad powers to spend federal money and established that the determination of what the general welfare meant would be left to the discretion of Congress. In its opinion, the Court warned that to challenge a federal expense on the ground that it did not promote the general welfare would "naturally require a showing that by no reasonable possibility can the challenged legislation fall within the wide range of discretion permitted to the Congress.". In South Dakota v. Dole, the Court in 1987 reviewed legislation allowing the secretary of transportation to withhold a percentage of federal highway funds from states that refused to raise their legal drinking age to twenty-one. In holding that the statute was a valid use of congressional spending power, the Court questioned "whether 'general welfare' is a judicially enforceable restriction at all."

Congress appropriates money for a seemingly endless number of national interests, ranging from federal courts, policing, imprisonment, and national security to social services programs, environmental protection, and education. No federal court has struck down a spending program on the ground that it failed to promote the general welfare.

Since providing for the general welfare means the concern of the government for the health, peace, morality, and safety of its citizens as Congress has so declared by enactment of so many laws as set out above, does Congress have the power to reverse or modify those laws when faced with the argument that such a cutback, modification or reversal would fail to promote the general welfare? In other words, since Congress has already defined the scope of providing for the general welfare, would a re-definition—at least in the absence of a factual record supporting it—constitute a failure to meet this constitutional mandate? I don't recall this argument ever made before in connection with any legislation, but it will be interesting to see how Congress addresses the federal social services programs that date to the 1930s. Remember, the Constitution doesn't authorize anyone else to provide for the general welfare; neither does it authorize Congress to delegate this power to another. The issue of privatization will no doubt spark these considerations.

Back to my missive. The regressives are so virulent in their opposition to Obama, they even take their challenge to his legitimacy as president to his birth, claiming he wasn't born in America. Again, despite undisputed proof of his 1961 birth in Hawaii, they dismiss all proof and rely on their beliefs. No wonder so many label these people as wing nuts!!! The vitriol that was spilled over Bush II's 2000 election he was finally awarded by the United States Supreme Court pales in comparison to the vitriol being spilled over Obama's legitimacy as president. The regressives conveniently forget that Obama received almost 70 million votes—almost 10 million more than the GOP's nominee, Sen. John McCain.

The right wing's effort to challenge the legitimacy of Obama's victory by putting the "most liberal" label on him naturally leads to the question of who is the most conservative president in our history. When the question involves social conservatism, historians recognize that this appellation is of relatively recent vintage, but the general consensus is George W. Bush. For those who wonder how Obama was ever elected, let me suggest to you how he managed to get almost 70 million votes. Historically, the prevailing view was that the Democrats got us into war, and the Republicans got us into economic depressions. Bush II gave us a double whammy. He got us involved in a war in Iraq based on lies, and his domestic policies led us to the worst meltdown since the Great Depression. With a track record like that, the Democrats were going to take the White House in 2008; all Obama had to do was get the nomination. We were going to have either the first African-American president, or the first female president had Hillary Clinton gotten the nomination. Of course, the votes cast weren't all pro-Obama votes; there were millions of anti-Bush votes in the mix. But evidently many people seem to have forgotten that.

I believe in helping businesses grow; I also believe in helping people in need. If the right wing truly doesn't want the government involved in their business affairs by way or reduced or eliminated regulations, then by all means they must be willing to give up the breaks government gives them so they can grow their businesses and their wealth. In short, they shouldn't have their cake and eat it, too. I also don't believe business should be given a free ride based on the historically inaccurate notion that the number of jobs supposedly created by a laissez-faire approach to business will outstrip profit-making as a prime motivating force. Businesses are designed to enhance the bottom line; they will employ only as many as absolutely necessary to maximize profits. And they will do everything they can to keep workers' wages and benefits (if any) low so that corporate profits and executive salaries and perks will be high. There is certainly nothing wrong with business focusing on the bottom line, but not when it becomes the primary motivating force to the exclusion of consideration of workers and their importance to those businesses, and the higher goal of acting in the consumer's best interests. Business leaders must never lose of the fact that without the workers, there would be no business to operate. Of course, the corollary is equally true that without business, workers would have no jobs. What this means is that, as is the case with government, business and labor must work together for the community by at least subduing the selfishness behind what's best for their own personal interests. However, with government blessing private companies as they move away from providing pension relief, and requiring workers, in planning their retirement, to place their faith in the risky, all-too-volatile market, the connection between employer company and employee is becoming more and more tenuous. I am concerned that we will return to a time when businesses used workers until they could work no longer, and then simply dumped them.

There is a theory that says history runs in cycles; events that we've gone through 50-100 years go will be repeated because human nature doesn't change and people don't learn the lessons of history. If we return to a time when workers' wages aren't sufficient to support a family; provisions for health care and retirement are not at least partially within the domain of employers; workers who become ill or injured and can no longer work are left with no lifeline to fall back on; or workers who complete their careers are simply cast aside as obsolete, we will see the reaction in the form of work stoppages, labor strikes, labor violence, etc., that we saw in the 1920s-1930s. At least, this is what our history tells us.

While both major political parties would love nothing better than to have simultaneous control of the White House and both houses of Congress, history shows that government operates more efficiently, and more positive action is taken on behalf of the majority of the population, when one party controls the executive branch, and the other controls the legislative branch. Such a situation forces all factions to compromise, because one party checks the other to create balance. The reason Ronald Reagan was able to accomplish much during his tenure was because of the close working relationship between him and House Speaker Tip O'Neill. The name-calling, fear-mongering and demonization today preclude this type of working relationship between the president and speaker of the house. If the GOP truly wants to return to the past, the

Reagan-O'Neill relationship would be a good place to start. But, of course, the right wing isn't talking about that kind of return to the past.

Intransigence will continue to control government action until we the voters put an end to it. Unfortunately, we see more and more candidates pledging to go to Washington (or their state capitol) not to debate but to ram their doctrinaire beliefs into law. When Obama took office, he vowed to compromise, and continued this message even as the GOP moved further and further to the right and vowed not to compromise at all. When has rigid doctrinaire beliefs founded on a particular religion's doctrine ever carried the day in our country's history?

Ours has always been a nation built on tolerance; recognizing and applauding religious, ethnic and cultural differences; and working hand-in-hand to build a better, brighter tomorrow. What happened to this nation? Now, it seems all we see is one group pitting itself against another; where one claims superiority over another; where one claims to have all the correct answers to society's ills while the other perpetuates them; and on and on. When the individual was part of the American community, we put our collective shoulders to the grindstone and lifted ourselves to become the most powerful, educated nation in history. Now, it seems we're focused less on the community and more on the individual with this glaring caveat: only those individuals who believe a certain way and act a certain way are praised, while others who are different are cursed and vilified. History teaches that we succeed only when we share and work side by side; without this sense of community, we will remain a divided nation. The consequences of this division are (or certainly should be) self-evident.

As I see the economic picture of our country, I am distressed at the increasing concentration of wealth at the top of the economic ladder. I am disheartened at the increasing role big corporations play in the formation and execution of government policy, and the coziness between government and lobbyists. This is not a Republican or Democratic issue; both parties are beholden to their special interests. Greed is a nonpartisan corrupter that stems from the "I've got mine; you get yours" mentality driven by the dark side of human nature. I don't want anyone to assume that I'm giving the Democrats a pass here; they have engaged in conduct that I find both troubling and questionable in protecting their interests. They place too much emphasis on pure entitlements and, by doing so, create too much of a dependency on government rather than individual initiative. At the risk of being repetitive on this point, our government—both parties—must rise above human nature and come together as Americans and enact legislation that is helpful to those who, by their actions, are most deserving, as well as those who, through no fault of their own, are temporarily in need or permanently incapable of helping themselves, without creating a "world owes me a living" entitlement mentality. To those who preach traditional American values; remember that the history of our nation is one in which we help others when they are down so they can get back on their feet and lead productive lives. While I don't believe it was ever the intention of government to create a pure entitlement society, as with so many good deeds, what started out as a positive program to help people has, over the years, been extended and stretched so broadly that what existed at the beginning is hard to recognize today. As the saying goes, no good deed goes unpunished.

I'm not suggesting that we go back to a time where help for the legitimate needy is abandoned; indeed, just the opposite. What our governmental leaders must do is to use common sense and logic to reach pragmatic and realistic solutions that help those who need it, and punish those who take advantage and engage in greedy, self-serving behavior. Perhaps I'm being far too idealistic on this, but I believe that we can help those who need it and simultaneously punish the greedy and corrupters as well. To believe otherwise is to admit that there's nothing we can do to prevent greed and corruption at the highest levels of our government. I have to believe we're better than that.

I am saddened by the inaction of government in its failure to address serious societal problems solely because there is no economic benefit to Big Business or Wall Street in doing so. Pouring more and more money into questionable programs with less and less oversight concerns me greatly. And I am troubled by the increasing corrupting influence of big money on candidates, elections and the development and implementation of policy. With big corporations and super political action committees able to contribute unlimited, obscene amounts of money to candidates, you can be certain of one thing: this money is not being given to promote "good government." My concern is that, in the name of jobs creation and improving the business climate, a Republican congress and president will cut or eliminate all regulations that Big Business claims is stifling them, such as EPA regulations that serve to eliminate toxic wastes in our air and water; regulations that provide for a safe workplace; as well as other regulations that will adversely impact the nation's health, safety and welfare. By all means, eliminating regulations may serve as useful function, but certainly not when health, safety and welfare protection is sacrificed to any extent.

There is one issue on which we see how Big Business, particularly Big Oil, impacts policy-making. That's on the subject of global warming. While there are scientific studies that show that global warming is real and is affecting weather patterns, there are those who say global warming is nothing more than a trumped-up issue pressed by the virulent environmentalists, or "tree lovers" as the anti-global warming groups like to label them. Casting aside those who dismiss the claim with labels, let's look at the logic. With more than seven billion people inhabiting the planet; and with more and more noxious gases from vehicles and industrial plants being emitted into the atmosphere, it just doesn't square with common sense that these emissions have absolutely nothing to do with our weather patterns or the atmosphere in general. What the anti-global warmers point to is cold temperatures in the winter as evidence of their position, believing that so long as we have cold weather, global warming can't exist. These so-called experts miss the point.

Global warming includes strange and inconsistent weather patterns—whether it be cold when it's supposed to be warm; rainy when it's usually sunny; incredibly hot when it's supposed to be generally cool, and on and on. We've certainly seen stranger and stranger weather patterns; for example, high temperatures in northern cities during the winter months; incredibly high temperatures in the Mideast in June; heavy rains in usually drought areas; drought in usually wet areas; tornadoes in December, etc. And here's the real kicker: what if those who with righteous indignation disregard all claims of global warming are wrong? How do we correct their error, assuming we have the time and resources to do that? In short, can we afford to wait and see if the anti-global warming groups are right—or wrong?

Businesses that rely on production of goods and services that require emitting noxious gases and other poisons into the air and water obviously want to remain in business and keep costs down so as to maximize profits. Are we to believe there are no consequences to life or health from these emissions? I believe it defies logic and common sense to believe that the emission or more and more pollutants into the atmosphere has absolutely no health or environmental consequences at all. I don't believe that hiding our heads in the sand or simply ignoring the issue will make it go away. It seems to me that it would be a better use of our resources if we take some of the billions we're currently giving away to foreign countries whose friendship with us is, at best, questionable, and use some of that revenue to assist in helping Big Business deal with noxious emissions. Of course, ultimately, it's up to those that pollute to clean up their act. Perhaps requiring them to use a portion of their expanding bottom line to implement with deliberate speed effective emission controls or risk business license suspensions/revocation will do the job. Those who do pollute our air and water should do so at peril of huge personal fines, loss of business license and jail time for executives who recklessly permit such actions.

Billions of dollars are being spent to elect presidents, senators, members of Congress, governors, state legislators, etc., for two reasons: to have access to people of power and to secure favorable legislation and other favorable government treatment. No one gives big bucks to a candidate without expecting something in return. Quid pro quo is human nature; you wash my hands, I'll wash yours. The Citizens United decision of the United States Supreme Court, which holds that corporations and the wealthy are free to contribute unlimited amounts to political campaigns, only adds to the high incentive for corruption. With PACs, SuperPACs and Citizens United, corruption will only increase. If you want to know where the corruption is, follow the money. Any legitimate effort to curtail or eliminate corruption in government must begin with ebbing the flow of money. Corruption will continue to plague our government until money is, in one way or another, removed from the political equation or substantially controlled by strong criminal penalties. Under the current scheme, there is no level playing field for the vast majority of the people whose voices want—and need—to be heard. Supreme Court Justice Antonin Scalia, speaking on the subject of the Citizens United decision, said Thomas Jefferson would love this decision because it allows for more free speech. This disingenuous common overlooks the obvious: today speech is meaningful only if the amount of money behind it is substantial. If a candidate is receiving millions from a very few donors at the very top of the food chain, and the $10s and $20s from others, who do you think that candidate will listen to once elected? He/she will naturally be beholden to the large donors' personal interests. That's only human nature. The others will be tossed a bone now and then just to keep them quiet, but the benefits of government will go to the wealthy. Where the playing field is grossly uneven, the meaningfulness of free speech is compromised.

Whether it be Wall Street, multi-national corporations, Big Oil or the military-industrial complex, we see corporate greed going virtually unpunished because of their influence on government officials. Government gives special legislative and executive agency favors in the form of tax benefits, subsidies, exemptions and do-not-stop cards for tax havens; contracts, handouts and bailouts; and virtual immunity for executives who commit illegal acts that cause meltdowns, stockholder losses, investor losses or other harms to the public. We see Wall Street executives on the merry-go-round, bringing their bottom-line profit-making approach to government, only to return to their previous companies or another similar company as lobbyists. I am distressed that the political parties pander to the super-rich and pay scant attention—if any—to the middle class, and literally ignore the poor. There is a vicious cycle at play here in which, in return for campaign contributions and other benefits (some of questionable legality and of dubious morality), elected representatives will provide tax breaks and other gratuities for the wealthy and Big Business interests—in return for which the wealthy will be given greater or additional breaks, in return for which .... and on and on it goes. This is crony capitalism personified. Crony capitalism is an economy in which success in business depends on close relationships between business and government officials; and is demonstrated by favoritism in the distribution of legal permits, government grants, special tax breaks, or other forms quid pro quo. It arises when political cronyism or favoritism spills over into the business world; and where self-serving friendships and family ties between businessmen and the government influence the economy and society to the extent that it corrupts public-serving economic and political ideals.

There is a way to address aberrant conduct by public officials, and it calls for the removal from office through the protracted process of actions brought directly by the people themselves based on misfeasance, malfeasance and nonfeasance of office; and it's called the recall election process. We've seen examples of this in California with Arnold Schwarzenegger defeating incumbent Gray Davis in a 2003 gubernatorial recall election, and recently where the governor of Wisconsin prevailed in a recall election. Certainly a recall election is expensive, but democracy was never meant to be cheap. All jurisdictions should have a procedure in place for conducting a recall election. There should be clear conditions under which a petition for the calling of a recall election can be submitted; clearly prescribed petition requirements; a verification process; a candidate nomination procedure; and the setting of an election by the appropriate election official. There should be a requirement that no more than one recall be held during an official's term. In Florida, we have a constitutional provision that allows for the initiative, or a process by which the voters themselves can use the petitioning process to place a proposed constitutional amendment directly on the ballot. While our conservative legislators have done just about everything they can to make this process more and more difficult—and based on some of the amendments, there is justification for some of these restrictions—the fact remains that this triggering mechanism is part of Florida's organic law. Why not provide for a similar triggering mechanism to remove someone from office who is not performing his/her duties in the public trust? Why should the voters have to wait and suffer the vagaries of such public officials for a full four years before being able to act? Why should it only be up to elected officials to determine whether an elected official should be removed from office?

Since the conservatives say they won't raise taxes on the super-rich, and that they want to cut taxes "for everyone," let's hold them to their promise of equal treatment across-the-board. This necessarily includes closing all special loopholes and exemptions from taxes on the super-rich. While the right wing would call this an increase in taxes on the rich, why not call it what it is: removal of special tax benefits and privileges not available to the rest of the public. Everyone pays the same percentage of taxes across-the-board. No more tax havens. Just a flat tax rate for all; everyone pays the same rate on their gross income. No deductions of exemptions for anyone. Right now, the tax code is riddled with so many exceptions, exemptions, deductions, etc., that the average American can't possibly comprehend our tax law, except perhaps for the fact that the wealthy who gain on trading stock pay at a tax rate of about 15% while those who make the same as salary pay at up to 35% Why not just simplify the monster called the Tax Code? Of course, the conservatives respond by saying that eliminating breaks for business and the wealthy will remove incentives for businesses to grow and provide jobs. This is utter nonsense. Back in 2007-8, these pro-business, pro-wealthy loopholes and exemptions existed, and we had the worst economic meltdown since the Great Depression. This alone demonstrates the fallacy of the conservative argument that allowing the accumulation of wealth at the top of the food chain will lead to the creation of more jobs. The trickle-down theory has been discredited, yet those who are blind to history's lessons seem to want to go back to that approach. Or maybe they just want to return to the good old days of George W. Bush!!

Why can't we go even further and repeal special substantive breaks given to Big Business and no one else? Really level the playing field. Do you think this will ever happen, no matter how much candidates talk about equality, etc.? No way.

Here's another example. During the first three years of Obama's administration, do you remember the oil companies' bottom-line reports? They were reaping their largest profits in history. How could this happen when the economy is supposed to be tanking? I'll tell you. Big Business will protect its bottom line, even to the point of not hiring and thereby requiring more and more production from fewer workers without increasing wages or benefits. Big Business is quite efficient at doing what it can to rid itself of oversight and worker protection laws sought by the Democrats when they know they get a better deal (translation: a freer hand) with the Republicans. Hence, keeping the level of unemployment high works to businesses' economic advantage.

After all, we do have a managed economy. The question is: who's really managing it, and for whose benefit?

What creates jobs is strong competition on a level playing field that grows a workforce, but with big corporations and Big Business squeezing out mom-and-pop businesses, we're moving inexorably closer to economic monopolization. Under this type of economy, fewer and fewer do better and better. If only one or two companies produce a product, then they share in the profits with no other competition. My daughter and son-in-law own a small business, and they spend far too much time filling out forms and doing other required functions unrelated to their business. Unlike big companies, they don't have a staff to handle the paperwork; the time they spend on paperwork takes away time from earning enough to pay staff and make their business grow. Conservatives want to get government out of the way of business, but evidently not small businesses. This appears to be equally true for the Democrats. Again, I hold both parties' hands to the fire in their collective failure to move the country ahead by allowing small businesses to focus on growing. After all, if they're allowed to truly grow, they'll be more inclined to provide competent service and products as opposed to the much more impersonal corporation that is far more able to diffuse accountability. It's a win for the consumer and the small business as well. Maybe that's the problem for politicians who are in the pockets of Big Business.

With high unemployment, job scarcity and more and more foreclosures, corporate profits—including Big Oil's—continue to reach unprecedented heights. Gas prices continue to fluctuate, always with the trend toward higher and higher prices, with government saying there's nothing it can do because the prices are set by supply and demand. Sure it is; Big Oil demands higher profits, and we supply them. Imagine that; our federal government says it can't do anything to regulate gas prices at the pump because they're beyond government's ability to address. And government expects everyone to accept this feckless rationale. I don't. Clever company spokespersons say it's all about "economic forces at work." What nonsense; it's about people who make the rules for us, and a private set of rules for themselves. Gas prices fluctuate by 10-15 cents per week; sometimes even more. Do you know of another product that has this much fluctuation in such a short period of time? I can't think of one. Why are gas prices treated differently from all others? Don't we have consumer organizations and anti-trust laws to protect the consumer—us—against what is tantamount to unfettered price-setting by the oil companies? Sure we do, but government won't do anything because Big Oil has contributed—and continues to contribute—mightily to members of Congress from both parties, as well as presidential campaigns. Does anyone really believe that the closeness we witnessed between Bush I and II and the Saudis was based on brotherly love and affection?

More and more private companies are getting huge contracts from states for performing public services that were formerly the province of government. We now have government of the rich, by the rich and for the rich. To prove my point, find out how many members of Congress are millionaires as compared to the rest of the country. Never mind, I'll tell you. One percent of all Americans are millionaires; 47 percent of the members of Congress are millionaires! Is this truly representative government? Our governments at all levels have lost sight of the fact that their ultimate purpose is to serve the people; business's purpose is to enhance the bottom line. I know I've repeated this over and over again, but it can't be stressed enough. The roles of government and business are strikingly different. If you remember nothing else, remember this point.

Congressional inquiries that are supposed to fairly and fully investigate Wall Street or Big Business criminal activities are a farce when the members of Congress doing the investigations receive campaign funds from the very companies they're investigating! Expecting complete and fair investigations into criminal activities by those who receive political contributions from the subjects of these investigations is expecting the impossible. The same is the case regarding supposed regulatory agencies, where we once again see crony capitalism at play. The government will, often in good faith, establish government agencies to regulate a type of enterprise. Of course, the members of that enterprise have a very strong interest in the actions of its regulatory body, while the rest of the public are only tangentially affected. As a result, it's not uncommon for current business officials to gain control of the "watchdog" agency and use it against competitors, as well as try to secure any other form of advantage that may be out there. Members of Congress and their families must be prohibited from having any interest whatever in the businesses these legislators are investigating.

Until early 2012, it was perfectly legal for members of Congress to trade stock on the basis of information available to them, but not to members of the public. Government officials faced criminal penalties for insider trading, but members of Congress exempted themselves from these laws. After the media made this knowledge public across the country, Congress passed a law prohibiting its members from profiting from insider information. But being adept at creating loopholes, Congress excluded the use of political intelligence from the law. Political intelligence is insider information which is passed out in hallways and lobbies, which information is picked up and then sold to those who can thereafter trade on it. Sounds like yet another clever way around this so-called prohibition on congressional behavior. There is something terribly wrong with any system that allows a member of Congress to leave office with a net worth of ten to a hundred times more than what he/she was worth when he/she was elected. Blind trusts and other means of preventing government officials from profiting from their office should be mandated. But remember this: when Congress closes one loophole, you can be sure it opens up another. It's our job to make sure that our representatives don't pull the wool over our eyes by loop holing us to their (and their wealthy supporters') benefit.

Lobbyists too often are in bed with congressmen and congresswomen and their staff, casually mentioning that when their time in Congress is over, they can always join lobbying firms. Where do those public officials' and public servants' loyalties lie when they're given this ticket? It's a merry go round for those in government to become lobbyists, and lobbyists to join government—just like corporate officials who go to work for government and then return to the private sector. Whose interests do these in-and-outers and merry go rounders promote? Their own!!! Until money as the lifeblood of politics is brought under control, corporate and government crimes will continue as the people continue to lose faith in their government. Prohibiting officials and employees from lobbying Congress for a period of time—say, three years—after leaving government would certainly help, but there are ways around such a restriction, such as allowing another to be the face of the lobbying effort, while the former government official does the spadework. Carefully drafted reporting requirements, and replacing administrative penalties with criminal penalties would at least make this subterfuge that much harder to conceal.

With government increasingly influenced by Big Religion and big corporate businesses, the logical consequences of the confluence of these forces don't bode well for our nation's future. The wall between church and state must continue to remain impenetrable; the corrupting influence of money must be strongly regulated; businesses must not be allowed to control policy for the purpose of enhancing their bottom line; government must not become the means of advancing a religion's social or political agenda. Requiring all government officials to live and work by the rules they apply to us would go a long way toward restoring some measure of faith in our government. And make no mistake about it: with increasing regularity, people are losing faith in their governments-federal, state and local. The core problem can be stated in a nutshell: as more and more money is spread around to dictate policy, the ability of the vast majority to truly influence government moves further and further beyond their reach. I don't have to tell you what the consequences are when the level of distrust and disgust reaches the low end of critical mass. It will take ultimate acts of statesmanship to navigate the churning waters born of the interplay of these societal dynamics.

I continue to be amazed at the disingenuousness and effrontery exhibited by government officials and corporate executives when they give the appearance of gnashing their teeth and grimace when they tell us they have "tough decisions" or "tough choices" to make. Tough for whom? Certainly not for them; they're the ones with incredibly high salaries, benefits not available to the general public, and golden parachutes. What you won't see is any effort on the part of these folks to reduce any of the benefits and perks they have. If those who have the authority to cut workers' salaries, hours and even jobs were honest and upright, they would set an example and cut their own salaries in the same proportion that they are cutting others, and cut the number of managerial or supervisory jobs at the same percentage as for rank-and-file workers. Cutting salaries and jobs for those who are actually working to protect their communities or fix roads and bridges instead of those who job is to push paper and decide whose salaries get cut and who gets fired, is the height of hypocrisy and sends the wrong message. When workers suffer cuts, but see others with big incomes getting a pass, there is justifiable anger and resentment. There should be zero tolerance for disingenuousness and hypocrisy in government. But if we don't act as a community in the face of such despicable conduce, then we have no one to blame but ourselves.

Let me give you an example of how this scenario of teeth-gnashing and hand-wringing works. Take a look at university presidents who are charged with cutting faculty and programs. Then, take a look at the contracts of university presidents—pick any university at random and use any search engine. You will find a six-figure salary along with a litany of perks—usually including a car and residence—and undoubtedly a golden parachute should that president resign. This golden parachute most often consists of at least a full year at the current salary, a guaranteed solid high five—or six-figure pension at the appropriate time and a tenured professorship at, or just below, the full presidential salary. Do you know of any middle-class person who gets such perks? I don't, either. So, when you hear about "tough decisions" having to be made, you can bet the mortgage (if you still have a home) that these decisions are about taking the financial scalpel to others—by cutting programs and jobs; reducing or eliminating pensions; reducing unemployment compensation benefits, etc. These decision-makers won't be adversely affected by their "tough choices" or "tough decisions"—it will be those who believe they are powerless to do anything about the real tough choices or tough decisions that will be forced on them. If the burden is real, then it's only right and proper that it be shared. To accomplish this, I would like to see a mayor, city manager, county and city commissioners, governors, senators, legislators, etc., show some leadership and take the same ax to themselves as they take to the workers.

It is imperative that our government leaders act as statesmen and stateswomen instead of trying to out-shout and out-label one another. We elected these people to work for us. And if they can't do that, then let's elect representatives who will. Bailouts and handouts to big business send the wrong message. and if those who run these corporations can't conduct business legally, honestly and ethically, they shouldn't be in business; they should be in jail.

Here's an interesting thought. In my online research, I came across a book by Psychologist Jonathan Haidt, entitled "The Righteous Mind: Why Good People are Divided by Politics and Religion." According to a review, Haidt examines the moral underpinnings of conservative, liberal and even libertarian viewpoints. He urges all of us to try to better understand the other's point of view and realize that good people are found expressing each of these three viewpoints. This requires sacrificing emotion and actually reading about the philosophical foundations for each one. Haidt's point is that compromise, common purpose and common decency must replace hardheadedness if there is to be positive action taken on behalf of the people who elected their leaders to do the public's work. Surely, this is a most difficult task, but it certainly beats the hate-mongering and vitriolic diatribes that permeate our political system today. Is this too much to ask for? I certainly hope not.

To keep business from its own excesses, I believe in effective and meaningful regulation, including the regulation of corporate campaign contributions. I can't believe our Founding Fathers ever anticipated the manner by which obscene sums of money are used to buy power and influence. Are there excessive regulations? Of course. Are there excesses in business practices? Again, of course. A government pledged to democracy, however, is ultimately successful only with the consent of the governed. If the governed demand effective and meaningful reform and true leadership and get heated rhetoric and inaction instead; if policy making is subject to the judgments of Big Business and Big Religion; if our tax dollars are spent to aid the crooked or incompetent, then sooner or later, the bubble will burst.

The next item is the last column written by reporter Charlie Reese of the Orlando Sentinel, who retired after a 49-year career. This came in an email to me, and has been making the Internet rounds for a while. It's such a great piece of writing that I'm providing it to you verbatim, because he asks the most logical and poignant questions about power and responsibility, lobbyist influence, and the con game played by both major parties.

545 vs. 300,000,000 People by Charlie Reese

"Politicians are the only people in the world who create problems and then campaign against them. Have you ever wondered, if both the Democrats and the Republicans are against deficits, WHY do we have deficits? Have you ever wondered, if all the politicians are against inflation and high taxes, WHY do we have inflation and high taxes? You and I don't propose a federal budget. The President does. You and I don't have the Constitutional authority to vote on appropriations. The House of Representatives does. You and I don't write the tax code, Congress does. You and I don't set fiscal policy, Congress does. You and I don't control monetary policy, the Federal Reserve Bank does. One hundred senators, 435 congressmen, one President, and nine Supreme Court justices equates to 545 human beings out of the 300 million are directly, legally, morally, and individually responsible for the domestic problems that plague this country. I excluded the members of the Federal Reserve Board because that problem was created by the Congress. In 1913, Congress delegated its Constitutional duty to provide a sound currency to a federally chartered, but private, central bank. I excluded all the special interests and lobbyists for a sound reason. They have no legal authority. They have no ability to coerce a senator, a congressman, or a President to do one cotton-picking thing. I don't care if they offer a politician $1 million dollars in cash. The politician has the power to accept or reject it. No matter what the lobbyist promises, it is the legislator's responsibility to determine how he votes. Those 545 human beings spend much of their energy convincing you that what they did is not their fault.

They cooperate in this common con regardless of party. What separates a politician from a normal human being is an excessive amount of gall. No normal human being would have the gall of a Speaker, who stood up and criticized the President for creating deficits. The President can only propose a budget. He cannot force the Congress to accept it. The

Constitution, which is the supreme law of the land, gives sole responsibility to the House of Representatives for originating and approving appropriations and taxes. Who is the speaker of the House? John Boehner. He is the leader of the majority party. He and fellow House members, not the President, can approve any budget they want. If the President vetoes it, they can pass it over his veto if they agree to. It seems inconceivable to me that a nation of 300 million cannot replace 545 people who stand convicted—by present facts—of incompetence and irresponsibility. I can't think of a single domestic problem that is not traceable directly to those 545 people.

When you fully grasp the plain truth that 545 people exercise the power of the federal government, then it must follow that what exists is what they want to exist. If the tax code is unfair, it's because they want it unfair. If the budget is in the red, it's because they want it in the red. If the Army & Marines are in Iraq and Afghanistan it's because they want them in Iraq and Afghanistan. If they do not receive social security but are on an elite retirement plan not available to the people, it's because they want it that way. There are no insoluble government problems. Do not let these 545 people shift the blame to bureaucrats, whom they hire and whose jobs they can abolish; to lobbyists, whose gifts and advice they can reject; to regulators, to whom they give the power to regulate and from whom they can take this power. Above all, do not let them con you into the belief that there exists disembodied mystical forces like "the economy," "inflation," or "politics" that prevent them from doing what they take an oath to do. [Remember rising gas prices I discussed earlier.]Those 545 people, and they alone, are responsible. They, and they alone, have the power. They, and they alone, should be held accountable by the people who are their bosses. Provided the voters have the gumption to manage their own employees. We should vote all of them out of office and clean up their mess!"

This is one of the best statements I've read on the current status of our federal government, which unfortunately too many states appear to be manifesting in the conduct of their own affairs. Because we keep re-electing members of Congress and supreme court justices have life appointments, whose ultimate fault is it that our federal government is tied up in gridlock? We have no one to blame but ourselves, for the American voters put these people in power, either directly or (via appointment) indirectly. Unfortunately, with politicians directly or indirectly dumbing down our education system; with more and more students incapable of thinking for themselves; with emotion rather than reason governing dialogue and debate; is it any wonder why voters complain they're confused about who stands for what? It is any wonder why political self-preservation trumps issue resolution? Is it any wonder that we keep returning the same people to Congress election after election after election? Have you ever wondered why campaigns for office usually are June-to-August affairs; that is, from the close of candidate qualification to the first primary? Because these are the months most people are on vacation or, in cities that have large universities, college students are away from campuses. Studies show this generally keeps the more liberal vote down. No secret here.

Congress is a rich person's club. How did it get that way? Reese says 545 people are at fault; he's right, but it was—and is—the voters who put these people in their positions. It will take a sea change of culture to undo the harm that's been done over the past 50 years. My concern is that it may be too late and we're already condemned by not learning the lessons of history, especially how previous empires thrived and then became extinct. If there is time to re-make our government into one where the people's interests are the be-all and end-all, there isn't much of it left.

Here are a few phrases you don't hear politicians say, except perhaps after they leave office and look to make money on their memoirs: "I'm sorry." "I made a bad decision." "I made a mistake." If LBJ had come clean on Vietnam, lives might have been saved; the country wouldn't have been put through great agony; and he wouldn't have left office as a vilified president. Had Richard Nixon said these words, and admitted his conduct, he would have spared the country two years of agony and probably would have survived Watergate. If Ronald Reagan had done likewise, his administration wouldn't have been tainted by Iran-Contra. Bill Clinton wouldn't have put the country through Monicagate; and Bush II wouldn't have been trapped in the lies of Iraq and wouldn't have left office with the lowest popularity rating ever. And Obama might not have been elected.

Why do these officials, and so many others, have a problem demonstrating human frailties? Why are they so willing to engage in a cover-up from which they almost never survive, instead of just being straightforward and admitting wrongdoing? I believe people are forgiving, and when an official readily admits fault and legitimately seeks forgiveness, people will be more than willing to accept it and move on. When allegations of infidelity were launched against presidential candidate Senator Gary Hart, he challenged the media to follow him to prove this wasn't so. The press took him up on his challenge—and exposed Hart's conduct which cost him his political career. Why the likes of John Edwards, with all his wealth and fame, would be willing to sacrifice his name and reputation by first lying about his adultery and then trying to cover it up continues to amaze me. Didn't he think of the effect of his conduct on his late wife and children? Now, his children will go through life with the stain of being John Edwards' children, whose father lied and cheated. What a great legacy to leave his children! The most important thing a person can leave as his/her legacy is a spotless reputation and an unsoiled name. Those who are vested with the public trust and who are willing to toss their names and reputations in the trashcan without any consideration given to their family—as well as the people they represent—obviously have deep psychological and character flaws. We see men and women spend so many years going to school, getting a job, move up the ladder of success, run for office, etc., only to destroy their careers and lives because of weakness and an "I'm better than you" mentality. It's too bad we don't always know these things about our "representatives" before we choose our leaders.

This is as good a place as any to consider the adage that a person can spend 30 years building a solid reputation, only to destroy it virtually overnight. Sens. Hart and Edwards certainly are examples of this, but the most glaring example of recent vintage is Joe Paterno. Over 60 years of excellence in coaching and running a clean football program at Penn State is now wiped out because he was silent when he should have spoken. This doesn't appear to be a matter of hindsight alone; we're told he knew what Jerry Sandusky was doing, but was fearful of the adverse publicity about the football program. What doesn't make sense is that if he wanted to be sure his program remained clean, why he kept Sandusky around when all he had to do was to inform his superiors and then fire Sandusky outright. This certainly would have kept the program clean. By allowing Sandusky to remain on and around the campus, he and key administrators were at peril of a smoking gun that could go off at any time—and it did.

Taking away Paterno's wins was certainly unprecedented in and of itself. In the past, wins were taken away when the game itself was tainted by, for example, allowing ineligible players to suit up. In Paterno's case, no one claims that what was on the field was impermissible; the horrific conduct occurred off the field. Bobby Bowden, the retired FSU football coach who now sits atop the FBS as the "winningest" (there's no such word as winningest, the proper designation is "most winning," but because it's used so often, I'm taking a liberty here and using it) coach, is understandably not happy that he achieved this distinction in the manner he did. He—as well as any coach or manager, for that matter—believes that winning takes place on the field where both competitors have a level playing field. Where the field isn't level by tainted players or rules infractions that give one side an unfair advantage, win deprivations are proper. However, where the playing field is level, it's natural for a coach, manager or player to want to settle the issue on the field and according to the rules. Now, with the Paterno situation, everyone knows that the NCAA will take away a coach's wins if he commits horrific acts or failures to act during his watch, even if they occur off the gridiron.

As a lawyer steeped in constitutional law, however, I believe there is something wrong with the system that allows the NCAA to do what it did without the rudimentary elements of due process. Simply stated, due process means, for purpose of relevancy here, the right to clear notice of the charges, the right to confront one's accusers and the right to subject them to rigid cross-examination in full compliance with the rules of evidence. What might be allowed during the investigative stage—reliance on hearsay being the prime example—is not permitted once the issue reaches the adversarial stage where charges are filed and, in the administrative arena, a trial-type hearing is held. Paterno was accused, tried, convicted and sentenced without having a single opportunity to, through his family and attorney, inspect documents or question a witness under oath.

I recall what happened at Duke University a few years ago when several lacrosse team members were accused of rape. It seemed that people were running around helter-skelter accusing, charging, convicting and sentencing these athletes before the first witness was questioned. The university dismissed the students based on the accusation alone. Turns out that prosecutorial misconduct and a lying rape victim were at the root of the charges. The university had to pay out large sums of money to the students and reinstate them. This was the price for a rush to judgment.

I'm certainly not trivializing what Jerry Sandusky did; his crimes are horrific and he deserves to spend the rest of his life in prison; and his victims deserve every consideration of sympathy and assistance, and every penny that will be paid to them to try to bring a sense of closure to these young men. But the NCAA's rush to judgment action appears to have no support in any of its authoritative charter provisions. It simply took a general administrative statute and added its own after-the-fact interpretation to justify the sanctions. Had the NCAA decided to have all sports forfeit their wins, impose a fine of $100 million ($10 million per child who testified at the Sandusky trial), prohibit scholarships for 10 years, and prohibit participation in any bowl game for 10 years, there is nothing anywhere that would have prevented the NCAA from imposing them. In short, under its self-serving interpretation, it could have imposed any sanctions with complete impunity. To say that there was an institutional collapse on Sandusky justifying the sanctions is a gross overstatement; four people are accused of the cover-up. Four. That's hardly the stuff of institutional misconduct. In this regard, the NCAA acted like a Star Chamber, accepting as gospel the Louis Freeh report, interpreting its statutes in an after-the-fact self-serving manner, and basing its conjured-up sanctions wholly on that document. That's not how our legal system that guarantees due process is supposed to work.

Yet, according to the United States Supreme Court, in a case involving former college basketball coach Jerry Tarkanian who sued the NCAA, the NCAA is not a state actor and therefore is not required to afford due process in issuing sanctions. The NCAA regulates college athletics; polices numerous public universities' athletic programs; is authorized to sanction universities, players and coaches for violations of NCAA rules; and receives funds from public universities. There is a body of law that says that a state actor is one who operates at the behest and support of public bodies. There is a body of law that says that if a person is held up to ridicule or otherwise painted in a "false light," that person has a cause of action. I find it hard to believe that the long reach of the NCAA's unbridled power will survive much longer. Everyone is held accountable in some way or another; the NCAA can't be any different, unless its powers exceed those of every branch and level of government. Checks and balances are the bedrock of our system of government; the NCAA can't be held to be above this bedrock principle. The constitution and courts will be the final arbiter. How else can this association's authority be checked and the reasonableness of its actions determined?

And who exactly is punished by the NCAA sanctions in the Penn State case? Not the three Penn State administrators; they're no longer with the university and the NCAA sanctions have no effect on them. Surely, they have an effect on Paterno's legacy, but he's deceased and beyond the university's and the NCAA's reach. Here's who's really punished: the thousands of innocent players who now have no wins to show for their hard work and dedication to the university and football team. The current players and coaches. The hundreds of thousands innocent fans who literally had their football team taken from them. The millions of dollars that would flow into the university treasury to be used for university wide programs. The alumni, their alumni parents and grandparents. These people who are completely innocent are the ones who will suffer by these sanctions. The team—assuming anyone wants to play for Penn State over the next several years—will be an embarrassment up against the Ohio States and Michigans. If I were in charge, I'd voluntarily shut down the program and avoid on-field embarrassments until it can be competitive again. The effect of the sanctions is far worse than the so-called "death penalty" of shutting down a program.

If the NCAA wanted to do something truly worthwhile in addition to the $60 million earmarked for child abuse and sexual assault programs, it would have ordered the university to set aside a set sum into the millions of dollars for each of the 10 students, which sum would be deducted from any damages they obtain in civil suits against the university. That would have gotten money immediately into the hands of those who are the true victims. The sanctions against the football team hurts only the innocent now in charge of that program, and the players who know they can't be competitive. As the saying goes, two wrongs don't make a right. The university did a wise thing in storing Paterno's statute in some out-of-the-way place on campus. History has a strange way of working; a saint one day becomes a villain the next and a saint again down the road. Who knows what the final chapter will be for Joe Paterno? And when can it truly be said it will be written? Will there be a mellowing over time or will the vilification be permanent? No one can truthfully say now because emotions run high at the outset of any horrific situation.

Even those the NCAA's message is that never again will football take precedence on any campus, still, at too many universities and college, football is the be-all and end-all of everything collegiate. Certainly, both of my alma maters, the UF and FSU, have succumbed to this mentality, and have paid the price by NCAA sanctions. Yet, there remain football programs that are bigger than life itself—I don't have to name them for you. Just look at your newspaper. Of course, I can't imagine anything more shocking than harboring a child predator; but who would have thought of such a thing in 2010? How a college football coach who prided himself on excellence on and off the field; a university president and other top administrators chose to remain silent while a child predator victimized one youngster after another—all in the name of protecting the cash cow—is just beyond reality. They sacrificed those boys on the altar of the football god. I hope that those who suffered in silence for so long can find some peace now that the evil has been exposed.

Since the purpose of the NCAA's penalties is to send a clear message that the protection of the student is paramount, let's hope that more efforts are made to protect the student-athlete from concussions and other disabling injuries from playing football, and that the NCAA stands in the forefront of this effort—and provides medical care and financial assistance to any student who's injured playing football. Now, that would really send a message to the colleges and universities to buy the best equipment and take the best precautions to avoid insofar as possible these types of devastating injuries. The game itself must take a back seat to the health, safety and welfare of the players.

On to my next subject. Since I'm a former news reporter, I don't want the media to escape without some criticism. First, it seems to be verboten for there to be "liberal media bias" but somehow it's ok for there to be "conservative media bias." Fox News believes that because the major networks and CNN, among others, are biased toward liberalism, it's ok for Fox News to be openly biased toward conservativism. Wait just a second here; I though journalists were supposed to report objectively—at least, this is what I was taught in journalism school. But that was before Watergate, and after that self-proclaimed great victory for a vindicated press, reporters flexed their self-importance and took a sharp turn toward advocacy reporting, mixing opinion with fact. As advocacy became more and more in fashion, and with social networking gathering more and more steam, today any pretence of objectivism has just about given way to left-wing/right wing reporting/commentary. The difference today between news and views is like trying to bring into focus a blurred line. But here's an important point: media ownership is Big Business, and the owners want to make sure that what is reported doesn't offend the corporate sponsors or those political figures who the news executives deal with, frequently on a regular basis. This is more so with regard to TV news, since sound bites are such an effective communications tool. In short, media owners want to make sure that their reporting don't bite the hand that feeds them.

I read an article recently that one of the dying professions is that of newspaper reporter. As a former reporter who started his professional career working for two south Florida newspapers, I find this both sad and disturbing. One of the reasons newspapers are cutting back on reporting, or folding completely, is that fewer and fewer are actually reading the lengthy articles or think pieces. You would think that with the communications explosion over the last 20 years, people would want to read more, not less. This is not the case; readership is down, and sinking lower. Reading and thinking have been replaced to a significant extent with sound bites, buzzwords, short punchy phrases, social networking which is antithetical to think pieces, etc., all designed to convey a more emotion-driven message to the masses. What is gained via buzz words and sound bites, rather than by actually reading an in-depth article discussing the background of a news story, is not really knowledge but knee-jerk reaction. It's impossible to get the in-depth background of any significant news story from a two-minute TV report or a blog, tweet or Facebook post. It will take greater effort on the part of the public to arrive at the bottom line and "get the news" by reading more and more from a variety of dependable sources. But I see more and more evidence of emotion trumping logic on this point. If newspaper reporting—and newspapers themselves—become extinct, what will people rely on to get the news? The rush to become a newspaper reporter following Watergate has, in less than 40 years, dwindled to the point of watching a great calling die. What a shame.

One of the phrases that the media overuse is "A lot of people . . . ." Listen to how many times a reporter conducting an interview uses this phrase. If I were the subject of such an interview, I would immediately fire back "How many people?" If I got a vague answer, I would press on: "How many did you personally interview?" I would keep hammering away until I got a precise answer, or an admission that the reporter was just using a buzz phrase.

In every totalitarian state, the government controls the media. The only evil that equates with this is control of the media by one political party or one point of view. The media must never be beholden to any government, political party or point of view. They may editorialize, providing this is clearly identified. The media's role is that of a watchdog, checking government on behalf of the people in the discharge of their First Amendment claims. Watergate was a watershed moment for the media because they exposed corruption at the highest level of our government. Of course, there are those who stubbornly cling to their dislike for the media for what they did to Nixon, but the reality is Nixon brought about his own demise; the media just reported what they learned. Coverage of Vietnam was another watershed moment because aggressive reporting uprooted lie after lie about the strength of the enemy and the actual lack of success despite government reports to the contrary. The constant reporting of the war and events surrounding it led to serious questions about the necessity of our presence and the eventual withdrawal. It was also the press that unearthed the lies about the war in Iraq. There were those who believed the media were demeaning the military and our armed forces, thereby undercutting our nation by acting un-American, but these critics were focusing on the messenger and not the message. Rooting out corruption and getting to the truth is a badge of honor for the press; engaging in advocacy journalism is not. And criticizing the media for exposing government (as well as corporate) corruption, lies and other crimes does a gross disservice to our nation's bedrock commitment to a government of the people, by the people and for the people; and the media's role as a check on government.

I'm not aware of any candidate election in our country that isn't conducted on a majority rule basis except for president and vice president of the United States. It's as if democracy is fine for all state and local elections but not for the highest offices in the nation. Is there something wrong with popular election of the top federal officials? There was a time when United States senators weren't elected by popular vote. If it's now mandatory for senators to be elected by popular vote, why do we continue with the undemocratic unelected Electoral College making this decision for us for our nation's highest offices? Are we as a nation incapable of electing our president and vice president? Whatever the reasons were more than 200 years ago for this curious system, are they valid today? There are those who say that because the constitution provides for the Electoral College, it therefore follows that this method is an acceptable part of our democracy and shouldn't be changed. While true from a constitutional standpoint, it's also disingenuous from a purely democratic standpoint. I have no doubt that, at one time, people felt that way about the method of choosing senators, but the reasons for holding to that method were no longer valid, so we changed to popular vote. We pride ourselves on being the world's beacon of democracy, until we are compelled to explain that we don't elect our top national leaders by popular vote. Perhaps it's time to fully evaluate whether the Electoral College has outlived its purpose, and scrap it in favor of a direct national election.

Jobs, entitlements, government waste, work ethic, education and crime

Generally, I support the view that those able-bodied men and women who can work should work before becoming eligible for any entitlement program. For those who legitimately can't work, there must be programs in place that provide for a safety net so these people can live some measure of a meaningful life. For those who must take a job that they view as "beneath their dignity," I say it's better to work and earn a living than live off a handout. The problem that exists now is where a wage earner loses his job through no fault of his/her own and after diligent search, can't find a job at an income level that supports him/her at a level that allows for maintaining current lifestyle without selling his/her home, etc. In this circumstance, in addition to unemployment compensation, there should be a plan that allows for borrowing against one's retirement plan, and/or already paid Social Security or Medicare payments until the employee returns to his/her previous earning level. Handouts by themselves are destructive of the strong work ethic upon which this nation was founded and on which we pride our growth. Entitlement programs for the able-bodied must not become a way of life in and of itself. We must rid ourselves of this notion of entitlement for entitlement's sake.

By entitlement, I don't mean government pensions for current retirees, or Social Security or Medicare for retirees. Those who paid into these two federal programs during their working career, and accepted a lower income level than their private counterparts in return for a guaranteed pension, played by the rules then in place, and they justifiably expect their governments—federal, state and local—to play by the rules under which these retirees functioned in reliance on the good faith of their governments. Besides, government pensions are contractual rights between the government and the employee and are constitutionally protected as vested rights. Any effort to change the rules for those who, by age or infirmity, are unable to do anything about it goes against every principle of compassion and human dignity our country stands for, and should be vehemently opposed. I do believe that government has created excesses in certain pension programs—for certain elected and appointed officers and high-level employees, for example. For the vast majority of government workers, however, pension payouts remain relatively low. I also believe that Social Security and Medicare need to be reformed, but not on the backs of those current recipients who can't work and thereby can't adjust their lives to changes that adversely impact them financially. Lumping those programs into which people paid, with those that are based (at least supposedly) solely on need, is unfair, legally wrong and morally reprehensible. Only the mean-spiritedness and dishonest would even attempt to convince the public that all programs are identical. The paid-into programs are not entitlement programs; those that allow for payment based solely on need are entitlement programs. (Of course, if a plan involves demonstration of need, but payments are based on what an employee has paid into a retirement plan, or Social Security and Medicare, then the plan is no longer strictly an entitlement plan, in my view.)

To those private company executives who believe unions are the problem, I remind them that it's very difficult to tell a retiree that his private company pension should be cut or eliminated when they see corporate executives earning seven-figure incomes or receiving golden parachutes upon departure, and they see retired public and corporate officials earning close to their full salary—if not their actual salary—as their pension payments. I have to believe that there is a problem when ordinary workers see pension payments to former government and retired top corporate executives in the six-figure range.

At the same time the private sector is working toward eliminating pensions in favor of employees assuming responsibility for their retirement, the public sector is doing likewise, moving inexorably from a defined-benefit system to a defined-contribution system. Under the former, the government guarantees a pension payment based on a formula that takes into account position level, salary, and length of employment. Under this system a pension is deemed a contract impacting a vested right that the government can't reduce or eliminate without violating the constitution's prohibition against impairing the obligations of a contract. A defined contribution retirement plan puts the burden on the employee to take a portion of his periodic income and pay into a private pension plan, like a 401K.

With increasingly strident voices, state and local government officials contend that because of severe budget shortfalls, and the costs incurred in paying retiree pensions, the time has come to end government-funded pensions. If indeed public pensions are costing too much, exactly whose fault is that? In Florida, no union can force the government to pay pensions at a particular rate. If the state agrees to pay out pensions to certain public officials at extremely high rates as compared to the rates of rank-and-file employees, that's not the worker's fault; it's the legislature's and the governor's fault. Those who argue for ending government pensions in favor of a defined-contribution system extol its virtues by saying this will allow the employee to control the size of his/her nest egg for a long, comfortable life in retirement. They make it sound so much better than the current guaranteed payout to retirees. But, yet again, the devil's in the details.

First, the government-funded pension system is founded upon a premise that the rank-and-file employee will generally be required to take a salary that is less than his/her private counterpart in return for the guarantee of a periodic pension payment when that employee reaches retirement age and leaves employment. When you hear talking heads wax on about the switch to a defined-contribution plan, do you hear them mentioning increasing employees' salaries when the government will be off the hook for pensions? I don't either. Second, under the defined-contribution plan, employees will have to subject their nest eggs to the ups and downs of the stock market. For the employee or retiree, everything is fine with the 401K plan, or any other type of plan—until there is a meltdown or collapse as we so recently witnessed in 2008. I know several people who lost hundreds of thousands of dollars as a result of the Great Recession of 2008. If someone loses a significant portion—or perhaps all—of his/her nest egg, how is that person to survive if he/she is too old to be able to recoup the losses? Multiply this situation by tens or hundreds of thousands—or even millions—and you can readily see the impact on the nation. Will the government back or guarantee to protect that nest egg from exposure to the vagaries of the market, or corrupt business executives whose actions lead to a meltdown? I don't think so, either. Finally, will the government exempt certain public officials from the defined-contribution plan? Perhaps this will be the most interesting aspect of all, for if government officials are allowed to keep their current defined-benefit pension rates, what does this say about their confidence in what they're planning on imposing on the rank-and-file?

What is happening is that some in government—as well as some office seekers—are effectively trying to throw out the baby with the bathwater; trying to lump together those who are getting a comparatively low pension and Social Security payment with those who are collecting what is tantamount to their full salaries while in retirement. Just look at pension payments for judges, members of Congress, etc. Lumping all those retirees with modest pensions together with those getting extremely large pensions is manifestly unfair. Where there are excesses, let's work to bring them in line. This must be done, however, in such a way that harm doesn't fall on the most vulnerable while those who are reaping huge retirement benefits remain immune from any remediation.

By this, I don't mean to give unions a pass. As with any innovation born of necessity, excesses can turn a good thing on its ear. Unions were a mobilizing force for the creation of the middle class early in the 20th century. Unions helped end abusive working conditions and afforded protection for the worker. However, high salaries for union executives, increasingly high pension benefits for certain types of workers, abuse and misuse of union pension funds, retribution against workers who didn't always follow the union line, etc., caused unions to come under government scrutiny. Complaints were voiced to the effect that Big Unions were in bed with Big Business, with the workers bearing the brunt of the consequences. Labor is now coming under increasing fire from the right, and unions are giving their opposition ample ammunition. Breaking up the unions, however, gives business the upper hand—and history tells us what happened when this was our nation's reality during the Industrial Revolution. As with the formation of meaningful government policy, there must be balance in order for management and labor to succeed in assuring the growth of our nation. This applies to both the public and private sectors. The combination of breaking up unions and giving business a free hand will have disastrous consequences.

Today's campaigning is so much about what people will believe rather than what candidates and politicians are actually saying. Because belief now appears to trump issues, politicians can—and far too often do—get away with falsehoods simply because they can, and the public has a short memory span anyway. As for the GOP, there is no doubt where it stands on Social Security; it wants to privatize it and thereby force those paying into it to have at least a portion of their money go into the market. The right wing says this will allow for greater management and accumulation of retirement funds. And a significant number of people really believe this. But recent history shows that millions lost money during the Great Recession of 2008, and are continuing to lose money today via home foreclosures, etc. As in war, there are times when the first thing that is sacrificed in politics is the truth. Why won't those who want to privatize tell the whole story about risks of significant loss? I think we can figure this one out.

Of course, there are those who say what they're going to do and are criticized for doing precisely that. For example, Florida Gov. Rick Scott heeded the right wing line during his 2010 campaign, and upon taking office set out to do exactly what he said he would do. His poll numbers as he nears mid-term are below 50%. President Obama campaigned on passing a national health care plan, which he did after he took office with the largest popular vote in history. Now, he's vilified by the right wing for doing precisely what he set out to do. The startling aspect of the health care scenario is that the plan that ultimately passed was in substantial form what the GOP congress backed in the 1990s, and the one that passed in Massachusetts during Gov. Mitt Romney's term. What happened to change by 180 degrees the GOP's view of a national health care plan? I don't know the answer either but you can bet that what wasn't considered socialistic when the GOP proposed it is now steeped in the evil of socialism.

It's time to eliminate the useless finger-pointing, inflammatory rhetoric and the toxic environment in our federal and state capitals and get down to the serious work of providing meaningful jobs to qualified people who truly want to work; real classroom learning to children who arrive at school prepared to learn; real economic incentives that reward hard work; and the end of handouts and bailouts for the undeserving—including foreign countries that our government asserts are our allies, when in fact they are not. Friendship can't be bought, and expending our valuable resources on ill-gotten wars and friendship-buying only takes away resources needed to fix our infrastructure and meaningfully provide for the health, safety and welfare of our own. I believe our federal, state and local governments have the resources to provide for their people, if they eliminated waste and spent wisely. In short, I believe in the adage that there is always money for what government wants, and never any money for what it doesn't want. The ideal situation is for government's wants to meet the legitimate needs of the people. Far too often, when someone doesn't want to provide a service or product it can legitimately afford and that is needed, that person simply says: "We don't have the money for that," as if that settles the matter. Such a retort should be met with inquiry into budgetary facts that prove the contrary. Usually, those facts will be there.

We see examples of the waste of our financial resources again and again. The primary reason for this is found in the fact that government officials and corporate leaders are not spending their money; rather, they're spending other people's money—our money—coupled with the belief that they can do so with impunity. Taking the fact of spending along with this belief of the unfettered ability to spend, and we wind up with our money being spent with very little—if any—concern for real accountability. Right now, very few are ever prosecuted for breach of the public trust, cooking the books, or other examples of gross financial mismanagement. Just look at how few are being held accountable for the Great Meltdown of 2008 during which millions lost their jobs, homes and retirement funds! The reason given for not holding these people accountable is that these white-collar crimes are complex cases requiring vast expenditure of funds to prosecute. This is a lame excuse that people seem to accept. Where is the outrage from those who lost so much?

Greed, of course, is not limited to government or business; welfare greed must be eliminated as well. It's a function of human nature for people who are receiving government funds to do whatever is necessary to continue to receive those funds rather than working to earn them. Social services fraud, whether caused by doctors and pharmaceutical companies, or recipients milking the system, must be addressed by strong criminal penalties and jail time.

If our laws were drafted with more precision instead of adding paid-for loopholes and exceptions, making public officials and corporate executives, as well as social services recipients of taxpayers' dollars, strictly accountable for unlawful receipt and wasteful expenditures, and they faced significant jail time for aberrant conduct, perhaps we would make a dent in reducing the incredible amount of waste of our tax dollars. Jail time certainly would be a disincentive to overspend, cook the books or commit fraud. Our government representatives must "want" what's in the public's best interests, rather than in their own or their financial backers' interests. Unfortunately, it will take a social upheaval of cataclysmic proportions to unearth the culture of greed and self-aggrandizement that has permeated our government and spread like a slow-growing cancer over the years to undo the damage that's been done.

The next point arises personally from my daughter's and son-in-law's business in North Carolina and involves the work ethic. While their business is a success (despite the paperwork thrust on small businesses), they continue to have problems hiring good workers. In my discussions with other small business owners both in my community and in other locales, I see another pattern that I find disheartening—a precipitous decline in the work ethic and a concomitant decline in pride in producing a product or providing a service. I realize that I could be overstating the matter, but I see and hear enough to believe that this is not something to ignore or sweep under the rug. I see and hear a lot about the clamor for well-paying jobs with good benefits, and whether this is something in which the government or the private sector should take the lead. This overlooks an important point. There is a tendency to equate a job with work as if using one word automatically includes the other. There is a fallacy in this type of thinking, as there is a stark difference between having a job and doing the work. While I hear much clamoring for jobs, I don't hear any such clamoring for doing work.

My daughter complains that her employees arrive late, do personal work during business hours, call in sick after they're supposed to arrive at work, etc. They do this even after they're admonished for aberrant behavior; and when they're admonished, their typical reaction is that there's something wrong with the owners or managers. When I mention this to other family-owned businessmen and women, they echo my daughter's complaints. It's as if these employees believe the world owes them a living, and that if they lose their jobs, they can get unemployment compensation, or perhaps some other form of handout. I suppose they reason that if the government can pay farmers not to plant, it can pay people not to work. To the extent this attitude exists, it's counterproductive and destructive of the work ethic that built this country and is necessary to assure its growth. There is no entitlement to a job; there is no entitlement to a salary and benefits, or advancement, simply because a person exists. So that we don't throw the baby out with the bathwater, however, there must be drawn as clear a line as possible between legitimate government assistance on one hand, and pure entitlement on the other.

I believe in affirmative action only insofar as it corrects a specific and identifiable current wrong. I don't believe that affirmative action should be used as an open-door policy to attend college, or as a vehicle for a job handout based solely on trying to right past wrongs. Today, there is nothing that justifies giving anyone a status advantage in attending school, going to college, earning a degree and putting his/her skills to use in the job market. All that is required is a desire to learn, to work and to have pride in a job well-done. This attitude will always carry the day. To those who simply say that people who believe as I do are (insert the epithet label of choice) whose opinions therefore aren't to be considered, I say you've made my point exactly.

With profits as the primary motivating force, and with Americans refusing to take jobs that foreigners will, it makes sense in a Machiavellian way for a business to keep its labor costs down as it increases its bottom line. This serves as ample incentive for businesses to look overseas and at illegal immigrants for their labor force. If you want to know why immigration reform has met with such resistance, here's as good a reason as any. Isn't it easier to outsource jobs than it is to put up with so many obstacles to hiring here in our own country? The "wages, hours and other conditions of employment" mentality today appears to exclude the "dollar's worth of work for a dollar's pay" work ethic principle. The "wages, hours" mentality must change by merging it with the "dollar's worth" principle. By this, I'm not dismissing or doubting the serious need for substantive job creation and development of an effective plan to reduce unemployment or underemployment; clearly, government needs to respond in a bipartisan manner with a strong and long-term plan. I'm simply stating that a situation exists that needs to be factored into the labor conditions and dealt with as part of an overall plan.

After years of spending more and more on education and getting less and less a return in terms of a quality product, more and more governments are cutting education funding as a means of addressing tough economic times. The logic behind this is inexplicable. We used to pride ourselves on having the best educational system and highest quality academic product in the world; not any more. According to the Paris-based Program for International Student Assessment, the United States ranks 14th in reading, 25th in math and 11th in science. (As of this writing, I heard on CNN in August that we're now 27th in math.) Instead of gaining ground as a result of promises made a few years ago by our government leaders to improve education, the United States has fallen to 17th in the share of adults age 25 to 34 holding degrees, according to a report from the Organization for Economic Cooperation and Development. While we were first as of the 1970s, today our nation trails such countries as South Korea, Canada and Japan and, in fact, is mired in the middle of the pack among developed nations. This sends a message that other nations are outperforming us and causes us to ask whether the decline in our quality of education bears any relationship to the growing partisan divide in our country. It seems to me that if this decline also found in subjects like history and civics—and there are enough studies to bear this out—then any appreciation for historical contexts and civility in government action is replaced by raw emotion, name-calling—all the things that cut against open, honest debate, logic, common sense and compromise. This is absolutely unacceptable and should send a loud and clear message that we need to change the culture of learning if we are going to have any chance of regaining our leadership position in the world and become problem-solvers instead of rabid agitators.

In Florida, a single test offered by the state is the primary basis for gauging a student's progress. However, grades continue to show that overall, our students are falling further and further behind in writing, reading, math, science—the essential tools for succeeding in life. Instead of looking for solutions to the steady decline of student performance, those involved in the educational process play the blame game. Government and education administrators blame the teachers and unions; teachers and unions blame government and administrators. And round and round we go, with no legitimate effort at true problem-solving. Notice no one seems to blame the students. Government and administrators expect teachers to make kids learn. With increasing regularity, teachers' salaries and advancement potential are determined by the success of students on standardized tests.

Here are some education facts of life. Go to virtually any metropolitan newspaper and you will find a listing of jobs that go unfilled. There are two reasons for this: first, many believe these jobs are beneath their dignity; second, the qualifications for these jobs are beyond the education and skill level of potential applicants. On this first point, there is a reason why so many large companies look to foreign lands or illegal aliens for workers: these people will take those jobs that out-of-work Americans might pass on. Why would any large company struggle to hire people with a low work ethic when it can hire people who are desperate for work and will labor more diligently? There are government and administrative officials who don't have a clue as to how to teach or what transpires in the classroom. There are teachers who are incompetent and shouldn't be in the classroom. There are kids in school who don't want to be there; have no interest in learning; and are troublemakers who believe getting an education is a cop-out to society. For fear of harming one's self-esteem, we still have vestiges of social promotion. So-called education leaders take the approach that if the test scores are too low, simply change the grading system to make those low grades higher. In short, don't raise the bridge, lower the river. What absolute drivel!!!

If you think there's no problem with what's coming out of the public school system, listen to interviews and count the number of times you hear "ya know" or "like" or "man" or "so" or "I mean" or any other throwaway word or phrase that makes no sense. With increasing frequency, I hear people end their comments with a "so." What does this mean? "So" what? This is call lazy speech, and should be corrected and not tolerated. No business or government employer should have to hire someone who can't speak properly. It might work for pro sports or the entertainment world, but must not become acceptable in business or government. All-too-often, in an effort to solve a problem, instead of raising the bridge, we lower the river. This mentality is harmful to our country. High standards must never be compromised to accommodate lazy habits.

If you still don't think that our education system is producing a dumbing down product, think a moment about labels on bottles and other instructions on the use of products. You'll see warnings such as "Hot coffee. Do not place cup on lap while driving." There was a lawsuit about this several years ago in which the injured person actually recovered damages against a fast food company for failure to provide adequate warning that hot coffee when spilled while driving could actually burn the consumer. I saw the warning on a knife that said "Dangerous. Can cause injury" How about a medicine bottle that says "Take only as directed." I call this a result of the "Duh" generation because this expression and the gestures that accompany it are so accurately descriptive of a disdainful indication of something that is obvious.

Earlier, I mentioned the Texas GOP's opposition to teaching students to engage in critical thinking. This ultra-conservative mindset only serves the declining reliance on common sense and reasoned judgment, the dumbing down of our children and the education system generally, the increased rejection of objective fact and the resort to venomous language and even violence in settling arguments. While so many other countries are expanding their respective education systems to address global technology, industrialization and a global economy; educators here warn of the growing inability of our children to think, reason, question assumptions and reach well-thought-out results. Rigid adherence to raw beliefs is replacing common sense and rational thought. This lunacy, if left unchallenged and categorically rejected, is a sure one-way ticket to our nation's permanent decline.

The solution to our educational woes is really rather simple, but it will take overcoming political correctness, particularly the silly notion of protecting self-esteem. Establish clear fixed standards which are either met or not. If they're not met, the kid fails and is retained. If a kid wants to be a bum, and his parents (assuming he/she has parents or at least an adult guardian) can't get him/her to exercise responsibility, so be it. That's not society's problem, unless crime is involved, in which case it's off to jail to do real time. While there are programs for such youths, the reality is that some simply don't want to be helped, unless it's a no-strings-attached handout. Under this circumstance, they should get precisely what they're entitled to—nothing.

Get rid of incompetent teachers. Let the good teachers teach! Let administrators do the paperwork; don't dump the non-teaching paper shuffling on the teachers. Government and administrative officers must cease telling teachers how to teach, but make sure that what goes into the classroom is an educated and properly trained and prepared teacher. Teacher salaries are abysmal; if a quality product is the goal, then the people who are charged with producing such a product need to be properly compensated. Paying a bureaucratic paper-shuffler significantly more than a classroom teacher turns the process on its head. There is a systemic problem of paying those in the trenches less than those who sit in offices far removed from the field and do nothing more than shuffle papers and count beans. This must change. And above all, children must go to school prepared to learn.

This process starts at home and continues through the several grade levels. No free passes, no excuses, and no fear of hurting one's feelings or lowering of one's self-esteem by constructive criticism. Too many of our children are told that they're special simply because they exist. We are in a competitive global economy, and in order for our young to compete not only at home but with other countries, they must be able to deal with criticism and defeat. They must learn that taking the heat is a learning experience from which they should grow and become stronger. If children are taught that success is guaranteed without the necessity of dealing with stiffer and stiffer competition and not having to do hard work, then they will be unable to handle the competitive, demanding world they will enter. Children are certainly special to their family and friends, but not necessarily to society. They must succeed the old-fashioned way; they must earn it. If they fail, it's not society's fault.

Discipline and an appreciation for learning must begin at home and continue unabated throughout the school years. It is not the job of the school systems to do what was not done before the children first set foot in the classroom. If a child is unruly or disruptive, have the principal call the parent or, better yet, call the parent's employer and have that employer direct the parent to take care of the matter and don't allow the employee parent to return to work until the child is prepared to learn and ceases misbehaving. Children must come to school ready to learn, and no government system can accomplish this. Misbehaving children must not remain a disruptive force in the classroom. When one is bad, that child adversely affects the ability of the teacher to teach and the rest of the children to learn. That misbehaving child must be removed from the classroom until such time as he/she learns to behave in that environment. Children also must be taught the basics to make their way into the world. English, grammar, writing, reading, math, civics and history must be mandatory. The importance of education leading to work as a collective value must be instilled from the get-go; the relationship between a job and work must be made clear as a bell.

A job involves work; they go hand-in-hand. The more one works his/her job with dedication and pride, the better the benefits will be. I believe that there is too much talking the talk, and not enough walking the walk. People have to walk the walk to be successful. Success is meaningful only if the effort extended is significant. For those who come from another country to live permanently and work here, they must learn English. If an American were moving permanently to Italy, it would be expected for him/her to learn how to communicate in Italian; it shouldn't be any different for those who come to America. If a person chooses not to learn the native language of the country in which he/she has chosen to live, that should not be a problem thrust upon the citizens or government of that country.

If a person takes pride in his work, and looks to work as a challenge willingly accepted, chances are he/she will be successful, grow with the employer and realize increased earnings, benefits, etc. It all comes down to attitude, and if one's attitude towards work is one of entitlement or instant gratification, that is one person who shouldn't be hired. I have to believe that, despite the horror stories I hear from my daughter, neighbors and friends, there are decent people out there who truly want to work and have a sense of pride in their efforts; it's just a matter of finding them. I hope I'm right; I don't even want to think of the dire consequences for our country if I'm wrong. And for those who are truly looking for work, please dress appropriately. If you want your attire to make a statement, make sure it's a positive statement. Remember, the world doesn't owe you a living. Wearing baggy pants, jeans, etc., for a job interview and constantly inserting throwaway words and phrases certainly make a statement. It's "Don't hire me."

For those who take education seriously, go to college and graduate, there is another matter that I find disturbing: the growing number of college graduates—especially those receiving advanced degrees in law, medicine, etc.—who are carrying high five—and six-figure debt in the form of student loans. These graduates are leaving school with a heavy mortgage in hand along with their degrees, and little prospect of finding jobs that will allow them to pay down this huge debt, let alone get married, have children, and own a home carrying yet another mortgage. We're creating a debtor class the burden of which will fall on others if there is rampant default. At the same time more and more college students take on heavier and heavier debt, college costs are skyrocketing. This is forcing those who understand the importance of, and want, a college education to make a choice of either not going to college at a time when a college education is virtually the only way to assure a successful life, or borrowing larger and larger sums of money to attend college that will take years to pay off under the most favorable circumstances. The American dream of a college education is moving further and further away from reality for all except those who can afford stiff hikes in tuition and other costs, even as the job market becomes tighter and tighter. Yet, our government leaders don't appear to be taking this "which choice of poison do you want" dilemma of not attending college or taking out a six-figure loan very seriously.

When it comes to addressing the national problem of street crime (not the white-collar crimes that involve politicians, lobbyists, etc., who tamper with the process for their personal benefit), I don't believe we can overemphasize the importance of youth gangs. We bear witness to enough occasions where what people won't do by themselves they will do as part of a gang. It seems that the gang mentality serves as a convenient excuse to avoid accepting individual responsibility for deviant and, far too often, vile and horrific conduct. The solution, as I see it, is to break up the gangs by providing for severe and certain penalties, including jail time for juveniles separate from the general prison population; offering rewards as incentives for providing evidence leading to the capture and conviction of gang leaders; blocking easy access to guns for those involved in criminal gang activities; condemning and destroying property where gangs are known to hang out; providing alternative meaningful community programs and activities designed to dissuade youths from joining a gang; imposing penalties on parents designed to get them more involved in their children's lives; and developing other programs that act as a disincentive to get involved and commit gang-related crimes.

Any discussion of street and gang crime inevitably leads to three issues: gun control, the disproportionate number of minorities who are in prison for gun-related or other violent crimes, and entertainment's impact on crime. Let me start with gun control. This is the phrase commonly uttered by those who believe that any meaningful regulation of firearms such as weapons of mass killings like Uzis or AK-47s only serves to deprive Americans of their Second Amendment absolute fundamental right to bear arms. Strange, but you don't hear about insurance control or vehicle control, etc. Once again, those who use appeals to emotion have seized the upper hand in the debate by labeling regulatory efforts as "control." I don't view efforts at making these types of assault weapons, as well as weapons like them, difficult to access as depriving legitimate gun owners of their constitutional rights. Legitimate gun owners buy weapons for protection and collection purposes. I believe that common sense, logic and a deep concern for public safety demand that weapons that only serve to kill others and that are both currently legal and relatively easy to obtain (like assault weapons) should be carefully and tightly regulated. After all, the law permits the tight regulation of the insurance industry; why not stringent regulations on those who can possess and own firearms that are suited for one purpose and one purpose only—to kill as many people as possible?

The National Rifle Association is not the National Uzi, AK-47 or Glock Association; taking the NRA at its word in desiring to protect Second Amendment rights, then it must be equally true to its word regarding the necessity for those rights to be exercised in a responsible manner. Surely, the NRA and its membership don't believe that there should be no restrictions whatever on anyone who wants to buy an assault weapon. After all, the exercise of all constitutionally protected rights presumes that they will be exercised responsibly and with accountability. For example, a person exercising his/her First Amendment right of free speech is accountable under the laws of libel and slander. A person who yells "fire" in a movie theater will be held accountable for resulting chaos and injuries. If a person doesn't register to vote, he/she won't be allowed to vote. In short, the exercise of any constitutional right must be directly accompanied by a concomitant acceptance of responsibility and accountability. There should be no legitimate argument or doubt about this when it comes to the Second Amendment.

We can debate until we're blue in the face whether guns kill people or people kill people. But there is one thing on which no one can disagree—people with guns kill people. And the easier the access, the greater the risk. It's really that simple. How strange it is that those who rail against abortion are silent when it comes to regulating weapons of mass murder. And make no mistake about it; AK-47s, Uzi, Glocks and other similar firearms have only one purpose: to kill the largest number of people as quickly as possible. There are those who will deny a woman the right to choose (and thereby force abortions to the back alleys where they were until Roe v. Wade), but in the face of the mass killings of innocent people, there is no outrage—only silence. We've seen mass murders in schools, on college campuses, in malls, in the military and in movie theaters. While Second Amendment advocates defend possession of firearms, and argue that the focus should be on keeping guns out of the hands of those who, by their mental or physical condition, shouldn't have them—a point on which there should be no disagreement—the fact remains that easy access to such weapons is a factor when mass murder is committed by assault weapons. How much a factor can be debated again and again with no common ground reached.

There is yet another fact on which we should all agree. At the time the Second Amendment was adopted, there were no AK-47s, Uzis, Glocks, or any other weapon of mass murder that we have today. The framers of our constitution couldn't have imagined the type of weaponry we have today. If we look at the constitutional doctrine of original intent in determining the scope of the Second Amendment, we won't find these assault weapons in any text. Therefore, it is the height of disingenuousness to find via the original intent doctrine authority for ownership of these weapons of mass killings. If, however, the constitution is to be read in accordance with the times, then access to assault weapons today must be logically conditioned upon their need for a well-regulated militia, or military force. Allowing weapons of mass killings to be easily available to all adult members of the public doesn't square with either doctrine of constitutional interpretation.

Each time we witness an unimaginable massacre with assault weapons in our homeland, our leaders send condolences; call for swift and certain justice; and calmly assure that everything is under control and people are safe. Then, after the victims are buried and the flags at half-mast return to their normal position, we get back to our daily business without any meaningful discussion as to how we can truly avoid repeats. Are we really that safe anymore? How do you feel when you walk into a mall? Anyone can easily carry an assault weapon into a mall. How about a hotel? Restaurant? Supermarket? Place of Worship? Think of how easy it is for a gunman to walk into any of these places. How about your child's school? Get my point?

The sad and, indeed, tragic fact is that unless we are willing to sacrifice more and more freedom of movement and become much like Israel with guards posted throughout the country—a task made that much greater by the size of our country—we may be forced to admit that all we can do is hope for the best and pray that we don't see the worst. But what are we to tell the families of those who are killed by a mass murderer? What do we tell the injured whose lives have been permanently altered? Do we tell them there's nothing that our government can do to protect us, especially since we took strong measures after 9/11 by placing public safety at our airports and public buildings ahead of personal privacy considerations? While we can't set up security fortresses at every mall, movie theater, school, college, supermarket, etc., throughout the country, we may have reached the point where our government won't undertake any effort to better protect the public safety at places where people congregate, even though things can be done if we have the will and fortitude to do them. One thing that comes to mind that can be done on an immediate basis is to hire a plain-clothed security guard for each mall entrance, restaurant, supermarket, or during a church, synagogue or mosque service.

We, of course, must assume responsibility for increasing our level of caution and awareness of our surroundings at all times. If we see something out of the ordinary, we must treat it as such and either report it to appropriate authorities or remove ourselves from that area. In sum, it's up to each one of us to do our best to assure the safety of our family, friends and ourselves. But government does have a responsibility to stop the bickering and posturing and exercise some foresight into how we can better protect the public without creating a police state and otherwise fully depriving anyone of his/her constitutional rights. I've set out a few ideas below.

Unless calmer and cooler heads prevail, the confluence of four elements—easy access to weapons of mass killings; a gunslinger mentality on the part of a few; increased level of visual violence in the media and entertainment industries; and the fomenting of hate, anger and fear, especially by politicians who should know better—may continue to lead to more horrific mass murders in public places, especially in a down economy. Of these four elements, the most dangerous is the first one. We could tolerate a gunslinger mentality, media and entertainment violence, and fear-mongering and hateful speech, as long as there were no guns around or nearby. I think it's safe to say that there's a thin line between brilliance and madness; sometimes, a person who's brilliant just snaps. Add to this the process of "acting out" what is shown in the theater and in video games, and you have a potentially deadly mix. But even under this circumstance, it's far more difficult to commit a mass murder with a knife or the "Saturday night special" than it is with an assault weapon. In short, I doubt anyone with mass murder on his mind would succeed with a weapon other than a firearm of mass killings. Therefore, logic dictates that the focus must be on guns, more especially rapid-fire, multiple-rounds weapons of mass killings.

I know people have said that if they were present and had a weapon, they could take down the perpetrator and thereby save lives. That might work if one or two have a concealed weapon and know how to use it. But what happens if several are so armed? Or perhaps dozens in a school, mall, movie theater or other place where the public congregates? Can you imagine if dozens of teachers and administrators in Columbine High School had weapons, or if dozens in the Aurora movie theater had weapons in their possession? The loss of life from all the wild cross-firing would have potentially been much greater, with innocents shooting innocents. How do you arm the few without allowing the many to do likewise? I don't think allowing mass arming is a solution to mass murder.

By my reference to these four elements, I'm not suggesting that all must be present or that there aren't others, perhaps more subtle. What I am suggesting is that a look at each of these four is as good a starting place as any to make sense out of why there are people who commit mass murder with assault weapons. Perhaps there are sociological factors. Psychological factors. Whatever the underlying reason may be, and whatever the cost, these killings demand answers and action. It's simply inconceivable to me that there doesn't seem to be any major demand that we seek answers to this obvious question of why must we, who profess an enlightened society, tolerate easily accessible assault weapons and mass killings.

I see several versions making the rounds of Adolph Hitler's statement in disarming the German Jews: "The most foolish mistake we could possibly make would be to allow the subject races to possess arms. History shows that all conquerors who have allowed their subject races to carry arms have prepared their own downfall by so doing." I saw this quote after Columbine, Fort Hood, and all of the other cities of mass murder committed by an a deranged person with an assault weapon. Note the two points of commonality: derangement and an assault weapon. Psychiatry and alert citizens and law enforcement must take care of the first; the second is up to our elected leaders to take charge and address the easy access to these assault weapons, and the sheer number of weapons on the streets of our nation.

This quote from Hitler is usually cited by the pro-gun groups seeking to invoke the fear of the Third Reich in order to prevent any form of gun regulation. The points they miss is that no one is seeking to prevent gun ownership for protection and safety, and our government has no ulterior motive of committing genocide. The target is the assault weapon; the weapon of mass killings. These types of weapons on the streets of our nation are causing the death and maiming of more and more innocent men, women and children. There are almost as many guns in the hands of Americans as there are Americans; in fact when the adult population alone is considered, the ratio is more than one gun per person! Here are two simple facts: no nation has more guns per person than ours—well ahead of the rest of the world. The country that's in second place: Yemen. The United States ranks seventh in the percentage of homicides by firearms—with only Thailand, South Africa, Colombia, Guatemala and Zimbabwe ahead of us. (I would include Slovakia, except that its population is so small that percentage is of no import.) Imagine our nation being in the same category as these countries!! Forgetting every other argument on gun regulation, consider our ranking in comparison with other major civilized countries of the world. I simply don't understand how our beloved country could possibly be proud of this status that I find both deplorable and embarrassing.

Simply put, no one should be able to purchase from a storefront gun shop, or order online, thousands of rounds of ammo, weapons that can rapidly deliver this ammo, explosive material and body gear without anyone raising an eyebrow. There should be red flags all over any person who attempts to build an arsenal that allows him to literally prepare for war. Laws requiring background checks are meaningless unless the checks are detailed and significant. The business owner who's required to do this check naturally has the bottom-line interest in selling a weapon and making a profit. There should be some means to alert law enforcement when such obviously excessive firearms and related purchases are made.

After Oklahoma City, Columbine, Virginia Tech, Fort Hood, Tucson, Aurora and Wisconsin, what evidence is there that measures have been taken to avoid the next mass murder? In light of the reaction following the Aurora massacre, where there was almost no national sense of outrage over easy access to the arsenal gathered by a 24-year-old, we may be becoming hardened to these horrific crimes. Because we're witnessing more and more of these types of crimes, putting more and more innocent people—men, women and children CHILDREN—in fear of going to public places, are we now willing to accept these mass murders as part of our culture or as part of our pride in individual liberty and freedom? If the answer is yes, what does that say about us? If the answer is no, what shall we do about it? How shall we address the fact that a killer, legally possessing firepower not too long ago reserved for fighting war against foreign enemies, can strike our homeland at any time?

Rather than moving away from cavalier possession of destructive weaponry, we're moving closer and closer to a fully armed nation. 9/11 forever destroyed the notion that our homeland was invulnerable to a foreign terrorist attack; with the tragedies listed above, domestic terrorism is now a reality here. After the shooting in Tucson that left six dead and Rep. Gabrielle Giffords of Arizona fighting for her life, a study was undertaken which disclosed that there are more than 300 million guns of varying types on the streets of our country. Regardless of the pros and cons of gun regulation, shouldn't we be having a discussion of what to do so that we can live safely with 300 million guns on the street? This is the conclusion reached by Dr. Joel Dvoskin, a Tucson clinical psychologist who did a study of the Columbine teen age killers and led a forum following the Tucson shooting spree—a conclusion in which I fully agree.

Setting aside constitutional issues, do common sense, logic and reason tell us that mass murder is one of the prices to pay for our freedom? Aren't the freedoms of speech, religion, press, etc., founded on the freedom from fear? And can we be free from fear in our places of public accommodation, or on our public streets? The next time you walk into a mall, house of worship, supermarket or movie theater, can you be absolutely assured that there isn't someone there who has a loaded firearm, or even a mini-arsenal? There are those who shrug their shoulders and simply say that no one can guarantee anyone's safety at all times. Even assuming this is true, does this mean that nothing should be done to at least make it more difficult to commit such crimes? I believe with all my heart that we're better than that. At least, we had better be, because when people whose only crime is going to the movies are at risk, then we are all at risk. The naysayers and do-nothings argue that there's always going to be some nut who'll perpetrate such a crime, and there's very little—if anything—that can be done. But with each horrific event, we're losing more and more of our freedom from fear; we're becoming more and more afraid to be on our public streets, in our malls, supermarkets, schools and now movie theaters. What's next? people ask. What should our leaders tell them?

As with the aftermath of 9/11, the right of privacy must be balanced when the issue involves protecting the public from someone who orders items that serve only the purpose of mass murderer. The point here is that the laws governing ownership, possession and use of firearms must be so written so as to separate out the collectors and self-protectionists from those who would seek to obtain these military style weapons. To be sure, this is not an easy task; but such laws must become part of our criminal code and both rigidly and competently enforced to protect all of the law-abiding citizens, including gun owners and Second Amendment advocates, from those who, as a result of their medical condition or criminal background, for example, should be prohibited from owning any firearm in the first place. Suppose there was a convention of national leaders who were in the Aurora theater that fateful night? Could this have happened? If you believe they could have been in the Oklahoma City courthouse, Columbine high school, Virginia Tech campus, and the Tucson mall, then the answer is yes. Getting closer to home and being honest with yourself, you must ask where the next mass murder will be, and will you just happen to be there? For me, the bottom line is that the Second Amendment must be harmonized with the "general welfare" clause and the "necessary and proper" clause to allow congress to provide for meaningful regulation of weapons of mass killings. And yes, it's really that simple.

I believe someone who plans these unspeakable types of crime leaves some type of trail; unfortunately, the plain-as-day forewarning is usually found too late to save lives. We all need to be more aware of what people say and do; and if they appear out of the ordinary by defying our notion of common sense or reason, then there should be some duty as citizens to inform and be held harmless for providing such information to authorities. I realize there is some hesitancy, even fear, of "getting involved," but if law abiding citizens faced with obvious circumstances that call for some action decide to let someone else take on this responsibility, remember that one or more of these innocent law abiding people could have been in a movie theater or mall or any other place where people gather, with a gunman with evil intentions standing right beside them. For me, it's all about common sense access to firearms. For those who claim to have a better handle on how to deal with mass murder, take it up with your elected representatives. Shrugging shoulders or raising our arms in despair and saying to ourselves that there's nothing we can do if someone is hell-bent on mass murder is a horrible admission to make; our nation was founded on principles that make us better than that. Are we ready to sacrifice them?

There is one final point on this subject that deserves consideration. There are instances where the mass murderer is a loner who craves attention. When he knows he's on TV, or his picture is spread all over the media, he gets the attention he so desperately craves. What I suggest next requires the media to police itself. Once the accused appears in court and is seen on the TV news, and once his name appears in the print media, his picture and name are not to be used again. Knowing that some loner craving attention out there realizes he's not going to get it from the media, maybe—just maybe—lives will be saved.

The second point concerns the disproportionate number of minorities in prison. There are those who believe that because so many more minorities are incarcerated across the nation, racism continues to play a role in our criminal justice system. Others contend that the minority jail population is a result of the disproportionate number of crimes committed by minorities and, therefore, race or ethnicity plays no role. Both sides can point to statistics to back up their claims. The fact remains that minorities are more likely to be unemployed and poor. The reasons for this are complex and involve education, training for the 21st century, family background and instillation of a strong value system. Some efforts at resolution may be viewed as beyond the reach of government, but our government officials nevertheless are elected and appointed to address deep societal problems such as this. Rather than look for scapegoats, they should do what they're paid to do: work to solve problems. I have to believe there are enough creative people who can come up with programs that provide incentives as well as more direct means of substantively addressing the overriding issues regarding the relationship between poverty and crime, particularly among our youth. We need to find these best and brightest, and put them to work to address this relationship.

The subject of street crime also inevitably leads to a debate over the impact of "entertainment" violence on crime, which I alluded to earlier. With greater access to more diverse communications means; increasing forms of social networking; the exploding Internet; edgier music and music videos, particularly rap and hip-hop; and more and more violence on the movie screen, the debate rages over whether any of these examples of entertainment violence impacts the commission of street crime. In short, the question thus becomes whether this bombardment of violence leads to acting out on the part of impressionable youth. The answer is a difficult one, because the debate inevitably leads to a discussion of government censorship against our nation's rich history of abhorring censorship in any form. There are studies that show a relationship between entertainment violence and street crimes; there are also studies that show no such significant relationship. I separate myself from these studies; I find it hard to believe and manifestly illogical to summarily reject the view that impressionable young people bombarded with violence on TV, radio and in the movies are not at all affected and will under no circumstances ever act out what they see and hear. There is certainly anecdotal evidence of a connection, however strong or weak it may be.

Having said this, the question is how to deal with this issue in such a manner that no government censorship is imposed. For me, the answer lies in greater parental supervision along with increased education on the role of entertainment in our society along with the need to clearly distinguish between what we see in videos and on the screen on one hand, and the real everyday world on the other. The former is not reality; the latter certainly is. In addition, we need to encourage those who are responsible for the videos, movies and music to engage in self-regulation or careful editing in the name of the greater good of protecting the health, safety and welfare of the public. This self-editing must be done in a significant and meaningful manner; the current G, PG-13, R, etc., needs refinement to become more accurate in describing the conduct supporting the rating. To be sure, there is a never-ending tension between addressing this matter without imposing government censorship; however, it is a tension that must be dealt with if we're going to get street crime under control—particularly during hard economic times—while simultaneously being true to our constitutional imperative. And parental guidance must always be there to explain to children the difference between entertainment and the real world. The Internet is a powerful source of information, as well as information that shouldn't be viewed by the young and impressionable. Closer parental scrutiny and self-regulation are the means of addressing Internet, video and related concerns. Of course, the relationship between media violence and acting out, in light of the Aurora tragedy, applies to securing weapons of mass murder as well.

War; History; Iraq and Afghanistan; Islamic Fundamentalists and Political Correctness; and Foreign Aid.

I think it's a good idea to start this point by defining what is meant by war. Most dictionaries define "war" as an organized, armed, and often prolonged conflict that is carried on between states, nations or other parties typified by extreme aggression, social disruption, and usually high mortality. War should be understood as an actual, intentional and widespread armed conflict between political communities, and therefore is defined as a form of political violence. War has also been defined as an act of force to compel the enemy to do another's will. This is fine for dictionary purposes, but for me, war is the ultimate societal breakdown by those who claim to be civilized. Nations don't make war; people do. And how strange it is that, recognizing the devastation of war and then supposedly doing everything possible to avoid war because it admits of the a breakdown, we have over many years developed "rules of war," such as the Geneva Convention of 1949 and its progeny, treating war almost as if it were a game. These rules of engagement define acceptable acts of war as well as well as war crimes, such as genocide. But isn't war itself a crime? If so, then "war crimes" is a classic oxymoron.

The adoption of rules of engagement presumes some sense of order agreed to in advance by potentially warring parties. But if war represents the ultimate breakdown of order, how can there be rules? And if there are actions defined as war crimes, then doesn't this effectively mean that there are different levels of war, with some being crimes and others not? Are there levels of war of which we are unaware? If war represents the absence of common sense, logic and basic morality, how can those who engage in war develop rules and define war crimes separate from war itself? If war means to destroy the enemy, then how does parsing the degrees of war make sense? For me, war should never make sense; it is an admission that Mankind is not all civilized—and in the 21st century, with our history books littered with wars, including one that was to be "the war to end all wars," we repeatedly witness the horrors of the ultimate goal of war: destruction and subservience by survivors. Albert Einstein said WW IV would be fought with sticks and stones. We have the weapons to make his prediction come true. How sad and frightening this is.

A brief study of both world and American history as it pertains to warfare over the past 200 or so years reveals a startling pattern. Even as nations met and agreed to various treaties designed to recognize and protect human rights, or the rights of Man, wars continued to be fought in order to impose one's racial, ethnic or religious superiority over others. Even within nations, one group would historically seek to gain superiority over another, even to the point of removing that group from the face of the Earth through genocide. Just look at Iraq, where Sunnis and Shiites continue to battle, and the wars with the Kurds. All three live within the borders of one country, yet these groups don't consider the others to be part of one nation. When the leaders of such nations such as Chile or Romania were called on the carpet by international justice and human rights tribunals, the Pinochets and Ceausescus claimed national sovereignty; that is, as presidents, they were as sovereign as their nations themselves and therefore beyond the jurisdiction of the international community. While heads of state have some level of sovereign immunity for actions within their nations, this claim of absolute sovereign immunity was eventually rendered inapplicable to human rights treatment and, as a result, dictators and despots who kill or maim their own are subject to the judicial processes of international law. The Nuremburg trials certainly demonstrates this. I could go on and point out other examples of racial and ethnic cleansing within nations, as well as wars fought among nations based on racial and ethnic superiority—Hitler's Germany and its Aryan supremacy being the most glaring and horrific example—all since the advent of the 20th century, but I believe I've made the point as to war's general recent history.

Our nation's involvement in recent wars reveals an added element. (I know that under our constitution, only Congress has the power to declare war, so legally only WWs I and II fit into this category. I don't know if anyone really cares for this distinction without a difference. To me, foreign enemies shooting at us and us shooting back, all with the same purpose in mind, is war. Our constitution, however, makes the definition of war whatever Congress so declares.) If there is one lesson we should have learned from World Wars I and II through Korea and Vietnam, it's that our nation stands ready to fight a war so long as the people believe in the cause. This was easy during WWs I and II. Then, it was war to prevent nations from gaining dominance over others, including ours. Vietnam was an entirely different kind of war. We engaged in a jungle war against an enemy that knew how to fight a jungle war; an enemy that could send waves upon waves of committed communists willing to die for their cause. We were outnumbered and fighting their kind of war, a war of attrition. The communists' losses far exceeded ours, but loss of life didn't matter as much to them; their mindset was to wear us down. We're not used to fighting long, drawn out wars. Our involvement in WWs I and II each lasted less than four years; Korea lasted about three. Vietnam dragged on for over 10 years before we exited as Saigon was overrun. That war simply wore us out. Our patience grew thin. Then we learned our government was deceiving us all along. The war in reality ended when the nation no longer believed in the cause. We spent billions of our own money to fight that war, but we didn't learn history's lessons. This was the first time Americans actually questioned the legitimacy of a war. It certainly wasn't the last.

Iraq was not a war pitting one nation against another; it was postured as a war designed to eliminate Saddam Hussein because his weapons of mass destruction posed a threat to us; he had killed many of his own countrymen; and we had to take out the terrorists that attacked us on 9/11. We and our coalition had to prevent Saddam from using his weapons against the free world and allowing al Qaeda to grow and expand its sphere of influence. Or so the story went. The disingenuously labeled "coalition" that fought the war—tens of thousands of American troops and a handful from a few other countries; the weapons of mass destruction lie; the cruel joke of "mission accomplished" after which thousands more American soldiers died; the foolish notion born of the discredited domino theory that defeating al Qaeda in Iraq would prevent further attacks by radical Islamic groups elsewhere—particularly when there was no evidence of al Qaeda's presence in Iraq to begin with—created a disconnect, causing Americans to once again question the legitimacy of our involvement there. Finally, after fighting an urban guerrilla war—once again, the enemy's type of war—that lasted longer than either world war, we left, tired and worn out. Since we departed, the reports of bombings and internal strife there continue. The fact is Hussein, as bad and evil as he was, was a counterforce to Iran. With Hussein and his family out of the way, and the nation itself in disarray, Iran has a free hand to engage in inflammatory bombastic rhetoric and snub its nose at the rest of the free world even as it develops its nuclear program with Israel as its primary target. As a result, the Middle East remains an ominous tinder box that needs only a single spark to ignite. And al Qaeda continues to remain a threat.

Now we have a war in Afghanistan, where we're trying to defeat the Taliban and restore democratic stability. I don't recall that the Taliban had anything to do with 9/11. And trying to bring western-style democracy to a nation and area steeped in thousands of years of tribal war history isn't exactly an overnight proposition. We are fighting this war urban guerrilla-style—yet again, precisely the type of war the enemy is used to. Yet again, we continue to spend billions in another foreign venture as Americans yet again question the wisdom of this effort. According to a CBS News report, we have about 80,000 of our troops there, along with 40,000 from other countries, and over 300,000 Afghan troops that we are training to fight about 20,000 enemy troops. If this is true, there is something dreadfully wrong here. Why it takes this much to defeat such a small opponent should raise red flags all over the place. This long, drawn out struggle is sapping our nation's resources and patience. We witness Afghan soldiers killing ours. Support for this war dwindles daily. We give billions to Pakistan, our "ally," or so we're told. This "ally" housed Bin Laden for years, and after a successful raid that took him out, Pakistan challenged us for conducting that raid. This is friendship with an ally? We gladly give big checks—our money—to foreign governments to be our friend. Is this money well-spent? Could our taxpayers' dollars be better used to rebuild and shore up our infrastructure, and enhance the value of other programs designed to help us here in our homeland?

Today's war is far different from those in the past; it's not about nation-building as much as it is about religion and ideology, or perhaps I should say the perversion of religion and ideology. Islamic extremists want to return the Middle East to the Persian Empire. The type of war we're fighting in the Middle East does nothing to derail the Islamic militants; it only saps our resources and our patience. Since Vietnam, we've been told again and again that the enemy is weakening, growing tired, losing the will to fight, etc. There seems to be a disconnect between what we're told and what we get from our news sources. Money that could be spent rebuilding and shoring up our infrastructure, and generally strengthening the homeland, is being frittered away by trying to contain too vast a territory and too many waves of humanity. We are told that the enemy is just a few radical, misguided renegades. We've heard this line before. But if this is the case, why can't the world's most powerful nation dispose of these so-called little groups like a gnat on one's arm? And why are the governments and people of Iraq and Afghanistan not able to rid themselves of these small fringe groups without our assistance? Is it possible the enemy is far greater and more powerful than we've been led to believe? Is it possible there is collusion involved between these governments and the enemy groups? Our government lied to us in Vietnam and Iraq; could it be happening again? Remember, those who fail to learn the lessons of history are condemned to repeat them.

Here's one solution that has been offered by a growing number of government officials, military pundits and ordinary Americans. We leave the Middle East completely, pulling out all our troops and non-combat manpower. We tell the nations that if your own people and government can't stop these groups, then you have a problem that you need to fix; we've spent enough time and money, and lost far too many of our young men and women, fighting your wars. But as we leave, the president makes the following statement: "We're going home to take care of our homeland. We're going to make our country even stronger. Those companies that have profited from our war efforts will need to look elsewhere for revenue. A good place is infrastructure revitalization;

education with emphasis on math, science and technology; creation of good jobs that help grow our nation; just to name a few. And listen closely to what I now say so it's absolutely clear to all concerned. If any nation or group attacks any one of our true long-standing allies who have always been by our side through thick and thin, or our nation's homeland, we will find the source and, without further warning, we will bomb that nation or group until the mountains and jungles are deserts and the deserts are parched and bare. And if there is any further attack, we will, again without further warning, turn your cities into vast empty wastelands." Rather drastic, isn't it? But would this work?

This next point concerns Islamic fundamentalism and political correctness. Every now and then, we read or hear about Islamic fundamentalists becoming radicalized and infiltrating our military or universities—perhaps even our cities—posing as law abiding citizens just waiting for "the word" to strike at our people and institutions. This comforting news is usually not followed by any suggestions as to what we should do about this., sort of like the color code the Department of Homeland Security came up with shortly after 9/11 which only added to the fear factor because a color didn't come with instructions as to what to do. Political correctness dictates that we not profile minorities—African-Americans, Hispanics, Orientals, Muslims, etc. However, by analogy to the criminal justice system, if it is known that a perpetrator is Caucasian, it defies logic and common sense to arrest and include in a lineup African-Americans, Hispanics, etc. Profiling for the sake of profiling is one thing and I certainly don't support that; profiling in search of a suspect, however, is quite another. We may effectively thrown out the baby with the bathwater. If we have evidence of an Islamic fundamentalist operation run by Pakistanis at a certain location in New York City, does it make sense to seek out Orientals or African-Americans, etc.? Is profile avoidance in the name of political correctness a wise use of our law enforcement resources? I don't think so either.

In virtually all instances where horrific murders were committed in the military or on a college campus, there were signals that the perpetrators were radicalized and had issued clear threats. Yet, those who should have seen the signals either didn't recognize them or simply ignored or turned a blind eye toward them. This may well be the result of the education level of those in the front line of our early warning system. Earlier, I pointed out that with more and more money being poured into our schools, the product is less and less educated. If, again in the name of political correctness, security jobs are being given to those who are not fully capable of screening those who might well pose a clear and present danger, then the risks are great that someone will slip through the system. And it only takes one or, at most, a very few to ignite the fuse leading to a disaster. We must not only be vigilant, we must make absolutely certain that those who are guardians of our security are both responsible, competent and capable of truly being guardians.

My final point on this subsection concerns poverty in America and the amount of money we give to foreign countries. According to the Poverty Law Center, in 2010 46.2 million Americans lived below the poverty level, which is established at an annual income for a family of four of $22,314. That figures to one for every seven Americans. Contrast this with the report from a congressional oversight entity that says the United States remained the world's largest bilateral donor, obligating approximately $53 billion: $38 billion in economic assistance and $15 billion in military assistance in 2010. By comparison, the United States obligated $34 billion and $15 billion, respectively, in 2009. The $38 billion in obligated U.S. economic assistance went to 182 countries. Afghanistan received the most, approximately $5 billion, while Iceland received the least, just $83. The U.S. disbursed $30 billion in economic assistance and $14 billion in military assistance. Afghanistan remained the top recipient of total U.S. economic and military assistance—both obligations and disbursements—for a third consecutive year. Iraq had held the top spot from 2003 to 2007. Haiti was a newcomer to the list of top ten recipients (obligations), as West Bank/Gaza dropped to 14th.

Note the significance of this data. We gave 182 countries $53 billion in 2010, up from $49 billion the year before. We're doing this while more than 46 million people in our own country are living below the poverty line! Millions of children and their parents are homeless through no fault of their own. Why are we giving billions to other countries while so many of our nation's own—including children—are homeless? Where is the justification for this? Notice this also: we're giving this money to the governments of these countries, including the Gaza Strip and the West Bank, even as the Palestinians continue to threaten Israel's survival. Moreover, how do we know these billions and billions of our taxpayers' money is going for their intended purposes rather than lining the pockets of government officials as well as others who are less than friendly to us? How do we know there is no profiteering by these foreign countries? And how can we justify spending this kind of money while one in seven Americans lives below the poverty line, with that number going up even as the amount given in foreign aid continues to go up? There is something very wrong with this picture when so many Americans are in financial dire straits and our infrastructure is badly in need of modernization. I believe in the phrase "charity begins at home." I also believe that benevolence has its place, but that our nation is judged by how well it treats its own less fortunate. These numbers suggest an imbalance; we need to address this in a competent manner. I can understand that in a global economy, the importance of maintaining international relations is quite evident; still, couldn't we use a few billions of dollars to work on at least those social issues that address the needs of our children? Our infrastructure is crumbling; what about using a few billions of that money that goes to 182 countries to at least start rebuilding our infrastructure.

Government dysfunction; key definitions

Our government is on the receiving end of much well-deserved criticism. Our federal government is held in low esteem, yet those in whose charge we place our trust seem not to care. We hear and read about the need to "throw the rascals out." We condemn legislative stalemate and vow that, in the next election, things will be different. But usually they're not, for one simple reason. While we may agree to send all members of Congress into retirement, when it comes to our very own representative, it's another story. We seem to be incapable of admitting a mistake when it comes to voting for our own incumbent. Add this human nature reality to the redistricting and reapportionment process the primary purpose of which is to protect the incumbent, and we wind up with very few competitive races for the 425 seats in the U.S. House of Representatives. The same rascals we say we want to throw out keep returning. Congress has so stacked the rules against addressing the needs of the people that we have gridlock and threats born of a "my way or the highway" attitude. And who's paying for this arrogance? We are. It is said we get the government we deserve. There are serious societal problems that can't be addressed by gridlock or ideology; they require action, and government action requires consensus, not pomposity. If the two major parties demonstrate gridlock and chronic inability to meet the needs of the people, then the country is ripe for a third party.

While history has shown that third party movements generally fail, there have been situations in which a third party candidate made strong showings, most noticeably Alabama Governor George Wallace and, most recently, Ross Perot. A third party candidate would need to be independently wealthy or at the very least have access to the kind of money it takes to get on the ballots of all states and run a nationwide campaign. Government officials dependent on the ballot box do what they can to make ballot access as difficult for non-incumbents as possible. This is another aspect of human nature: self-preservation. The risk of a third party is that it would be captured by an ideologue who promises everything to everybody, but fails to deliver anything to anyone—except greater hardship for the less fortunate.

In Florida, we have term limits for both houses of the legislature; not so with both houses of Congress. For too many, being a member of Congress is a lifetime job of privilege. They are supposed to represent us; they are our servants. This is now largely a pipedream. Over many years, members of Congress have stacked the deck against their bosses—the voting public—and have made themselves the bosses. They no longer believe they need to demonstrate accountability. They believe the voters are stupid and have short—very short—attention and memory spans. Judging from our tepid reaction at the polls to their conduct and behavior, they're right. This is not a party issue either; this is a human nature problem in which the ultimate goal is self-perpetuation. The perks of Congress are wonderful; why should any member give them up and become short-term statesmen and women dedicated to doing the people's work?

One suggested solution is to eliminate the perks and require Congress, as well as all government officials, to live under the same rules that they apply to us. In fact, I've seen variations of this theme floating around the

Internet as a proposed constitutional amendment. This is a good idea, but its realization is impossible without a cataclysmic event that compels such action. I can't imagine what that would be. From the time perks started in the late 40s and 50s, the federal government has had over 60 years to build a system of perks for itself. The optimist says changing the playing field will take a long time at best. The pessimist says this will never happen. We do, however, need to change the culture of our elected leaders who believe in entitlements for themselves, but not necessarily for those who truly need them.

While term limits might sacrifice highly competent persons with vast institutional knowledge, it will also prevent those who believe their election is a gateway to a form of entitlement that they receive while serving from safely drawn districts for 20 to 40 years or more. Of course, amending the federal constitution to provide for term limits would be an incredibly difficult and time-consuming task at best—equivalent to a catastrophic political earthquake-tsunami-hurricane rolled into one—but perhaps it's time to consider this prospect. We're certainly not getting the kind of attentiveness that we should from our elected representatives. There are those who say we now have an Imperial Congress beholden only to Big Business, including Big Religion, Wall Street and Big Unions with deep pockets from which to give contributions and other benefits to legislators who will do their bidding. This is a sad commentary about our Congress, and a sad statement about us as well.

As a lawyer (I'm still an active dues-paying member of The Florida Bar) and resident of Florida's capital city, I closely follow the travails and machinations of my governments, particularly state government. The buzzwords and buzz phrases that are currently in vogue are: less government, limited government, less spending, liberal, conservative, individual freedom, individual responsibility, judicial activism, justice, reducing taxes, socialism and voter registration reform. At the risk of omitting some, allow me to define these terms as they are used today.

"Less government" or "limited government" means less regulation of business while keeping all breaks now available only to the wealthy while imposing more regulation of such things as a woman's choice to have an abortion, same-sex marriages, purchasing and use of contraceptives, and prohibiting government intrusion in the freedom to pray in public schools and other places where the public gathers. Exactly what prayers would be said isn't formally addressed. Do you believe the groups that support prayer in schools and public places would allow for prayers of different religions? I don't.

"Less spending" means less funding for predominantly social services programs and projects designed to help the middle and lower classes; and increased spending for the military and the military-industrial complex President Eisenhower warned us about upon leaving office in 1961. However, this phrase does not apply to block legislative earmarks for such items as bridges to nowhere, buildings that have politician's names on them, and other pet projects that allow legislators to "bring home the bacon" and secure large political contributions from the beneficiaries of these expenditures.

"Liberal" is any person—Republican, Democrat or independent—who disagrees with any part of the social or political philosophy and agenda of those right wing groups that now make up the GOP.

"Conservative" is any person who fully supports the political philosophy and agenda of the GOP's right wing—which is now the only wing of the GOP. The Grand Old Party as we knew it is no more.

"Individual freedom" means less government involvement in regulating Big Business while keeping special breaks intact, believing that if business is left alone, the wealth accumulating at the top will trickle down to the middle and lower classes. This phrase also means allowing Big Business to expand its influence in the formation of public policy, as well allowing for more religious freedom for individuals to espouse specific dogma in places such as schools, courthouses, athletic events, etc. This phrase doesn't mean more freedom for individuals to make choices about their bodies that affect no one else; personal lifestyles that affect no one else, etc. This mantra as used by the right wing means getting government out of their way, but having government direct how others choose to live; i.e., prohibiting abortion, and use of contraceptives, and banning gay marriages.

"Individual responsibility" means requiring those who receive social services assistance to assume more responsibility for their own lives and not rely on government to provide for them. This phrase, however, doesn't mean that people who have no health insurance should exercise individual responsibility by purchasing it. It's a person's individual choice whether or not to buy health insurance, no matter what the Supreme Court majority says. If a person chooses not to have insurance and is in need of health care, it will be paid for by those of us who have insurance—unless the government passes a law that says "no insurance, no health care coverage unless the person demonstrates current ability to pay in full." This is as good a place to comment on this subject, because it's used so frequently today. Individual responsibility has become a euphemism used by one who claims to be exercising it, to accuse another of lacking it. By saying someone else, or another group, opposes or lacks individual responsibility, it allows for the accuser to play the "blame game." It's easy to say "It's not my fault" when personal accountability can be ignored of diffused. Note how many people, when accused of something, blame virtually everyone or everything else but themselves; particularly those who claim support for individual responsibility. I've touched on this subject when I mentioned political leaders whose hands are caught in the cookie jar, those who commit crimes and are caught, etc., who quickly blame society, the economy, or whatever happens to be the reason du jour, except themselves. A politician who's caught taking bribes blames "unfortunate circumstances;" a murderer claims the victim made him angry; etc. If more people simply admitted to their human frailties, they—and everyone else—would be far better off. But it's not human nature to do so.

"Judicial activism" is uttered as an epithet—predominantly by conservatives—whenever the judiciary renders a decision that goes against their actions and beliefs. I suppose it's the opposite of judicial passivism. They believe that only they know what the constitution means, so when a decision goes against their agenda, the judges therefore aren't following the constitution; rather, they are legislating from the bench. They believe that whatever a conservative legislature passes and governor approves should be the final say; the judiciary has no role in superintending the conservative agenda, unless of course the judiciary agrees with them. Example: until June 28, 2012, United States Supreme

Court Chief Justice John Roberts was a judicial passivist because he could be counted on to follow in lockstep the true conservative line. However, his tie-breaking decision to uphold the Affordable Care Act—Obamacare—now places him in the role of a judicial activist. The notion that the only judicial activists are liberals or conservatives in name only is the height of incredulousness. If you want an example of judicial activism by conservative justices, see Bush v. Gore—a case that stands for only one point: the election of George Bush.

"Justice" in the criminal justice sense, means not only filing criminal charges, but having the accused actually convicted of his/her crimes, especially if the perpetrator is white and the victim is black. This word doesn't appear to be used very much—if at all—when both the perpetrator and victim are of the same race or ethnic origin.

"Reducing taxes" means cutting taxes in a manner usually measured by income level; providing virtual immunity from tax increases for the very wealthy; giving huge tax breaks to Big Business; and maintaining loopholes for the upper class. This goes hand-in-hand with reducing expenditures for programs that benefit the shrinking middle class and the legitimate poor.

"Redistributing the wealth" means no additional taxes on the wealthy; cutting taxes across-the-board; retaining current tax and other legislative breaks; and securing new breaks. See generally the definition of "reducing taxes."

"Socialism" is generally defined as an economic system characterized by social ownership and/or control of the means of production and cooperative management of the economy, and a political philosophy advocating such a system. When used by the conservatives, it's an epithet that means government control, regulation or operation of any program or activity that should be handled by the private sector. For those who are against anything that hints of socialism and are currently or will at some future time receive payments, government pensions, Medicare or Medicaid benefits, to be true to their opposition to any vestige of socialism as they define it, they must return such payments immediately, and/or let the government know they don't want to receive these socialistic payments under any circumstances. Who knows, maybe if enough people follow their beliefs on this point instead of engaging in rank hypocrisy, we can recover and retain funds to address the deficit; rebuild our infrastructure; maintain a strong defense that prohibits profiteering; help those who legitimately want to work get a job; and further provide for the health, safety and welfare for those in legitimate need.

"Immigration reform" means making sure that illegal immigrants who are working for companies paying as little as possible in wages and providing for little if any benefits, can remain in the country while those in charge look the other way; or simply allowing illegal immigrants to work and remain here for as long as they wish, doing whatever American workers won't do. With this ability, the question naturally arises: why should there be any laws governing illegal aliens? Let's see if our government bothers to answer this question. Additionally, it means purging voter registration lists of those who some officials think are illegal aliens based on records the veracity of which is suspect. The stated purpose of this purging is to prevent voter fraud, which according to virtually every study is almost non-existent, at least to the degree that justifies purging based on flawed data. Of course, we can all agree that illegals shouldn't be able to vote, but the devil's in the details. If the system by which illegals are identified is flawed to the point of risking the disenfranchisement of legally registered voters, then that system should be scrapped. If the system can be perfected to the point of disallowing only illegal aliens, no one should really object.

"Voter registration reform" means requiring voters to present proof of ID and/or voter registration cards and meet other conditions prior to voting. In practice, the cumulative effect of these requirements is publicly declared to prevent voter fraud; the reality, however, is that the purpose is to suppress minority voting. No one, except the party faithful, really believes that the conditions imposed by the GOP legislative majority in several states is designed to level the playing field. I suppose the rationale is that since the Democrats did the same thing when that party was in power, what's good for the goose is good for the gander. I don't recall the Democrats ever making it more difficult for the wealthy to cast a ballot, however. For me, I have no problem with a photo ID; allowing those to show up at the polls to vote solely on their word that they're registered defies common sense. And if it were just the photo ID at issue, it would be an easy one to address. If you don't have one, get one. You need an ID for so many other things, why not one for voting? While voting is a right, its exercise is not unfettered. A person wants an absentee ballot, he/she has to apply for one. Having some form of identification simply makes sense. But when the ID requirement is one of several hoops a prospective voter must pass through, it's worth taking an analytical view of these conditions to see if, in their totality, they burden one group of voters over another. What might appear perfectly neutral may, upon examination of the cumulative effect, impose an impermissible burden on the exercise of that right. Subtle burdens can be just as insurmountable as obvious ones.

If you're wondering why I've set out these observations, it's because each one of us has opinions that we are entitled to be made known to a wider audience. You don't have to be a politician, athlete, entertainer, or amass incredible wealth to have and share your opinions. If you allow the talking heads, the rich and the powerful to voice their opinions, the opinions of the vast majority of us will go largely unheard. You think people would listen to a Donald Trump if he weren't wealthy? Recall these great lines from the song "If I Were a Rich Man" from The Fiddler on the Roof: "The most important men in town would come to fawn on me! They would ask me to advise them . . . And it won't make one bit of difference if I answer right or wrong. When you're rich, they think you really know." What a great—and true—statement!! Just because a person is rich doesn't mean he has intelligence or is capable of addressing societal issues in a competent manner. All wealth does is provide a platform. This is equally so with the famous. Would people listen to an Alec Baldwin or a Sean Penn if they didn't have a built-in platform of fame? With so many avenues of expression available today, it's important to speak your mind. Writing a book is one way of doing this, and it's yet another way I've chosen for myself. There's nothing stopping you from doing likewise.

Ok, enough preaching. This will only get a concurrence from those with similar beliefs, and incur sharp disagreement from those who don't share them. But if what I've said makes you think, then I've certainly accomplished my goal with this section. If my comments are dismissed as the views of a liberal, well, once again, that makes my point precisely. And to those of you who believe things will get better once the right wing takes over Congress and the presidency, you're absolutely right. But for whom? For those who are in the middle or lower class and believe the answer to all of society's problems is for the right wing to take over our government, I say be careful what you wish for.

Now is the time to talk about my reaction as my big R day approached, particularly my panic attack, which I originally thought was far worse. I'll subtitle this section

Retirement Anxiety

As I said at the very beginning of this book, as retirement approached, I was facing my biggest fear: uselessness. I told my wife and children of this fear, and my daughter Amy offered comfort by saying that if I ever felt really useless, she had a little girl who would make me feel very useful. Avery was less than a year old at the time, and the thought of playing with her and watching her grow helped; but this fear continued to nag at me; a of the unknown. For as long as I can remember, on workdays I would get up at 6 a.m., wash and shave, comb my hair, make my breakfast, leave for work about 7 and be at my desk by 7:30. This required a great deal of discipline, but I chose this early arrival time because most of the lawyers and staff arrived for work around 9 a.m., and between 7:30 and 9 I could more often than not accomplish more in that time than I could the rest of the day.

There were many times I would go to my office on a Saturday, Sunday and holiday just to finish a task that could have waited for a weekday. I enjoyed the challenge of practicing law; of pitting my knowledge and skills against other lawyers. But I would soon be giving up this structure, routine and challenge.

I thought about having gone to school, worked, or both, for almost 50 years. I thought about how ordered and rather predictable my life was over this long period of time, and how that would change forever. I thought about what I would do with the days, months and years ahead; how I would fill up all of this free time; whether I would be able to meet my expenses and still have enough money to enjoy life; whether I would simply exist rather than live an active and productive life. I worried constantly. Night sweats. Insomnia. Digestive problems. Depression. The works. At one point, as I felt heavy pressure on my chest, I thought I was going to have a heart attack.

I tried to put on a good front, but the worry was wearing me down. I had become surly, snappish, and overall simply not pleasant to be around. What made matters even worse was that my wife, who was also facing retirement at the same time I was, somehow managed to have an air of confidence and purpose that was completely opposite of my demeanor and behavior. She accepted her upcoming retirement with joy and anticipation; I feared for mine.

With the worrying taking a physical and mental toll on me, at Harriet's urging, I agreed to see my primary care doctor, who recommended counseling. Needing to find some way to deal with, and hopefully get over, my fear of this upcoming change-of-life event, I agreed to counseling sessions. I even stressed at having to go to counseling sessions, believing that I didn't need to see a shrink. I quickly found out that counseling takes many forms, not all of them associated with psychology or psychiatry. The one I saw was a stress counselor—aptly named as far as I was concerned.

The first three visits were "getting to know you" type sessions during which the counselor took down my background and history—family, education background, work background, outside activities, recreation, etc.—and my fears. I was hyperventilating, talking as fast as I could to get it all out. I told her that I've always defined my life by work. When you meet someone, you usually ask "What's your name, where to do live, what do you do." So, for me, work was very important, and because of the value I placed on work, retirement for me created an identity crisis.

During our fourth session, the counselor told me that what I was experiencing was nothing new or isolated. Most people facing retirement have some degree of apprehension about the future, she said. My counselor made it abundantly clear that I control my attitude toward retirement, and, in summing up our previous sessions, tellingly said the following: "So, Mr. Waas. Let me see now. Except for your parents' difficulties, you had a good, relatively happy childhood; you attended a good high school and were active in various organizations; you went to college; received your undergraduate degree in journalism from the UF; worked as a news reporter for two years; went to FSU Law School; graduated in 1970; went to work; got married; have two daughters; have been happily married for 40 years; both of your daughters are successful; you have wonderful grandchildren; evidently you have enough income and investments for retirement; have no debts." When I answered "Yes" to each of her summary points, she said: "So, Mr. Waas, what exactly is your problem?"

What indeed. The wake-up call was received loud and clear. Thus ended my "therapy" sessions and my panic attacks. Literally overnight, I realized that I was the cause of my problems. People retire every day, and it was up to me to make my retirement years whatever I wanted this new phase of my life to be. For me, the half-empty glass became a half-full, or more accurately, completely full.

Why leave state employment? Florida's DROP System and Personal Finances

Why was I required to actually leave state employment on June 30, 2010? Fair question. At the time I was facing retirement, Florida had a somewhat unique retirement program under which a public employee (my wife was a school teacher with the Leon County, Florida public school system; I was a state employee for over 32 years) with 30 years of service, or age 62 with at least at least a specified number of years of employment service, could retire and thereby have his/her pension payment fixed as of the date of retirement. However, that employee could continue to work and collect his/her salary for up to 60 additional months with the government paying a monthly sum based on a statutory formula into a separate retirement fund set up for that employee. This program is called the Deferred Retirement Option Plan, or ironically named the DROP program. My "retirement" occurred June 30, 2005-just a few days before my 62nd birthday—and on the following day I entered the DROP. (Under this plan, one has to retire by the last day of the month immediately preceding his/her birth month.) My monthly pension payment was fixed as of June 30, 2005 at 27.5 years of government service multiplied by a statutory formula the explanation of which would only bore you with tedium, except that one of the factors in this formula is the average salary for my highest five years of income. Therefore, on that date, I knew exactly what my monthly pension payment would be when I fully retired. I also received a computer readout of how much money would be deposited into my DROP account at the end of each month, which I pasted inside my desk. Whenever I felt like I wanted to retire, I checked the list to see how much more money I'd accumulate if I stuck it out for a few more months. The monthly amount made the decision for me to stick it out for all 60 months.

(My wife "retired" in June 2004 and worked to 2009 when she could have fully retired under the DROP; however, this plan also allowed school teachers to continue teaching as long as the school's principal wanted to keep a teacher under annual contract, up to a maximum of three years. My wife decided to work one more year so she could retire at the same time I did.)

When I turned 66 in July 2009, I opted to take Social Security at the full amount. My wife began taking Social Security when she turned 62 in 2011. So, between my pension and full Social Security, and my wife's pension and her Social Security, we wouldn't have financial difficulties—providing the state and federal governments kept functioning relatively normally.

We didn't factor in our DROP money—the 60 monthly payments the government put into a separate retirement account for each of us which we both took as lump sums. That money joined our other savings and went with our investment counselors. Under the DROP program, it is possible for a person to retire and, with the passage of a fixed time frame, return to government employment. I know several lawyers with the attorney general's office who have done just that. None was in the position I was, however—having entered the DROP at 62, completed the five-year maximum and retired at 67. The others entered the drop years earlier, so by the time they reached 35 years with state government, they were between 60 and 62-really too young to retire, although they certainly could have. I retired at the oldest age possible under the DROP. Still, I suppose it would have been nice to have been asked whether I would like to return some day, but this never happened. And the answer would have been "no" anyway.

I give this financial information to you because one of the biggest fears for any soon-to-be retiree is whether there will be enough money to live in relative comfort for the rest of one's life, especially when taking into account rising medical costs. The fear of outliving your nest egg was certainly foremost on my mind; and with the state of our economy and the rush of Baby Boomers into retirement, the risk to current levels of Social Security and pension payments is not all that hypothetical. However, I've come to the realization that there is really nothing more that Harriet or I can really do about this, and if Harriet and I are adversely affected as a result of pension and Social Security changes (assuming government could alter vested pension rights protected by the constitution), what about the other tens of millions who depend on one or both?

In short, our loss (should there be one) will also be others' loss, which will come at great expense and much turmoil. I can't believe this will ever be allowed to happen. I realize my confidence may be shortsighted, but there is a certain level of comfort in relying on the federal and state governments to continue to provide the two monthly payments to which my wife and I contributed during our working years.

Fortunately, working for the state allowed me to have quality health care paid in full. Upon retirement, I was able to obtain medical care combined with my Medicare coverage that assured continued quality care at an affordable price. This is most important as a general matter since people are living longer and quality medical care is essential in assuring a decent quality of life in our later—very later—years. What you are about to learn about me makes having this insurance that much more vital in assuring a reasonably comfortable retirement.

Health Issues

If the truth be told—and the truth is what this book is all about—I probably couldn't have worked beyond the end of the 2010 calendar year. The reasons are wholly health-related. While my genetic line is fairly good for some things—cardiovascular, for example—the main inheritance from my parents was their arthritic conditions. My mother had osteoarthritis, my father had both osteoarthritis and rheumatoid arthritis. Both were also obese. When I was a child, my father would constantly complain about cold and rainy weather, accurately predicting both because he said he could feel the bad weather "in his bones." I had no idea then what he was talking about; I certainly understand this today. While my arthritic condition is the main reason why continuing in the workforce beyond my retirement from the state would have been very iffy at best, a description of my health issues will shed further light on this assessment.

I recall my father telling me that I didn't walk until I was four years old. While the inguinal hernia I was born with was a factor, it wasn't the only one. According to my dad, every time I tried to walk, my legs would shake and down I'd go. Finally, at four, I started to keep my balance. Although I have no recollection of ever being tested as a child for neurological problems, and have been tested as an adult with no neurological pathology, I do wonder whether I had residual neurological problems as a child that exacerbated my orthopedic problems that developed much later.

Knowing I was going to a desk job from law school, I began an exercise program right after graduation in 1970 that served me well; after my bout with childhood asthma, I was not obese, and would not allow myself to ever become chronically overweight. (Ok, I could stand to lose a few pounds, but that's far different from the kind of epidemic of obesity we read and hear about every day, especially with regard to young children.)

The debilitating effect of arthritis, however, is another story. Although I had eight shoulder surgeries—including two rotator cuff repairs and two restructuring operations—both knees scoped, and several trigger fingers taken care of, overall I was doing relatively well until I reached 62, when I had to have my right knee replaced. For the first time, I had to take a rather extended leave of absence from work to recover and rehabilitate not only my knee, but my leg and overall health as well. There is a tendency for people unfamiliar with joint replacement surgery to believe that all that's necessary is to take care of the surgical area. Not true at all. Major surgery affects the entire body, and that's what must heal when undergoing joint replacement surgery. While I was out of my office for three weeks, I had Harriet go to my office twice a week to pick up my mail; I would contact my secretary to let her know what needed to be done; and I had access to my office computer from home so I could draft documents for later filing. Fortunately, during this period, I had no court appearances or filings to worry about. I don't like idleness; I wanted to work and accomplish as much as I could around my recovery. Usually, when a person is out of work for an appreciable length of time, the burden is shifts to co-workers during that absence, I wanted to avoid this at all costs; my co-workers had their own assignments, and I was quite capable of handling mine. Fortunately, nothing slipped through the cracks during my absence. Timing is everything.

Shortly after getting over this surgery and getting back to work, I found out that I had prostate cancer. Now that was a shocker, because there are absolutely no symptoms—at least in the early stages of this disease. I felt fine, but my PSA levels were continuing to rise. (I won't explain what this is, except that the level is determined by a simple blood test. Men, get your PSA tested annually, and make sure you have a good urologist.) My urologist recommended a biopsy, which revealed no cancerous activity. However, because my next PSA result showed another climb, he recommended a second biopsy six months after the first one, which is not the normal thing to do. Bingo! Prostate cancer. Earliest of stages. I received this news from my doctor while working. Needless to say, his call shook me to my shoes. Was I scared? I was petrified. My life literally flashed before my eyes. How could I have cancer when I felt so good? I sat at my desk just staring into space. I know I looked like hell because my secretary came in and asked whether I was ok, saying I looked like a ghost.

After a few minutes, I called my wife at her school and left a message to call immediately. She was the first one I told; that wasn't a pleasant experience, but she gave me her usual reassurance that we would do whatever it took to deal with this. I then called my doctor to set up an appointment within the week to discuss "options." He wanted both my wife and me to be present. I knew this wasn't going to be a pleasant visit.

Then came the hardest part of all—telling my daughters. Telling your children you have cancer is both painful and hurtful; although they tried to hide it, I knew that the pauses and sniffles was their way of dealing with this unexpected serious news. Children naturally want to help, but children are scared and feel helpless when first dealing with what is a life-threatening diagnosis for a parent. I told my girls that I would fight this, and that the doctor told me that because my condition was in its earliest stages, it was both treatable and curable. That made them feel better; it certainly made me feel better.

Let me digress here for a moment and explain how important it is to have a good urologist. After my doctor found the cancer and before I had the surgery, I had another PSA test and, for the first time, it showed that my number had dropped a few points. Had my doctor not insisted on the second biopsy, the assumption would easily have been that all was fine and that I didn't need that second biopsy. This would have meant that the cancer would have had at least six months to grow before my next PSA test. And as long as my PSA levels didn't go up, I wouldn't have had a further biopsy. Prostate cancer is treatable and curable so long as the cancer doesn't spread beyond the prostate gland itself.

The degree of its spread beyond the gland makes the disease more and more life-threatening. I could easily have gone one or two years without having the disease detected. Looking back, I could have been a terminal case within a few years.

Before my first appointment, I read everything I could about prostate cancer. Risks. (Wow!) Side effects. (Wow, wow!) So, by the time of my appointment, I had at least a rudimentary understanding of what I was facing. My doctor explained the biopsy results. ("Is there a possibility that I had a false positive?" "Uh, uh." Can't be blamed for trying.) He talked about "watchful waiting." Waiting for what? My condition to go away? Get worse? Not a good option. Implanting of radioactive seeds? No way. If that fails, there's virtually no backup plan. Freezing the prostate? I still have a cancerous growth in me that could potentially spread even after this treatment. Another not-so-good option.

I then asked the questions you're not supposed to ask: "What would you do in my situation? What would you recommend if it were your father?" My doctor said that it was my decision, but then volunteered that if I weren't planning on having any more children (I was 63; let the Hollywood stars in their 60s have children—not me.), I should have it removed completely. I asked the doctor what my situation would be if I did nothing and the cancer continued to grow. He gave me five years, and the last year would be extremely painful. That was all I needed to hear; 10 weeks later, it was out. It's amazing how quickly you can make a decision when your options are severely limited, like really having none at all.

After my diagnosis, I was obligated to tell my supervisors, as well as co-workers. After all, they were going to find out anyway; they might as well hear it from me. Within a few days, I began getting phone calls and office visits from friends, co-workers, colleagues and even neighbors telling me they heard about my situation and would I like to discuss it with them, since they had all been through it.

What a revelation it was for me to learn that quite a number of people I know had this removal surgery and had beaten this dreaded silent and potentially fatal disease! I quickly found out how important this prostate cancer network is in coming to grips with the disease and, far more importantly, its treatment and cure. Yes, cure, as I am now more than five years past my surgery and my PSA readings continue to be zero. I now visit my urologist once a year—typical for a prostate cancer survivor. I won't list all of those who provided wise and comforting advice and counsel during this difficult time, in part because I can't remember all of them, but I am ever so grateful to them. Thanks, guys.

Since my bout with prostate cancer, a couple of friends of mine were given the same diagnosis, and I found myself giving them what I had received—sage advice. It's a great feeling to be able to provide for them the way I was provided for, and I will do this gladly should I become aware of others who need friendly counsel from one who's "been there, done that."

I was out of my office for about 10 days, during which I again had no court appearances or papers to file. Harriet again picked up my mail and I did my work via telephone and access to my office computer from home so I could compose documents for filing when I returned to my office.

Although my co-workers didn't know it, I wore a catheter to work for several weeks. Strapped to my left leg. Not a very comfortable way to work, but absolutely necessary. After the catheter, I had to wear Depends for a few weeks until my, uh, system adjusted to its new configuration. You see, where there were once three gateways between my bladder and the outside world, there was now only one—and that "one" takes time to adjust to its new role as sole gatekeeper between the inner and the outer world.

This was only the second time in my life that I had to wear a catheter, at least as far as I can recall—and I would think this is something I would easily recall. Actually, you don't "wear" a catheter. Rather, it's (for lack of a better word) jammed into your most private possession. I know this sounds squeamish; believe me if you've never had this experience, it is. And if you've had this experience, you know exactly what I mean.

The first time was when I had my knee replacement surgery. Funny, no one told me that this would be necessary. I now know why. Ok, here's the story. When I woke up from the surgery, I lay in my bed for hours. Then, I realized that I hadn't gotten up to go to the bathroom, and what's more, I didn't have any feeling of a need to get up and go. This was puzzling, and as I put my arms under the covers, I felt something rather strange. It seems that there was this plastic tube running alongside of me. I reached for it and traced its path and tried lifting it. Rather heavy, I thought. Then came the eureka moment as I held up this plastic bag full of rust-colored liquid. Reality and fear merged in my mind. OH, NO!! I dropped the bag and traced this plastic tube to its other end. Reality and fear hit like a ton of bricks. OH, NO!!! OH, NO!!!! OH, NOOOOOO!!! Oh, yes!!!!

I called the nurse and said, what's this? (Now, this was a foolish question; I knew it, she knew it; but where there is shock, logic and common sense take a vacation.) Doctor's orders, she said. "But that's only for one or two days. Once you're out of bed and begin walking, it comes out." I found out the next day how "it" comes out. Here are the instructions for removal of a catheter. The nurse grabs the plastic tube and says "Take a deep breath. Now, expel your breath slowly." YEEEEOWWWWWW! OH, MY GOD!!!!

This first experience with catheter removal helped me deal with the second following the (here's the description of my cancer surgery) radical prostatectomy. Doesn't this sound exotic? Following this surgery, the doctor told me all went well, that my prostate was on its way to the pathology folks; there didn't appear to be any further cancer activity beyond the prostate itself (The biopsy confirmed the doctor's original opinion.); and that I was on the road to recovery

Not so fast! Turns out I was too optimistic about the recovery part. One of the side effects I generally experience following surgery is scar tissue formation. I had this following my major shoulder repairs and knee replacement. Scar tissue for these orthopedic surgeries isn't so bad; exercising usually causes scar tissue to break up and dissolve.

With prostate surgery, however, it's a far different story. Scar tissue forms on the outside of the last gateway I mentioned previously. That is, the area between the end of the bladder and, uh, the connection to the outside world. When scar tissue forms over this area, what's in the bladder can't reach the outside world. I will spare you the intricate details, but on four occasions, I was rushed into the emergency operating room literally with minutes to spare before my bladder would burst.

Picture in your mind driving to the hospital after calling your doctor and telling him you can't deposit your bladder's holdings into the appropriate receptacle. This happened to me four times!! Each time after additional scar tissue was removed, I had to wear a catheter for ten days. So, that's a total of 40 days of additional catheterization. Needless to say, I wasn't a happy camper. Not by a long shot (pun intended).

I have to believe that what finally got me over these scar tissue episodes was the doctor's instructions that if it happened again, I would have to insert the catheter myself. Picture that one!! No way!!

For those of you who wonder how scar tissue is removed under these circumstances, well, I'll tell you. For those of you who are squeamish, skip this explanation. You see, you're stripped naked, placed on the operating table, legs apart, and then sedated. Before going under, you note this long, thin tube with what looks like Roto-Rooter blades on the end that, when inserted, is used to cut out the scar tissue—and that is the end of my explanation. You can easily figure out what happens between sedation and waking up. However, for those of you who are morbidly curious, it's not unlike having a colonoscopy—YOU'RE GOING TO PUT THAT TUBE WHERE???!!!!!! Only this particular Roto-Rooter tube doesn't go where the colonoscopy tube goes. Oh, you're already figured that out. Good; then I don't have to explain any further.

There is one other matter that must be considered when undergoing radical prostate surgery. Until the muscles heal and the one gateway between bladder and the outside world is properly functioning, any form of straining—coughing, laughing, etc.—will cause, uh, some leakage. So, for awhile, one must protect against such possible embarrassment. When a friend or colleague who had been through this would ask how I was doing, I'd respond by saying: "It Depends." This is an inside joke (literally) but having a sense of humor is vital as recovery continues. Because of the side effects from the surgery, I had to, uh, be careful of the potential for leakage for about three months. Fortunately, today this entire episode is relegated to the past. I'd say it's all behind me now, but that's my response to having had a colonoscopy.

Since I've mentioned the subject of colonoscopies, let me digress a bit here because I just had my five-year reunion with my gastroenterologist. For those of you who've had a colonoscopy, you can skip this and the next three paragraphs; you're already most familiar with this important diagnostic procedure in the fight against colon/rectal cancer. For those of you who haven't yet experienced this, allow me to explain what is done. If you're over 50, doctors recommend that this be done every 10 years (it used to be five for everyone, and still is—but only if a person has a family history of colorectal cancer. My father died from this, and my mother had non-cancerous polyps removed, so I remain in the five-year cycle.) Here's the chronology for me. As I get close to a five-year age from 50 (55, 60, 65, 70 etc.), I get a call from my doctor's office. I will be given a date for the procedure and a prescription for a bowel preparation (what a great phrase) that I must take the day before my scheduled appointment, along with instructions not to eat anything of a solid nature; I must restrict my intake to liquids only, and only certain kinds of liquids—nothing red or purple. The prescription consists of two six-ounce bottles of liquid and a 16 oz. cup. The instructions say to take one bottle of liquid at 8 a.m., pour it into the cup and add water to the 16 oz. line. This mixture must be swallowed as fast as humanly possible because the taste can only be described as absolutely horrible; like mixing dishwater with cod liver oil, mineral oil and bitter lemon. This must be followed by two 16 oz. glasses of water within one hour after the mixture is swallowed.

I felt a bit bloated after drinking 48 oz. of fluids in such a short period of time. Who wouldn't? But that's nothing compared to how I felt after that. The last time I had a colonoscopy, the doctor recommended a preparation product that was called Golightly, I believe. If that was the proper name, it was one of the most misleading names I've ever seen on a medical product. There was nothing about going "lightly" that I experienced, so I hoped this newer product would be less difficult to deal with.

I was wrong. About an hour after consuming the medication and water, I began to feel what folks in San Francisco or along the Pacific Rim must feel at the onset of an earthquake. What happened can best be described by the Drano commercial. You know that one where the Drano is poured down the drain and you see the sludge forcibly jettisoned from the clogged drain. Well, this is precisely what happened, and not from my sink drain. I spent the morning hours recalling that Drano commercial several times. And 12 hours later at 8 p.m., I had to repeat the process. All in all, I didn't have a great day-before my, uh, procedure.

That bowel preparation prescription should be named the Big Bang Theory in liquid form. If the energy of these two six-oz. bottles could be harnessed, we could easily replace the atom bomb with a much more deadly device. The black holes in the universe could be blown open by harnessing the full potential of this two seemingly innocent bottles of ultimate power. The colonoscopy itself is nothing compared to the preparation for it.

On the day of my five-year reunion, I was led into the holding area; given a gown that, judging from where the holes were, was manufactured by alien beings with many arms; told to remove all clothing and put them in a bag and lie down, then fitted with an IV and told to wait. I was wheeled into the colonoscopy room where I was told to roll over on my left side, bring my knees to my chest and lean forward so that my backside was close to the snakelike tube that was hanging from a pole. I was told I would be sedated and . . . . the next thing I recall is my doctor telling me all went well and that he would see me in five years. While I try to find as much humor as possible in having this done, it doesn't detract one bit from the seriousness of the reason for going through this. I know some who didn't, and are no longer here. I also know some who didn't and are now dependant on a colostomy bag. For me, it's worth the inconvenience of the preparation for the peace of mind that follows. Even if the news is not good, the earlier the problem is caught, the greater the chance for survival. Like prostate cancer, colon or rectal cancer is treatable and curable if found through early diagnosis. Ten years ago, my doctor found two pre-cancerous polyps and promptly removed them. Enough said. Please, have this examination done as prescribed by your physician. This can very well be a lifesaver.

I think physicians who perform colonoscopies have to have a great sense of humor. That has to be the reason the "instrument" used for this purpose is called an endoscope. Hmmmm. I know my gastroenterologist has a sense of humor; he enjoys hearing the story of how vague and indirect he is with instructions, since he's always using innuendoes. Bada Boom! Or that he should move his practice to New York because that's in the Upper U.S. (Think Italian accent.) Or asking him how are things? "Looking up." Hmmmm again.

All this is medical background leading up to the "surgery from hell" that I had after retiring, and which ultimately led me to conclude that I would probably not be able to work again, at least for quite a while.

During the last three months leading up to my retirement, I noticed that my arthritic flare ups—neck and back pain, hand and shoulder stiffness and discomfort—were becoming more frequent and lasting longer with higher pain levels. The anti-inflammatory and pain medication I had been taking for over 25 years was providing less and less relief. Exercising was leaving me with more and more soreness and pain. I also saw a pain management specialist for anti-inflammatory and pain medication, and for periodic injections. But the steroid injections that used to provide relief were becoming ineffective. Although the arthritic pain was getting worse, I was nevertheless able to continue working right up to my retirement. I'm certainly grateful for that.

Over the years, I've had X-rays, MRI and CAT Scans of my neck and back. I saw the big words like spondylosis, spondylitis and stenosis on my diagnostic reports, and looked them up, but didn't pay too much attention to them. I figured these just meant aches and pains. As I left my employment, however, the aches and pains were getting worse. Sleep became more and more difficult; walking became problematic. I was having migraine-type pain over my left ear, and had developed shooting pains in my neck and upper back. Even though I had an L4-L5 (that's lumbar) fusion a few years earlier that I really don't consider major surgery, the pain and stiffness in my lower back and thighs were becoming constant.

I thought that retirement would mean less stress and therefore less pain, but the pain level continued to intensify even as my life was becoming less and less complicated. I finally visited a local orthopedic surgeon who specializes on the spine and was told I needed a new and complete set of diagnostic tests on my upper (cervical) and lower (lumbar) spine, since I had not had either in a few years.

After I had these tests run, I returned to my physician who took a look at the results and, with eyes as wide as saucers, told me what I needed to have done surgically he couldn't do in Tallahassee because he didn't have the staff or the facilities. He asked me whether I wanted to have pain or mobility in my neck; I couldn't have both. That was a shock. He said he would refer me to the University of Miami orthopedic department. I was given the UM physician's name and, upon looking him up on Google, found that he was the chief of the spinal deformity section for the hospital. Spinal deformity!! Oh, my!! I went back and looked at my diagnostic reports—I noted with great interest the words "degenerative spine disease." Reality check; my spine was deteriorating. Picture a tree with wax dripping from the several branches. This is what my upper spine looked like—with the dripping wax being calcified bone spurs. In short, my spine was a mess.

When I arrived for my appointment at the UM, the orthopedic surgeon told me he does about two a year of the kind of major spine surgery I needed. Considering his 25 years as a surgeon, he had only done about 50 of this particular kind of extensive surgery. He reviewed my file and my test results, asked me to describe my pain, and told me that a cause of my migraine-type pain was degeneration at C1-C2-dangerously close to my brain. Before he would do surgery at that level, I would need a steroid injection to see whether surgery that high up in my neck would even temporarily alleviate my pain, but he warned me that this had to be done by a physician who had done this relatively infrequent type of injection before and it had to be done in a hospital setting. When I asked why, the doctor said that if the exact location were missed, the needle would go into my brain—and I'd either be paralyzed or more probably never know it. How wonderful!! I returned home, made an appointment with my pain manager who told me he had done this type of injection many times but usually where an auto accident was the cause. I had the injection and felt a temporary subsiding of the pain—a good sign that the surgery might work. I scheduled the surgery for April 2011. Harriet and I went to Miami two days before the scheduled surgery. We were told to expect to remain in Miami for about two weeks. We rented a room two blocks from the hospital at a facility that catered to families and patients who had to remain for an extended stay.

We met with the surgeon the day before the surgery and, after describing what he was going to do, told us he was obligated to lay out the risks. He said "You could die; you could become a quadriplegic or a paraplegic; you could have a stroke; there are risks." He did point out that he had never experienced any of these with his patients, but he had the duty to inform me of what I could be facing. I told him that none of these would make me very happy, and then I asked him what the bad news was. Might as well try to keep a sense of humor about this.

The night before my surgery, I told my wife that the girls get my rings, except my good friend gets my Masonic ring. Yeah, I was nervous, very nervous. I really didn't sleep well that night.

Next morning, however, as I checked into the hospital, I felt a strange calmness. I just didn't want to hurt anymore. Then the parade of nurses and staff began. IVs. Antacid pill. Sedation pill. Waiting. Waiting. Finally, the staff came for me and took me to the OR. (That's operating room for those who've been lucky enough to avoid one.) The last thing I remember at this point was how bright and cold the OR was.

I didn't know how much time had passed when I began to regain my faculties. I recall the incredible pain in my neck and back, and that I felt as if I were lying on a slab of ice. I recall asking for a nerve block to eliminate the pain (a nerve block does just that; it blocks the nerve from receiving pain signals), but was told by the nurse that a nerve block can't be given for above-the-waist surgery. I remember saying "Now you tell me!" I asked why I was lying on a bed of ice. The nurse answered "Because you had extensive surgery." As if I couldn't figure that one out. I did learn the truth, however: I wasn't imagining lying on a bed of ice.

As my faculties returned to some degree of normality, I felt a neck brace wrapped tightly—very tightly—around my neck. I also noticed a #$%&#% catheter attached to me again. Then the nurse held up a mirror and I saw a brace that had to come right out of a Star Wars movie wrapped around my neck with a front extension to my sternum. I was told I would have to wear this day and night (even when showering, which I could do only with assistance) for about four months. Oh, joy!

I was given two braces, so that the one I had to wear was always dry. During showering, the pads that were attached by Velcro to the plastic brace would become saturated with water and soap. After showering, the pads took a half a day to dry.

Because I had trouble sleeping with the uncomfortable and cumbersome brace, the doctor said I could shift to a soft collar, but only at night. Even with that, I couldn't sleep in my bed for four months. I had to sleep in my recliner, and sleep was difficult even then. I had to jam pillows all around me so that I wouldn't pitch forward while sleeping. During this four-month period, sleep was limited to a couple of hours at a time. When I say this was the surgery from hell, I'm not being overdramatic. This was by far the roughest physical experience I've ever had to endure.

Immediately after the surgery, I was placed on a morphine pump for the first three days, so much of what I remember is necessarily in a time warp. On the third day following the surgery, I recall my surgeon telling me what transpired in the operating room, including my, ah, complication. First, he told me that I had nine vertebrae fused—my entire cervical spine (C1-C7 in medical terms) and the first two vertebrae in my thoracic (mid-back) section (T1-T2). This, he said, will affect my mobility. (He was absolutely right, as I am unable to turn my head more than 10 degrees left and right, and I can't lower my head at all. I tell my friends that I would make an excellent Frankenstein monster for Halloween or a costume party, although my preference is the Tin Man from The Wizard of Oz.) He also told me my recovery time would be from 12 to 18 months. Just what a benevolent Type A impatient person wants to hear. Then he told me of my "complication."

I was told I spent more than 13 hours on the operating table under general anesthesia. Now, I understand this is a long time for any person to be anesthetized, let alone a patient who is 67. It's not that the operation itself took that long; it was what happened to me on the operating table that impacted my time out. As it was explained to me, I was placed on a table that rotates, so that while I was originally placed lying on my back, I was actually anchored onto the table and rotated so that I was flipped over. With my back fully open for surgery, my head suddenly and accidentally slipped out of its anchor. I can just picture this: my back is splayed and my head is hanging down. My wife told me the doctor said he had two assistants working feverishly to get my head back into place while he stabilized my back to prevent further splaying. I'm glad I slept through this complication. Fortunately, it was a no-harm, no-foul situation, as the (here it is again) complication didn't affect the outcome and my vital signs remained strong and steady throughout the 13-hour procedure/ordeal.

Well, you ask, what did exactly the doctor do to my neck and back? Ok, I'll tell you. Spinal fusion is just that; I now have rods, bolts and screws in my neck and upper back holding my upper spine in place. On the X-rays, my neck and back show up looking like the Eiffel Tower. I have more metal in my neck than I am worth-literally. The titanium has a market value greater than the chemical composition of my body. If I throw in the titanium in my right knee, the metal in my body is worth that much more than I am. This doesn't exactly fill me with confidence and joy. What I really need is a spine transplant, but medical science isn't there yet. I suppose my spine could be removed, but then I'd look like Jabba the Hutt (Star Wars fans know who this is.). I'll now tell you why quality health insurance is absolutely vital. When my medical providers' statements arrived, I added up the total cost for this surgery—hospital stay, surgeon fee, anesthesiology fee, etc., etc. etc. My only payment was $250 to the hospital. The total cost covered by my insurance carrier: over $200,000! In my next life, I want to be an orthopedic surgeon. Unfortunately, in this life, I get light-headed when I see the sight of blood, especially my own.

Another condition I've been diagnosed with since retirement is permanent hearing loss. Two forces were at play to bring this about. First, a report issued by a medical journal a few years ago found that those who took non-steroidal anti-inflammatory drugs over many years suffered varying degrees of hearing loss. That's me to a T, as I've been taking NSAIDs to help with arthritic pain and inflammation for over 30 years. Second, I developed muffled hearing in my right ear after flying home from Michigan in September of 2010. I've seen two ear, nose and throat specialists who told me there was no pathology, and even inquired of my orthopedic surgeon who fused my neck to see if he was aware of any pathology that explains my sudden muffled hearing condition. He said he wasn't aware of any, and the X-rays and MRI scans revealed no pathology. I went to an audiologist who, echoing the ENT specialists, assured me that this condition would have occurred anyway, as I had significant hearing loss in both ears before this flight. So, as a result, I now wear a hearing aid in my right ear. I have one for the left, but vanity prevents me from wearing it. Besides, I can hear well enough and sound is balanced enough using just one. What did you say? Just kidding.

On the subject of vanity, I find it strange that people will think nothing of someone who wears glasses (I don't, except for reading fine print), but with a hearing aid, sometimes, when someone knows I'm wearing one, I can just feel the "oh, poor guy" pitying directed my way. I guess this stems from the time that deaf people used large horns or hearing aids the size of a cereal box, or use of a hearing aid was equated with being "deaf and dumb." Today, hearing aids are so technologically advanced, that unless you actually know a person is wearing one, or you're actually staring at a wearer's ears long enough to notice, you really can't tell someone is wearing one. I have the behind-the-ear type that has a thin, almost invisible plastic wire the tip of which is inserted in my ear canal. There's a computer chip in the aid itself that is programmed specifically to my hearing loss. I have three settings that I adjust by pressing a tiny button on the aid; one for small group meetings, a second for larger groups in auditorium or luncheon settings, and a third for watching television or movies.

I've had to point out mine to most of my friends before they realized I was wearing one. I'll admit it's tough to overcome the perception of a stereotype, even after I've been told repeatedly that I'm putting entirely too much emphasis on a hearing aid use stereotype that no longer exists. Perhaps they're right; even with such a stereotype, I'd certainly rather hear what someone is saying than pretend and miss conversations. I got tired of saying What?" too many times. What made matters worse is that, because Harriet spent 37 years in the classroom, she knew she could never outshout the kids, so she learned to speak low, forcing the kids to be silent so they could hear her. Well, whenever I'd say "What," she would repeat what she said at the same volume level as before, which only made repeat myself. Although I told her many times that she would have to repeat what she said louder or I'd miss it, old habits die hard. Hence, the greater my need was for a hearing aid.

Once you get over the perception-driven vanity and convince yourself that there is no shame in wearing a hearing aid, it's amazing how much better you feel. Besides, with all the noise pollution from boom boxes, etc., a whole generation will be facing the very real prospect of hearing loss down the road. The more people who wear hearing aids, the less vanity will play any role. Still, I don't wear that second hearing aid very often. I figure maybe people are just trying to be nice, and wearing both just doubles the potential for stereotyping. To try to maintain a sense of humor about this, I tell my friends that one advantage I have is that because I have the latest state-of-the-art computer-driven device, if I turn a certain way at precisely 10:15 p.m. in my backyard, I can pick up sounds emanating from distant planets. I've actually had a few folks believe I was serious about this. Still, at times, I feel as if this thin wire leading from the aid to my ear is a big as an underground utility pipe, but that's just part of the vanity issue I can't seem to fully disregard.

There is one aspect of my hearing loss that adds some humor on almost a daily basis. Harriet has no real sense of smell. Her olfactory lobes simply don't function well. However, she has the hearing of a cat. While my hearing is deficient, I have the sniffer of a bloodhound. On more occasions than I can count, she'll say "Did you hear that?" "Hear what" is my usual answer. I'll say "Do you smell that?" She'll say "Smell what?" My reply: "What did you say?" Oh yeah, you have to have a sense of humor. We've installed sensors that pick up smoke just in case I'm not at home. The alarm is set so that it can be heard in neighboring counties, so I'll hear it. This is how you make accommodations for hearing and olfactory deficiencies—and get a chuckle out of it.

My purpose in setting out in rather precise detail my medical history is not to engage in a pity party or curry any sympathy. All in all, I'm very lucky to have made it this far on my own two feet. (Ok, so I have one artificial knee.) I only want to show that even with these physical difficulties, it is entirely possible to enjoy myself in retirement after completing a rewarding professional career. Even before my orthopedic problems kicked in big-time, I already decided I didn't want to keep working until I literally dropped. I know lawyers who were found in their offices with their heads on the desk, victims of heart attacks in their 50s. I very much wanted to leave work while I still could enjoy my life, and that's precisely how it's worked out for me. And Harriet, too.

Another reason for this detailed description is that I can truly say (and my friends have said this, too) that I am a bionic man. While I have a fixed chronological age, my right knee is only a few years old. I absolutely will not die from prostate cancer. My shoulders are in their 20s now. The six trigger-fingers I had repaired are less than 10 years old. My thumb joints are less than five years old. My neck and upper back are babies by comparison. So, you see, when I'm asked how old I am, I answer "which part of me are you referring to?" I believe it was the late, great actress Bette Davis who said growing old isn't for sissies. Damn right on that one!

My more than 25 surgeries remind me of the song "That's Life" (how appropriate) by Frank Sinatra. Perhaps you know the words to that part of the song that goes "I've been a puppet, a pauper, a pirate, a poet, a pawn and a king . . . ." Well, with all my operations, I've been prodded, poked at, stuck with, cut open, stitched up and rehabbed. I've got huge scars on my right knee, abdomen, neck and upper back, both shoulders, etc. My attitude was—and is—that so long as the doctors can patch me up and send me on my way with some measure of a normal life, then I'm all for this cutting and pasting. You might think that undergoing all of these procedures (that the word nurses usually use; it's so, well, antiseptic. Why can't they simply say "operation, where the doctor is going to cut you from there to here, and you'll have tubes running out the wazoo, including a catheter; and there will be a bedpan at your side. You DO know how to use a bedpan, don't you?") would demonstrate courage. Nope. I just don't like pain, and if surgery is the only way to potentially reduce or eliminate pain, I'll take that chance every time.

I do think, however, that a little more "truth in surgery" would go a long way toward . . . . wait a second, maybe it's best not to know everything.

This might scare people out of having an operation they need. Patients are told to ask questions; my admonition is be careful what you ask for.

All of these medical issues taught me something about myself. Arthritis and pain go hand in hand. If you spend any time watching TV, you will undoubtedly see ads for many pain medications that supposedly rid you of stiff, painful joints; chronic low back pain; neck pain, etc; And if that doesn't work, there are always prescription pain killers. Notice that all ads include the words "temporary relief." That's because there's no such thing as permanent relief.

Let me level with you on the matter of pain medications. Over-the-counter pain medications don't work with my severe spinal arthritis condition, and NSAIDs and opiates no longer work for me, and have serious side effects that can easily turn a patient into an addict. While there are other methods of reducing pain—physical therapy, injections and surgery—the unfortunate fact is that with a severe orthopedic condition, there will always be some level of pain. I've taken medications, done physical therapy, had steroid injections and major surgery, and I still hurt. It's the classic "some days are better than others" situation.

The key in dealing with chronic pain is pain management; and that's where I am now. The most important lesson I've learned through all of this is that pain is also affected by what you do and your attitude. In short, the mind plays a vital role in pain levels. If I am by myself at home, I will focus on my pain more than when I'm out and about with others. Whenever I attend a meeting, go to a movie, or even become engrossed in a book or TV show, I'm too busy to think about my pain level, and I actually feel better. When I'm with my children and grandchildren, the pain level drops precipitously. Gee, I wonder why? No, I know why: I'm laughing and enjoying myself. My attitude is that if I let pain get to me, it surely will. So, if I keep busy and focus on doing the things I can do, and use physical therapy, injections and OTC medication as an aid rather than a cure-all, I will be able to control my pain, at least to extent where I can tolerate it. I can't say for how long, but it beats giving in to it.

My advice, therefore, to all pain sufferers is to do everything you can on your own without medical prescriptions to lessen pain's affect on your lifestyle. Even if you're hurting, go to a movie, take a walk in a mall, visit family and friends. In short, do what you enjoy doing, and I believe you will find that you will actually feel better. I know this works for me—at least, right now. There are times I just don't want to get out of bed or leave my recliner; that's precisely the time to get up and do something. I'll take a walk, even if it's just to stretch my legs. Lying down or sitting for a prolonged length of time is the worst thing anyone who suffers chronic to severe pain can do. The key is movement!!

Now comes my disclaimer: to avoid any untoward consequences for dispensing medical advice, what I've said on pain management is not, I repeat NOT, medical advice. This is just a common-sense realization resulting from personal experience. Therefore, there is no liability on my part for imparting this information. Just trying to protect myself here. Lawyers will do that, you know.

If there is a silver lining to all of my medical issues, it's that the more serious conditions that hit me after I retired could have happened five, 10 or even more years ago when work was vital to me. Back then, I had my daughters' education and weddings to pay for, dance and acting lessons, a mortgage, car payments—the usual bills that just about any family of four will have. If I had to take disability retirement, my ability to provide for my kids would have been severely impacted. We had Harriet's income as a teacher, but you know how underpaid teachers are. So, I am thankful that I was able to complete my career and earn enough to provide for my family.

I mentioned previously that I joined a health club to avoid obesity and the inactivity of a desk job, and began an exercise regimen that was fairly regular and consistent for 40 years. My doctors tell me that having this steady exercise program most likely helped me forestall the onset of severe arthritis. I had hoped that exercise would have prevented this condition completely, but genetics played a heavier role. Still, if it had to be, it's better to have to deal with this condition now than back then.

Again, my purpose is dwelling on my medical history is not to show bravery or engage in the melodramatic. In fact, I'm a real sissy when it comes to pain. If I could tolerate pain better, I might not have opted for so many "procedures," but I'm pretty much like most people when it comes to pain. After all these operations, however, I sometimes feel like Adlai Stevenson did after losing the presidential election to Dwight Eisenhower when he said: "I'm too old to cry, and it hurts too much to laugh." Laughter is its own valuable medicine, however, so I'll do everything I can to laugh at what life has in store for me, trying to make lemonade out of lemons, and if making others laugh makes me laugh, well, so much the better.

A few years ago, my struggle with arthritis combined with the need to keep a positive attitude through humor, led me to take the lyrics of a popular song of the 1960s and create my own set of lyrics. The song is Neil Sedaka's "Breaking up is Hard to Do" that I renamed "Getting Old is Hard to Do" which I actually had copyrighted. I sent my lyrics to his agent, and received an email letting me know that Mr. Sedaka actually liked my version. Imagine that!

For you who are musically inclined (and those who aren't), here it is:
(Chorus: Down doo-be-doo fall down, a downa downa down doo-be-doo fall down, a downa downa down doo-be-doo fall down, getting old is hard to do)

Please take these pains away from me
Arthritis leaves me in misery
All these aches just make me blue
Oh, getting old is hard to do.

Years ago, I had no pain
Now I think it's just so insane
After all that I go through
Yes, getting old is hard to do.

I said that getting old is hard to do
Hard to hear, and hard to chew
Don't say that this is my fate
Don't tell me getting old is all that great.

I won't give in, I'm a stubborn guy
No need to give a reason why
Joint replacements and orthopedic shoes
Yes, getting old is hard to do.
(Repeat chorus)

Ok, so it's not exactly Johnny Mercer, Neil Sedaka, Paul McCartney, Carole King—or even Moe, Larry and Curly. (Actually, considering what passes for lyrics these days, perhaps my effort isn't all that bad.) I find taking popular songs and writing new lyrics rather enjoyable. I've done this for a few for friends, and they appreciate it, or at least they tell me they do.

I call this next brief narrative a few of my pet peeves that relate to health issues. The first is born of the fact that as one gets older, the need for medications increases. Several years ago, there was a great and scary crisis in the pharmaceutical industry over instances of tampering with over-the-counter Tylenol, which led to several deaths and illnesses. To prevent tampering, the manufacturers placed tighter controls over the dispensing of medications. And tighter lids. Much tighter lids. Now, you'll usually find a cellophane wrapper around the top that is literally bonded to the bottle, and once you work your way through that level of protection, there is usually a cover that is glued to the top with tiny tabs on the side that are supposed to allow for easy grasping and quick removal of this cover, or a cover with one side raised so that the plastic can be pulled to remove the cover. On the latter type, this is at least the theory. In fact, when that tab is pulled, the tab comes off, often leaving the cover in place. That's when I reach for the pair of scissors or nail file to puncture the top and use the hole I created for removal. For those in their 20s, 30s, 40s and even 50s who have some weightlifting training, removing the cellophane might not be a difficult chore, and if you have fingernails an inch long, getting the cover off the top might not be so hard. But remember, those who have most need for these over-the-counter medications (or vitamins or supplements) are in their 60s and beyond. Some may not be former weightlifters or have long fingernails.

I believe that before any package of this type is made available to consumers, every CEO and other corporate executives of these companies must first pass a test of opening their own products without the assistance of a pair of scissors, nail file or knife. If they can't do this within, say, 30 seconds, this so-called protection for the consumer should scrapped in favor of a more consumer-friendly method. And while they're at it, these big shots who are 60 and over should also be required to read the instructions printed on the bottle in two-point type. This should be required without the use of a magnifying glass. The eyesight of those who are the biggest users of over-the-counter medications are not 20-40-somethings with the eyesight of an eagle; for the most part, they're AARP eligibles or senior citizens with diminishing eyesight. Those responsible for the manufacturing of these products certainly don't have the ultimate consumer in mind; it's time they do.

My second peeve stems from an overzealous reaction to Florida's legitimate problem with some doctors who overprescribe pain medications. In a classic case of lumping good physicians with bad ones, the regulations on those doctors who overprescribe for pain—so-called pill mills—have lumped legitimate pain specialists in with these pill mill operators. Because of my arthritic history, I occasionally need pain medication, especially during flare ups. But the paperwork imposed on the legitimate is hurting their ability to practice medicine. With increasing frequency and regularity, government, as well as insurance and pharmaceutical companies, are seeking to effectively take away or usurp the practice of medicine from the doctors. I have many friends in the medical community and, without exception, they tell me horror stories of insurance companies that refuse to pay for what the doctor believes is a medically necessary procedure because the companies don't believe the doctor; and pharmacies that refuse to fill doctor-ordered prescriptions because the pharmacist believes that the prescription isn't necessary or proper or constitutes an over-prescription of pain medication.

If the practice of medicine is turned over to the government or the suits who sit in an office far removed from the doctor and have never seen or examined the patient; and if the pharmacists who've not examined the patient can second-guess the physician's treatment protocol, then the patients are at increased risk for serious medical problems with accountability diffused among the suits and pharmacies. From my conversations with others throughout the state, what I hear from my doctors is not isolated; rather, it's an increasing pattern. One of my doctors tells me that he asks for names when he's told that he can't treat or prescribe; this way, he can tell his patients specifically who objected to the doctor's choice of treatment and medication. This usually leads to a change of heart in deference to the treating physician; the point here, however, is that doctors must be allowed to be doctors, and the suits and pharmacists mustn't be allowed to practice medicine.

My final peeve might well be ascribed to my hearing loss if it weren't for an article I read recently that addressed a bill authored by a member of Congress prohibiting television stations from increasing the decibel level for commercials. This tells me it's not my hearing at all that's the problem; it's the gurus who run the television stations allowing advertisers to increase the volume on their commercials the purpose of which is to get the viewers' attention. How many times have you had to adjust the volume on your remote when the program that you are watching comfortably suddenly shifts to a commercial that's now blaring at you? I find I must adjust the volume downward, only to have to increase it when the program returns. In addition, I've noticed that the many channels also have differing decibel levels, so if I'm flipping from one channel to another, I'm constantly adjusting the volume. I find this quite annoying. Do you have this same problem?

The legislation I'm referring to was designed to keep the decibel level constant for both programming and commercial. This makes good sense; unfortunately, this legislation went nowhere. Why? See my previous comments about businesses seeking any way possible of getting their messages to you; in this particular case, no matter how loud or obnoxious they are. It appears that loud, obnoxious commercials sell, otherwise, businesses would cease doing this.

My reason for this narrative is that experience is both a great teacher and molder of personality. We're all a product of our experiences, and these medical issues certainly affect who I am. This discussion also constantly reminds me of my biggest fear now: immobility. Every time I see those commercials advertising scooters or the "Help me. I've fallen and I can't get up" device, a wave of panic washes over me. I tell myself, however, that I will continue to do everything I can to avoid such a fate. While it's certainly true that Man proposes; God disposes, God is very busy, so if I can help Him by doing everything I can to control my activities and attitude, I will. My retirement plans are what they are and I will do everything I can to see that they come true.

There is one other medical-related observation that I believe needs to be made. Have you ever gone shopping at a mall and forgotten where you parked your car? Have you ever forgotten where you placed something, like your keys, glasses or umbrella? Come on, admit it. When this happens to a young person, no one seems to pay any attention; but when it happens to an older person, the reaction is quite different.

At the beginning of this book, I mentioned the different recollections Harriet and I have of our courtship. Some people might attribute this to a memory decline brought on by the aging process. After all, as I inch closer to 70, I suppose I'm easy pickings for those young whippersnappers who believe that senility awaits me—as well as all others who are beyond middle age. I have an entirely different take on memory lapses or loss, however. To describe my theory, I use the computer as an analogy. Picture a computer with lots of memory capability but little information inputted. When the computer is asked to recall information, it can readily produce it in a nanosecond. But as more information is inputted into the computer, it will take a nanosecond or two longer to retrieve a particular piece of information. The human mind works pretty much the same way; it stores experience and knowledge throughout one's life.

At age 20, there is not nearly as much information stored in the brain as, say, age 40 or 60 or 80. So, if at age 20, one is asked to recall an event, it's naturally easier to retrieve it from the memory bank. When a person is asked to retrieve an event at age 60 or 80, the brain has stored that much more experience and knowledge in the memory bank, thereby requiring additional time to retrieve it. See how easy it is to explain memory lapses? Every time I can't find my car, keys, cell phone, wallet, glasses, etc., I know precisely the reason why. It's certainly not, uh, uh, you know.

To test my own memory, for reasons that escape me, I remember the exact day I had my tonsils removed—March 5, 1956. When my daughters were little and lived at home, I would remind them of my "anniversary," after which they would roll their eyes. Now, I do this with Harriet, and she rolls her eyes. The reaction doesn't bother me; to me, it's proof I still have all my marbles—even if they're aging.

I suppose I should have warned you not to read this section on my medical trials and tribulations on an empty stomach. If you didn't and it, uh, upset you, I apologize, although a lot of good that does right now, eh?

This book is also about the joys of retirement, however. So now is the time, and I'll use the title below, to discuss

Retirement: Two Big Myths, A Few Facts, And My "Plan"

During my last few months in the workforce, the message I was given repeatedly by friends and colleagues was that I had to have a "plan" for retirement. I was told that the average lifespan for someone who retires without a plan is about 2.3 years. The reason for this, it was explained, is that the body will shut down if there is no purpose to life other than to sit in front of a TV, eat and sleep. Well, I don't know if this is true, but I'm now past that 2.3, and don't feel as if I'm bored out of my mind.

I did do one thing in anticipation of a more laid-back type of life: I created my Man Cave. We have two family rooms in my home; the second was an add-on about a year after we built our home in 1985. For almost 25 years, that second family room was hardly used. However, about five months before I retired, I decided I wanted to set up this room as my retreat. Harriet readily agreed; so we got rid of the furniture in our original family room; moved the furniture from the addition into the original family room; and bought a leather recliner, couch and two-seater, along with a large HDTV, computer, printer, computer table and chair for the add-on. The computer sits right next to my recliner. Two French doors separate the two rooms; when the doors are closed, my Man Cave is virtually soundproof. I sit in my recliner to watch TV or read, and work on my computer when I'm not watching TV. I don't want to leave the impression that I'm a couch potato; I don't spend a lot of hours in my Man Cave; but the time I do spend either watching TV or using my computer is very relaxing. And if I decide to go to my patio and lie in my hammock, I can do that as well. I leave the hard work to others now; I'm having a great time doing precisely what I want to do. And no, I don't have a refrigerator in my Man Cave, although I admit the thought has some appeal. I do have a bathroom with a shower, however. During my first four months of my rehab from my neck and back surgery, that shower proved to be a godsend because I couldn't lift my legs to get in the bathtub in our bedroom.

Frequently, when asked what my retirement plan was, I would also be asked what hobbies I had. I really have none, nor have I ever had any. Years ago, I bought one of those paint-by-the-number sets, thinking this would make a decent hobby. Well, I finished the painting in about an hour. Thus ended that "hobby." While I enjoy reading about famous people, and enjoy a good religious history-based murder mystery; I have no interest in collecting stamps or painting, or anything that for me is unproductive time. This type of activity just isn't my cup of tea. I am by nature an impatient person, and anything that requires patience is off the table. But for awhile, I did have a plan early on that I thought would be a very good hobby.

While growing up in New York, I attended a lot of hockey games at Madison Square Garden. My dad's hotel connections got us into many sports events. Baseball games at Yankee Stadium and the Polo Grounds. My favorite, however, were New York Rangers games. I just loved when the fights broke out. Flash forward to the mid-1990s in Tallahassee. I never would have expected Tallahassee to be a hockey town—until 1994 when a minor league team in the East Coast Hockey League relocated to Florida's capital city. Harriet and I immediately bought season tickets right over the penalty box for the visiting team. Needless to say, we heard a different game than most of the fans. If I dared repeat any of what we heard, this book would be censored; but we learned lots of interesting things about players' families and bodily functions. We began going out with the coaches and players after home games, and with friends Art and Ruth Smith traveled to hockey games as far west as Lafayette, Louisiana; as far north as Indianapolis; as far south as Ft. Myers and as far east as Jacksonville. Because of my zeal for the sport, I created a piece of jewelry that I called the Puck O' Luck—a pin shaped like a four-leaf clover with the leaves circular like hockey pucks, and a hockey stick for the stem. I had this item trademarked, and sold them in Tallahassee, Pensacola, and Jacksonville. I still have several of them.

Over the seven-year history of the Tallahassee Tiger Sharks (minor league teams tend to move around quite a bit), Harriet and I collected a lot of hockey memorabilia and decorated our original family room with pucks, signed hockey sticks, etc. We've kept our family room virtually untouched since the team left for other venues in 2001. Our sports memorabilia make for a great conversation piece, and an equally great decor. Even though the minor league team is long gone, we still occasionally travel to Pensacola and Columbus, Georgia, for a game. To this day, I prefer to watch a hockey game than any other sports event on TV or live. Thank goodness for the hockey network!! While I don't watch much TV, what I do watch are hockey games first, then other sports events. To this extent, TV is a form of hobby and hockey games are part of my retirement "plan," although not like it was when I had my very own hockey team to root for.

About this same time, I embarked on another sports activity that I thought would be a good hobby as well. I started playing slow-pitch softball for a team in a city league. I was in my early 50s and thought that the exercise would be good for me and, judging from the ages of some of the players, something I could do in my 60s and 70s. One of my teammates was Arden Siegendorf, a former state trial judge from Miami who moved to Tallahassee and went to work for the AG's office. We became friends and he filled me in on his softball exploits going back over 30 years. One day, we had lunch and I took a paper napkin and figured out that if he averaged so many games per year and had so many hits per game over more than 30 years, he would be close to 10,000 hits. I joked that this is more than Pete Rose or Ty Cobb had combined. We started an actual countdown to the night he "got" his 10,000th hit. Shortly thereafter, an article with a banner headline appeared in the Tallahassee Democrat legitimizing his 10,000th hit. This is a classic example of taking suppositions, forming a hypothesis and legitimizing the latter based on the former. Arden went on to play several more years and was inducted into the Softball Hall of Fame.

As for my softball career, well, because of my great fielding abilities, I was the catcher. That's the position that's usually filled by someone who has a lot of trouble getting the ball into the glove. That's a perfect description of me. I think this was a result of having men who were 6' 2" weighing over 240 pounds storming home plate to take out a 5' 9" 175-pound catcher. I guess there was an element of fear in being laid out at home plate. During one game, I turned to catch a foul ball and wound up having my first surgery for torn cartilage in my right knee. I euphemistically played softball for five years before realizing that it was much safer and smarter for me to leave the game to the more athletically inclined, and look for something more my style—like reading, traveling, exercising where I control the equipment, etc.

Ok, it's R time!! June 24, 2010, my last day in the office! The first thing I did after arriving home on my last work day was to reset my alarm clock from 6 a.m. to 9. There was no reason for this, as I certainly wasn't planning on getting up precisely at 9 a.m.; it was just something that served as a symbol—the first experience of my change-of-life.

The second thing I did was not go to bed at 10 a.m. For all my work years, I was an "early to bed, early to rise" person. My father instilled in me a belief that if I slept late, I might miss something; I didn't believe I would miss anything if I got a very early start each work day. Instead, that first night, I stayed up until after 1 a.m. watching a baseball game. So instead of the usual startled alarm-driven wake-up at 6, I slept comfortably and woke up on my own at 9:30. By the time I shaved, dressed, had breakfast and checked my computer for email and news, it was nearly lunchtime. Then, Harriet and I went grocery shopping and by the time we got home, got the groceries unpacked, and read the mail, it was nearing 4-almost the time I left for home when I worked. (I liked a 7:30-4:30 workday; this allowed me to get a lot of work done before the "crowd" arrived and avoid both morning and afternoon heavy rush hour traffic.)

I quickly learned a big myth about retirement. One of my main worries was how I would replace roughly 10 hours a day I spent in the workaday world. This 10-hour "replacement" issue is a myth. First, by going to bed later and getting up later, I'm cutting this time by three hours. Because I'm not rushed in shaving, dressing, eating breakfast, reading the newspaper, etc., I'm spending at least an extra hour doing these things. So, that's four hours so far. If I have lunch with friends, that's a two-hour session rather than the one-hour lunch period I had when working. That's five.

Plus, I really wasn't devoting 10 hours to actual work. Here is a not-so-dirty and not-so-little secret. Government lawyers have computers in their offices, and while they're supposed to use their computers solely for government work, the reality is that the Internet is easily accessible from these computers. Do you think that government lawyers never check the Internet for news, etc., etc., etc.? Do you believe that all government employees never use their computers to check personal items on the Internet?

I spend about one-to-two hours a day on my home computer. I will not admit that I spent that much time, or anything even approaching that time, on my office computer. Actually, I'm not admitting to using my office computer for anything other than government work. What I am saying is that .... well, I think you get a reasonably clear enough picture. The ultimate fact remains that the need to replace 10 hours each day is a Myth—with a capital M.

So, let's say, for argument's sake, that the number of replacement hours is really eight. I've already accounted for five and haven't really done anything worthwhile yet. Therefore, only three more hours to go. If I read a book, go to the gym, walk in the mall, etc., I've just burned two of those hours. If Harriet and I go to a movie, I've burned all three. Again now, I'm assuming eight hours. It might even be less, right? And I've not even addressed travel and organizational activities. More on those a bit later.

Another thing I realized along with this replacement of hours myth is how work actually controlled my life. For the 50 years or so that I worked and/or attended school, my schedule was always-ALWAYS-controlled by someone else. I had to get up each morning on schedule so I could be in class on time and make it to my next classes on time—time set by others. When I was a newspaper reporter, I had several deadlines to meet during each day—deadlines I had no control over; I either met them or would pay steep consequences. Fortunately, in my two years as a reporter, I never missed a deadline—and that's the absolute truth.

As a lawyer, there are deadlines in which to file papers (usually 10, 14, 20 or 30 days), hearings and meetings to attend, etc., all to accommodate someone else's schedule. The deadlines are set by rule of court, judges themselves, agency personnel, and on and on. Meeting with staff at 9; meeting with agency lawyers at 11; strategy session at 1; hearing in court at 2; post-hearing session at 3-and on and on it went. You get the idea.

With retirement, however, schedule setting is entirely up to me. I choose the time I go to bed. I choose when to get up. I choose when to shave, dress, have breakfast, read the newspaper, use my computer, have lunch, watch TV, read, etc., etc., etc. Since I share my activities with my fellow retiree, Harriet, believe it or not, there is always something to do.

A few months after we retired, we planned on taking a Panama Canal cruise. Unfortunately, the dates we set for the cruise were interrupted by the need to have my neck and back surgery in Miami. Other "planned" vacations also had to take a back seat, as my recovery period precluded any vacation travel. We are now planning cruises and vacations for 2013 and beyond.

Although I had gone on cruises to Mexico and Alaska, my love for cruises really began in earnest when Harriet and I went on our first family cruise in the Caribbean. And by family, I don't mean Harriet, my daughters and me. As many as 17 went on one or more of them. My brother-in-law Jim, his wife Lori, their sons (my nephews) Marc and Jeff; Marc's wife Jackie; Lori's two sisters and brothers-in-law; their children; and Lori's parents. We agreed to go our separate ways during the day and get together at night for dinner. Although legally we're not all related to one another, we had a lot of fun with great people.

The second myth is the need for a retirement plan. While it's important to have things to do, a fixed day-by-day plan is unnecessary. In fact, the unpredictability of retirement is a positive thing. If every day is planned, it won't be too long before boredom sets in. There are days when I have nothing planned, only to get a call or email that triggers an activity. I've also found that staying home isn't a curse of retirement, so long as there is something to do beyond watching TV (unless it's hockey or a ballgame). I have yet to spend a weekday watching TV. First of all, daytime TV leaves much to be desired. Second, if I'm going to spend a day at home, there are books to read and things to do around the house. In short, there's always something to do even if I decide to stay home. If I go out, there's shopping, the malls, movies, etc. Then there's that "honey-do" list so many soon-to-be retirees talk about. Harriet and I have been on the go so much that we've yet to get to the "honey-do" list. We still want to paint our bedrooms, but haven't had the time.

In making travel plans, there are two types of travel I look forward to beyond vacation trips: visiting my kids and grandkids, and traveling with my Masonic friends and brothers, and my Masonic activities. Let me tell you about what it's like for me to be a Mason. I'll do it this way:

The Masons

In the next section of my book, I discuss positive thinking, values and leadership. The reason I included a section devoted to these is that they are embedded in the value system of Freemasonry, and Freemasonry is a vital part of my life and I wanted to share these important points with you.

Before discussing my involvement in the Masons, I believe a brief description of what the Masons are will be helpful. Those of you who are Masons, of course, know the answer. But for those who aren't, the Masons are a fraternity; one that espouses a system of morality that is explained allegorically and illustrated by symbols. A reason for this method of teaching is that people tend to remember better by associating a thought or idea with something else rather than by direct or rote instruction. To become a Mason, a man must profess a belief in a Supreme Being, however manifested. The Masonic fraternity is made up of Christians, Jews, Muslims—it doesn't matter what one's personal religious beliefs may be. The system of morality espoused by the Masons is as old as ordered civilization itself; but what makes the Masons so different is that the fraternity has been around in one form or another for hundreds of years; its rich history is that of famous men who contributed to the founding of our country. Indeed, our nation's bedrock governing principles are founded upon the principles, precepts and tenets of Freemasonry. To see firsthand the impact of Freemasonry on our society, go to any public library and ask to see publications on this subject, or go to any search engine and type in Masonry or any combination of words with Masons or Freemasons in it. You will find books lining many shelves, and over 700,000 online sites.

Masons take men of good character and make them better by instilling in them a system of values that has stood the test of time. In addition to possessing and preserving a fundamental belief in a higher being, Masons also instruct others to do what conscience dictates is good and right by others; to share in their respective gifts and blessings; to educate others about these time-tested values; and to make absolutely certain that each one does his part to assure the passing down from one generation to the next these values, and by doing so, preserving our way of life. Masons also share a common commitment that takes many forms—dependability, honesty, accountability, trustworthiness, and similar conduct, all directed to basic common sense human kindness. One noted writer on the subject of Masonry offered the following which defines a Mason most directly and eloquently: "A Mason is a man who does all the good he can, in as many ways as he can, in as many places as he can, to as many people as he can, for as long as he can."

Masons historically have been leaders whose moral compass is found in the words of the Declaration of Independence, the preamble to the Constitution of the United States, and other writings that are an integral part of our nation's history. History teaches that where oppressed people seek freedom, you will find the Masons. When there is a cry for justice, you will find the Masons. When liberty and democracy are imperiled, you will find the Masons. Throughout history, the Masons have fought against despots, dictators and demagogues. Over the years, my personal value system has become more and more refined as a result of what I've learned-and continue to learn—as a Mason. Being a Mason is not a part-time job; it is a lifetime commitment to learning, growing as a man and sharing; always remembering that a Mason is judged by the good deeds he performs for the benefit of others.

In 1981, while in private practice, I knew both of my partners were Masons, but I never said a word to them about this, and they never discussed this with me. One day, Paul Lambert told me he just attended a Masonic legislative breakfast at the Capitol. At that point, I asked "How do you become a Mason?" It was as if I had opened a flood gate. "You don't know how long I've been waiting for you to ask," he said. Shortly thereafter, I received phone calls, a petition to join a Masonic lodge, and instructions that I had to follow carefully and precisely. I found out later that to become a Mason, you had to initiate this; no Mason will ever extend an unsolicited invitation to join this fraternity.

As I mentioned when discussing my family history, my grandfather Leo was a jeweler. He worked out of his efficiency apartment and wore an apron that had a symbol printed on it that I found quite unusual. I was 15 when I asked my grandmother what that symbol was, and she said it had to do with his friends. My grandfather never mentioned this symbol to me. Turns out he was a Mason, and the symbol on his apron was the compasses and square that is the familiar symbol of the Masons. I simply didn't know my grandfather was a Mason during his lifetime. My father wasn't a Mason—probably because he never thought of asking his father what that symbol meant. I now know that at least two of my grandfather's brothers—my granduncles—were Masons. If only I knew then what I know now!!

Getting back to the beginning of my Masons story, my petition was accepted, went through the various ceremonies, and I became a Master Mason in October 1981. I quickly began participating in various Masonic functions, as well as working my way up the leadership ranks until, in 1991, I was elected as head of my lodge, with the title of Worshipful Master and the Masonic designation for life of "Worshipful." Two years later, I was elected secretary of my lodge, which is in reality the most intensive job in a lodge because of the litany of responsibilities for making and maintaining official lodge records, interfacing with the Grand Lodge of Florida, handling vouchers and receiving and recording payment of all bills, taking and keeping minutes, and generally doing what a secretary of any organization usually does.

I was appointed by several grand masters to serve on the Grand Lodge Panel of Attorneys, providing legal advice to Grand Lodge officers. I also joined a couple of what are called appendant and allied Masonic bodies—the Scottish Rite Masons (who are 32nd degree and 33rd degree Masons) and the Shrine (you have certainly heard of the Shriners).

By the end of 1999, however, I was becoming burned out from the intensity with which I was involved in fraternal activities. My workload was also picking up; my daughters had moved away and were involved in more and more activities which in turn involved more out-of-area travel for me; and I started to miss lodge meetings. Missing one meeting made it easier to miss a second, then a third and, before long, I had become inactive in all Masonic organizations.

By 2005, with retirement looming on the horizon, Harriet began to worry (she told me much later) that because I had no hobbies or other outside interests, I would become a couch potato retiree with barely little—if anything—worthwhile to occupy my time. Our girls had their own lives and we couldn't visit them every time the spirit moved; we would justifiably outlast our welcome in very little time.

One day in 2006, a Mason who also worked out at the same gym as I came over to me, introduced himself and asked whether the picture that hung on the wall in my lodge was me. My lodge hangs a photo of every Past Master (that's the designation of one who has served as Worshipful Master) on the wall in the lodge's social room. I said it was, and he proceeded to ask why I hadn't been in lodge for so long. I gave him every lame excuse I could—burned out, too busy, lodge meetings were boring, etc.,—and he backed off. Every time I would see him at the gym, however, he gently but persistently persuaded me that that I would enjoy the fellowship and that I should return. I thought about this, talked it over with Harriet, and finally agreed to return to my lodge. My intention was simply to enjoy the fellowship of my fraternal brothers, have dinner, stay for the business meeting, and return home. At the first meeting I had attended in five years, I was overwhelmed with emotion when I was greeted as a long lost relative. The genuine warmth of my fraternity brothers' welcome was very moving, and I will forever be grateful for their kindness.

Turns out, however, that my cajoler, Jim Olsen, had other plans for me. One of the highest offices a Mason can have is that of District Deputy Grand Master (DDGM). There are 34 Masonic districts that make up the Grand Lodge of Florida's geographical distribution (there are also 10 zones). Each DDGM is solely responsible to his appointing Grand

Master, and for all intents and purposes, is THE grand master of his district in the absence of the Grand Master himself. As such, the DDGM is the highest ranking Mason in his district during his year of service. Well, Jim just happened to be the incoming DDGM, and within one month of my return to my lodge, he asked me what district committee I wanted to chair. I literally picked one out of the air and thus I became a district committeeman.

Thanks to his efforts, and because of my previous work in Masonic education and having become proficient in the ritual work of the fraternity, I was named District Instructor in 2008 and 2009. He was also instrumental in my being appointed DDGM in 2010 with the lifetime Masonic title of Right Worshipful, which is the second highest title or designation that can be given to a Mason. Only the Grand Master himself is given the highest title "Most Worshipful" which he carries for life.

One of the primary duties of a DDGM is to make a formal visit to each lodge in his district twice during his term of office. There are 10 lodges in district number 7 which encompasses Tallahassee and extends from Havana in the north to Carrabelle in the south, and from Monticello in the east to Chattahoochee in the west, or a geographical area consisting of roughly 75 miles by 70 miles. He must complete a report on the functioning of each lodge, thereby making certain that the lodge is following all of the Grand Lodge requirements as set out in the digest of Masonic law. He must also appoint up to 12 district committeemen whose duty it is to assure that the Grand Lodge programs are properly functioning within the district. Yet another duty—and the most time-consuming—is to host and be responsible for a Grand Master's official visit to the district.

This involves making hotel arrangements for Grand Lodge dignitaries and providing in-room gifts for them as well as getting a block of rooms for others who will travel to Tallahassee for the event; inviting public officials; preparing and sending out invitations and monitoring RSVPs; selecting a location to hold the dinner and another for a formal lodge meeting; planning the layout of the tables according to Grand Lodge protocol; planning the menu; getting staff to help with the dining room setup; cooking and serving dinner; breaking down the dining room at the conclusion of the dinner; arranging for a program for the ladies; preparing a written program for the dinner itself; providing for microphone arrangements at the head table and off to the side for the Grand Master to receive fund-raising presentations and personal gifts; and seeing that the formal lodge meeting after the dinner is conducted properly and without any hitches.

The Grand Master looks to one man to assure a successful visit—his appointed DDGM. I've seen others who had unsuccessful visits try to blame their committees or others he depended on to pull this off, but a Grand Master will not accept this. I believe that the prevailing view is that if a man can pull off an official visit, he can do anything as a Masonic officer. I am thankful to so many who helped make my handling of this important dinner-meeting annual event a successful one, but particularly Charles Elul, who volunteered to handle the printing of invitations and RSVPs and dinner program, microphone set-ups, and dinner preparation for a few Past DDGMs and willingly did all of this for me. He also had water available in the lodge room for all of the guests.

I thoroughly enjoyed serving as DDGM. Being appointed to this position is one of the highest honors that can be given a Mason. While it takes a lot of work to do the job properly, the job, for me, was truly a labor of love.

I was named vice-chairman of the highly influential jurisprudence committee for 2011 (this committee is also made up of all living Past Grand Masters) and for 2012, was appointed to the Grand Lodge office of Grand Orator. There are six elected Grand Lodge officers and 13 appointed officers, so I am in rarified territory. With this latest appointment, I am a Grand Lodge officer of the Masons of the State of Florida for 2012-2013. Thus, in five years, I went from being inactive to appointment to one of the highest offices in the Florida Masons. The Grand Orator gives the Grand Oration at the annual Grand Lodge session usually held at the end of May. I will deliver the Grand Oration in May 2013.

Truthfully, I began working on my speech even before I knew of this appointment. I had given speeches on Americanism, patriotism, positive thinking, leadership, etc., to Masonic groups over the years. I was on the debate teams in high school and college. I had been a member and officer of a Toastmasters Club and had hosted a number of civic and social events. I was retired and looking for something to do one day, when it occurred to me that I could take my previous speeches, combine them, add new points, and wind up with a good grand oration. So, this is what I did. By the time I received my appointment letter from the incoming Grand Master in December, 2011 my grand oration was written and tweaked more times than I can recall. As a result, I don't have to worry about writing my grand oration; from installation in May 2012 to May 2013, I get to wear a beautiful jewel, collar and apron signifying my Grand Lodge office at Grand Master's official visits to the districts throughout the state, as well as other formal visits by the DDGM, and when attending any lodge on my own, including my home lodge. It's a wonderful feeling of pride and contentment to be so recognized by your fellow Masons. As grand orator, I follow some distinguished Florida public officials who served in this office, such as former governor and U.S. senator Spessard Holland, former congressmen Don Fuqua and Michael Bilirakis, former congressman and Florida treasurer and insurance commissioner Bill Gunter, former Florida secretary of state and U.S. senator Dick Stone, former attorney general and secretary of state Jim Smith, and federal district judge Bill Stafford. This certainly doesn't hurt the ego department, either. I believe a speech of this nature has to be more than a talk; it has to set a tone. It must inform, educate, challenge, inspire and motivate. Whether I achieve these goals or not will be judged by the audience; but I will certainly give it my very best effort.

Jim Olsen also re-involved me in the Scottish Rite and made sure I was involved in the newly formed Grotto. In 2012, I was head of the Scottish Rite consistory (denominated as the Master of Kadosh) and the Grotto (denominated the Monarch). These are called allied or appendant bodies because one must first be a Mason and member of the Grand Lodge and a particular Masonic lodge in order to be a member of one of these additional organizations. I also served as president of the Masters and Wardens Association in 2011, a group made up of Masons from all 10 lodges in my district.

A primary reason for my change in retirement travel is that, with the offices I had and have with the Masons, there is simply no time for Harriet and me to take an extended vacation. This, plus the arrival of Amy's son—my grandson—means postponing our vacation travel plans until 2013. Because of the reasons this time, however, we're perfectly content with this temporary hold on our vacation getaways.

My original plan in returning as an active Mason therefore didn't work out as intended, but I'm certainly not complaining. In 2006, I thought my Masonic career was essentially over, and I was ok with that. After all, I was Worshipful Master and secretary of my lodge, and served on the Grand Lodge panel of attorneys for several years. Turns out that the best was yet to come. I am deeply indebted to my cajoler, and all the brothers who eagerly welcomed me back and helped me along the way. This is what Masons mean when they talk about friendship, fellowship and brotherly love. I certainly had more than my share.

In 2007, I learned that several Masons in my lodge volunteered as part of their charitable efforts to work in a haunted house every October for about three weeks or so leading up to a Halloween night finale. My curiosity being piqued, I visited this haunted house to see what it was like. It's located on State Road 12 in Havana, Florida, just a few miles north of Tallahassee, and is called "Castle Dread. Terror on 12." It's on private property owned by Sammy and Debbie Tanner, who run the operation.

Each October, the outside area behind their residence is turned into a "graveyard" filled with Styrofoam head stones that have such sayings as "Jack and Jill went up the hill; Jack fell off the hill; Here lies Jack without Jill." The haunted house itself is located behind their residence and the graveyard, and has over 20 separate rooms with manikins and other pneumatic, animatronic, and robotic "things" you might find in a haunted house, and some you might not because they're too macabre. Add to this mix 20 or more live actors and, trust me on this, you have one very intense, scary haunted house.

The first three years of my participation, I ran the "Hellavator" that took visitors to, well, you can figure out where. I dressed in a tuxedo (purchased from Goodwill for $25), black shoes, top hat, white gloves, white makeup with black circles around my eyes, and took on a schizophrenic manic-depressive personality. I had a ball doing this, particularly dealing with people's reaction. The Hellavator never really went anywhere, except to rattle around and give the feeling of up-and-down movement caused by a pneumatic device. I had about 45 seconds to do a manic-depressive schizoid routine; I had a great time with this character. The ham in me just rolled out.

For my fourth year, I played the Dead Godfather, again in tux only this time with a white tie, black gloves, black fedora, pencil-thin moustache, ghostly white face and a makeup bullet hole in the middle of my forehead. I sat at a table with a strobe light that gave off a loud popping sound that I triggered at just the right moment, surrounded by mannequin skeletons, one playing a piano. I used such phrases as "Bada Bing Bada Bang. I'm gonna make you an offer you can't refuse." The hardest part was to keep myself from laughing at people's reaction.

My third role—the one I played in my fifth year and continue to play now—is that of the haunted house's proprietor, Tobias Dread. Tobias' story is that his wife was murdered and son kidnapped, which caused him to snap. He wears a satin robe, a top hat and carries a cane. He sits in the middle of his library and when visitors arrive, they're greeted by Tobias jumping up, pointing his cane and saying "Murderers!! Kidnappers!!! You killed my wife! You kidnapped my son! My friends in my castle will take care of you, you evil people!" I'll bang my cane on the walls, yelling "You evil people, you, you" and then I'll throw in "you lions and tigers and bears." Invariably, I'll get an "Oh, my" to which I'll follow with "I'll get you, my pretty, and your little dog Toto, too" as the visitors run into the next room, which is just as scary, perhaps even more so, than mine. I get a great laugh out of people's reaction, but I know that the visitors' laughter is a nervous one. It's possible the haunted house will change locations in the future; that won't matter. It's what's inside the house that makes for a most fascinating—and frightening—experience.

The "Hellavator" Operator

The "Dead" Godfather

Tobias Dread Master of Castle Dread

These roles actually allow me to have the unfettered freedom to create a character. Maybe I should have done more with this. I did do a couple of plays with my daughters when they were taking acting lessons, and I was an on-screen paid ($75) extra for an HBO movie about the 2000 presidential election, entitled "Recount," as well as having a speaking role in an FSU film production. Wait a second here; I was an actor! Being a lawyer trying to convince a judge or jury requires some acting skills. I suppose there is a blurred line between being a Jack Nicholson or a Clarence Darrow. And now with my permanently stiff neck, I'm also available to anyone needing a Frankenstein monster or a Tin Man. (On the latter, here's a true story. While in Orlando in 2012 for the annual session of the Grand Lodge of Florida Masons, I came across a vendor who is an artist and had made a Tin Man out of used cans. This piece of artwork has sardine cans for feet; a funnel for a hat with a tin heart clipped to the funnel; fruit cans for legs and arms; tomato cans for its body and head; pieces of tin for ears and nose; and eyes from a doll. This is a one-of-a-kind item that stands about 20 inches high. Sure I bought it; couldn't resist it .... and it now hangs from a wicker shelf in my Man Cave. If I can't find humor in an otherwise serious matter, then I'm in trouble.)

Harriet also plays roles in the haunted house; from a witch to a widowed old lady, with a voice that could shatter glass. We make quite a pair at the haunted house. Thank goodness we've never been stopped by law enforcement while driving the 12 miles from our home to Havana. We'd either provide a good laugh or wind up in jail, or in some institution. For the first time, the haunted house will be located in a Tallahassee mall named, well, the Tallahassee Mall. It will still be creepy and scary no matter where the house is located.

Harriet is thrilled with this Masonic turn of events. We travel extensively when the grand masters make their official visits to the several districts. It feels good to get dressed to the nines and visit with Masons and their wives from all over Florida. As a result of my return to my fraternity, Harriet and I have a new and expanding group of friends. The Masons network is large and I'm proud to be a part of it, and we're proud to get to know fellow Masons and their spouses. I can honestly say without any reservation that being a Mason has made me a better man and has fully enriched my life. If you ask any man who is a Mason how he views the fraternity, I have no doubt you'll receive a similar response. The fraternity's oft-repeated goal/slogan is to make good men better. I couldn't put it any better.

As I mentioned previously, although I really didn't have a retirement plan as such, except for visiting family and traveling on our own, the Masons actually have taken a lion's share of our time. This is a wonderful thing for Harriet and me. The Masons' ladies have their own activities and Harriet is very much involved in the volunteer work the ladies perform. We are, in that regard, a Masonic team, and we will both be involved in the Masons for as long as we can.

There is one more point that needs to be made regarding the Masons. There are those who purport to be experts knowledgeable about the fraternity who claim that the Masons are devil-worshippers and anti-Catholic. This is pure unadulterated nonsense. One of the appendant bodies is York Rite Masonry. Its focus is more on Catholicism than any of the other Masonic organizations, although one doesn't have to be Catholic to become a York Rite Mason. Those who stubbornly cling to such notions about the Masons only demonstrate their ignorance and refusal to be dissuaded by the facts. I won't dignify such drivel by any further commentary on this matter. Those who believe such BS don't deserve to have anyone pay attention to such absolute drivel.

Now, back to retirement. What I found so amazing about myself shortly after I retired is how I actually took to it. After more than 40 years in two high-powered, intensely combative and stress-filled professions, journalism and law, I had no problem quickly adjusting to a much slower pace of life. To be successful in these professions, I believe you have to have "fire in the belly." There has to be a part of you—a big part—that actually enjoys conflict, confrontation, very high highs and significantly low lows. And I thrived on all of this; I enjoyed the combative nature of these professions. I loved the challenge of breaking a news story and seeing my byline in newspapers; and winning cases, especially the high-profile ones.

Because I had family, friends and Masonic activities awaiting me, I believe it was that much easier to rapidly jettison a pace of life that was highly stressful, hectic, frenetic, helter-skelter, in favor of a pace that is calm, tranquil and orderly. The advantages of retirement revealed themselves rather quickly: no work stress, no conflict, no worries (financial or otherwise), no aggravation, no pre-trial or pre-hearing sweats, no stomach-churning, no deadlines, no writing notes to myself at 3 a.m., no late-night calls, no sleepless nights. You get the point.

Taking all these factors into account, it is no wonder how that burning desire to excel in my chosen profession—that "fire in the belly"—is now extinguished. I simply have no desire to practice law again. I know many lawyers who began practicing before I did, and who are still at it; and if they're happy, that's really all that matters. I've just found other ways to be happy. Will that fire ever return? I really don't know; but it would take the right opportunity at the right time for me to give up the wonderful freedom and independence I now enjoy. I don't have to pretend that the decisions and actions of a manager or supervisor represent intelligence and wisdom when, in fact, too many don't. I don't have to kowtow to anyone because my employment status might be affected. I'm free to say what I want and do what I want, answerable only to my family. To me, retirement is truly an absolutely liberating experience.

There is another aspect of retirement that is absolutely fascinating, but it requires being a grandparent. It's what I call the flashback syndrome. It really started for me when my daughters were pregnant. I would see them waddling around, having their centers of gravity altered on a day-by-day basis, and have flashbacks to the time Harriet was pregnant with our girls. Now, when I see my grandchildren play games or say something funny or poignant, or simply be the children they are, I'll see my daughters as little children once again. I recall the many moments I simply stared at Lani and Amy during their pregnancies and they would catch me staring. They would ask what I was staring at, and I'd answer "nothing," but I believe they knew. I was seeing them as little children once again, playing games with me or talking to me as only a three-four-or-five year-old or whatever age they were can.

A friend of mine told me that as you get older, all you have are the memories that grow and grow in number. That's certainly true; but I also have a closeness with my children and grandchildren that allows me to not only have both memories and flashbacks, but continue to make new memories and add to the flashback moments. There is a difference for me between the two. A memory can be recalled at any time; a flashback occurs when I'm with my family. If one of my grandchildren does something that my daughter did as a child, I'll have that particular flashback. Of course, that might lead to a more elaborate memory. Still, it's great to be able to recall events of the past that are similar to events today. This, however, requires a frame of reference—a foundation that can only exist if you're a grandparent. Hooray for grandparenthood!!!

Positive Thinking, Values And Leadership

My reasons for including a discussion on these three points were previously mentioned and will be more fully explained later in my book. For now, however, I want to share these points with you for whatever value you may choose to give them.

By far, the most important thing I've learned since retirement is that I'm in control of my destiny. Too often, we tend to focus on the negatives in our lives, rather than the blessings we have and for which we should give thanks. The purpose of this section is tore-emphasize the point that success in retirement depends heavily on one's attitude. Let me begin this section with an experiment. Visualize for a moment a 12 oz. glass. Now fill that glass with 6 ozs. of water. Do you see a glass half-full or half-empty? Your answer to this simple question says much about you, for it reveals whether you give in to human nature or try to rise above it.

Simply put, human nature dictates a tendency to take for granted the good things in our lives, focusing instead on the negatives that befall us just about every single day. How many times have you told yourself "I can't do this" or "If I try this, it will only lead to failure?" Each one of us faces stressful situations every day. At times, we feel consumed by them; but while we can't always control events in our lives, there is one thing we can definitely control, and that is our attitude toward dealing with them.

The first order of business is to eliminate negative thinking and focus on the positive. Negative thinking is a self-fulfilling prophesy. If a person believes something won't work, chances are he or she will be absolutely correct. If, however, a person believes that, through hard work, even the most difficult challenge can be overcome, then there is a good chance it will be. For me, I would rather try something and fail, than do nothing and guarantee failure. It's important to view each challenge as an opportunity.

Willie Nelson, the famous country singer and songwriter, said "Once you replace negative thoughts with positive ones, you start having positive results." Sir Winston Churchill was one of the great leaders of the 20th Century, twice prime minister of Great Britain who led his country to its "finest hour" in WWII. He said: "A pessimist sees the difficulty in every opportunity; an optimist sees the opportunity in every difficulty."

Do you focus on negative thoughts, or are you a positive thinker? Do you see difficulty in every opportunity, or do you see opportunity in every difficulty? Industrialist W. Clement Stone said "There is little difference in people, but that little difference makes a big difference. The little difference is attitude. The big difference is whether it is positive or negative." Motivational speaker and author Zig Ziglar said "Positive thinking will let you do everything better than negative thinking will." Henry Ford said "Whether you think you can, or that you can't, you are usually right." Each one of these five men was of entirely different backgrounds and in different professions and vocations; yet they had one thing in common: All were eminently successful in their respective endeavors. You don't need me to tell you why they were successful, but I will. Positive thinking.

Author and speaker John Hawkins has written on the subject of the difference between losers and winners. He says there are seven basic differences. Here they are:

1. Winners are optimistic while losers are pessimistic.

I've covered this one already, but I can't emphasize this point enough. Even under the worst of circumstances, a positive attitude can only help the situation. While an optimist may be accused of not being realistic or engaging in pie-in-the-sky wishful thinking, pessimism or negativism never serves a beneficial purpose.

2. Winners do things losers won't do.

Oftentimes, it's the people who go to almost unthinkable lengths who manage to make it to the top. Thomas Edison, one of our greatest inventive geniuses, reportedly tried more than 1,000 different substances as filaments before he found the right one for the light bulb. Ross Perot and his wife both worked and then lived off his salary while they saved every cent of her salary to fund his new business. These are people who went to extraordinary lengths to reach the top and they did it instead of complaining that "life is hard" and just giving up

3. Winners fail more often than losers.

The loser tastes defeat and quits. The winner gets knocked down and keeps on getting back up. Winners have "been there, done that, and got the t-shirt"—so when they're in that same situation again, they've learned from hard experience what to do and what not to do. Losers, on the other hand, fail, decide it's too hard, and quit before they've ever really gotten started.

4. Winners know what they're trying to do while losers go with the flow.

No person just shows up one day and becomes a CEO, astronaut, or Olympic gold medalist. As a general rule, it takes a lot of effort, planning, and grunt work to be exceptional at anything. Even if you just want to be a great father or the best friend you can be to another person, it helps a lot to know that that's what you're trying to do. Since it's so rare that anyone turns out to be "accidentally" great at anything over the long haul, it's very important to figure out what you're trying to do and what you want to accomplish.

5. Winners take responsibility for their own lives while losers point the finger elsewhere.

It's not society's job, Wall Street's job, or the government's job to take care of you. That's your job. Winners take responsibility for what happens to them, their own lives, and their future. If you're waiting for "society" or the "government" to show up, fix all your problems, and make you into a success, you're going to be in for a long, long wait.

6. Winners work harder than losers.

You know the famous story of the young man who asked a stranger how to get to Carnegie Hall. The answer: "practice, practice, practice." No person is ever going to become a champion at anything working 40 hours a week to get by and then spending the rest of the week kicking back in the La-Z-Boy watching TV. (Unless you're retired, of course. Then, you can kick back any time you want.) As Thomas Edison said, success is 10% inspiration and 90% perspiration.

7. Winners ask. Losers wait to be asked.

It's amazing how fearful people are to ask; they think they will be thought of as stupid or ignorant, or worse. Yet, asking is the simplest, most efficient, and potentially most rewarding action a person can take. If a person doesn't ask, people will assume he or she already knows, and this is when a person is at the greatest risk for failure, because if a person guesses, chances are that guess will be wrong.

So, positive thinking leads to positive results; negative thinking leads to negative results. This common sense reality is nothing new or novel; it's simply a matter of keeping the importance of positive thinking foremost in your mind. The great songwriter Johnny Mercer said it well when he penned this famous line from one of his most memorable songs:

"You've got to accentuate the positive, eliminate the negative, latch on to the affirmative, and don't mess with Mr. In-Between."

The importance of a strong system of values.

Earlier, I pointed out that, as we look beyond our borders, we see violence, destruction, poverty and selfishness even as we hear echoes of freedom and liberty. Here at home, we see corruption and greed at the highest levels. We pride ourselves on being the wealthiest nation in the world, yet we see poverty and neglect as our nation continues to slide further and further down the list of most educated countries in the world, along with a declining standard of living for more and more people as fewer and fewer realize the American Dream. In fact, polls show that more and more believe they will never live this dream. And yet again, we hear the echoes of freedom and liberty. There is a disconnect, however, between what we see and what we hear. We also learn about the powerful, rich and famous engaging in abusive, destructive and even criminal behavior. So many of them are held up as role models who are fawned over, praised, pampered and literally have everything one could ever hope for. Because of their status as "special" people conferred on them by fans, etc., these "special" people believe that the laws and moral code that apply to us don't apply to them.

Of course, while we witness this type of aberrant behavior, we also see many good things exemplified by the work of organizations and individuals that ease the horrors of international strife and domestic turbulence. The critical overriding question, however, is that even in the midst of the performance of good, humanitarian deeds, why we have these storms and struggles both around the world and here at home.

I have no doubt each person can come up with one or more reasons why there are these horrific examples of inhumanity that contrast sharply with extending a helping hand to a fellow human being. For me, however, there is a single word that captures and explains this divergence, and that word is values—our system of beliefs that promotes devotion to Deity, hard work and a strong positive work ethic; a system that teaches respect for and tolerance of others, particularly those who are of different races, religions and political and social beliefs; of caring, sharing; practicing the Golden Rule, etc. What we find in those who for all their fame and wealth, suffer the trials and tribulations I've previously mentioned is the absence of a moral compass, for without it, there is no value.

This should be obvious. We should know that basic, common sense morality, dignity and human kindness are neither secret nor mysterious. This is why we try to emphasize the vital importance of a deep and abiding commitment toward other members of the human family, more especially our families and friends. This commitment takes many forms—dependability, honesty, accountability, trustworthiness, and similar conduct, all directed to basic common sense human kindness. What I'm referring to is not novel; it's to those principles/values that have stood the test of time. A strong value system has as its source a feeling of belonging, being part of something meaningful, something that provides for a sense of accomplishment. No one is an island. Personal happiness lies at the heart of a strong value system. To be happy, we must belong to something—a family, a community, a club, a fraternity, a religious organization, or some other group. We are, after all, all social beings.

It is only when we lose sight of our moral compass that the dark side of human nature takes over and leads to the kind of storms and discord I've previously mentioned. We as a society really have only two options. We must rise above the temptations of greed and self-aggrandizement, or we will surely fall prey to them and suffer the consequences. The re-emphasis on a strong moral code must not, however, be the value system of a particular group seeking to impose its system on others; it must be one that has a common core that appeals to all, regardless of one's faith or background. We must strive to find common ground and promote a value system or moral compass from that common foundation. Until this is done, I see a downward spiral. Competing moral values has the same adverse impact as competing religious doctrines. If one clams to be better than another, it's impossible to find the common ground necessary for compromise and peaceful co-existence. We can put our head in a hole in the ground like an ostrich and make believe that nothing bad will happen; we can whistle past the graveyard and kid ourselves into believing that all is well, or all will be fine someday if we just wait it out. But unless we make a conscious commitment to put the common good above personal gain, and act accordingly at all times, nothing will be done to lessen or eliminate the conditions that could easily be self-destructive.

Earlier, I mentioned the issue of "traditional American values" and "traditional family values." I assume those who mention both are talking about the same thing, but without defining these terms, usually they mean whatever the speaker wants them to mean, literally in Alice-in-Wonderland fashion where the Cheshire Cat intones that words mean whatever he chooses them to mean; no more and no less. Communication is a two-way street; there must be no disconnect between speaker and audience. Otherwise, there is the great risk of misinterpretation or as that famous movie line says "What we have here is a failure to communicate."

While these points raise serious issues, I hope all of us can agree that we need to come together and develop a broad consensus on what constitutes our traditional American (family)values, and then by our actions be true to all of them.There really is no acceptable alternative. If you believe my assessment is wrong, think of the reasons why and see if they are logical and based on common sense.

We must not let events control us.The good news is that ultimately, we have the ability to control events by our words and, far more importantly, our deeds.The realization of this, however, will take both dedication and hard work. But the work must be done; the status quo isn't working, so it must be replaced by positive action. We have the right to speak our minds and organize to accomplish what's best for our country. We have the right to petition our government for redress of grievances. These two precious rights pave the way for those who aren't part of the "inner circle" to penetrate it and make absolutely certain that those in power or positions of influence act at all times for the common good, rather than solely for personal gain.We expect our leaders to lead, but they must lead wisely, with common sense and with a laser focus on the common good. If this is done, we'll be ok.

If you find this too preachy, I ask you not to criticize the messenger and thereby dismiss the message. Focus on the message. If you find any point(s) of agreement, talk to your friends and neighbors. That's how words turn into action.

Leadership

At the outset of this discussion, I don't profess to be a leadership expert; however, I've certainly seen enough people who functioned in leadership positions, and I've run enough organizations, to have an appreciation of what works and what doesn't, and what constitutes good leadership what type of conduct results in leadership failure. I touched on some of these during my discussion of my years with state government. Here are some more precise aspects of what I view as the overarching principles of effective leadership. (I will refer to "he" throughout this discussion, but the points here apply equally to women.)

Thousands of books and articles have been written on the subject of leadership. The common theme of these publications is that a good and effective leader is a beneficial force for action, helping others to develop and act to accomplish clearly defined goals. The key is not leadership for its own sake, but effective leadership that is measured by action, and not mere words. This is so because leadership exists by law and in fact. One who is put in charge by election is certainly the lawful leader, but if he fails to command the focus and attention of those who have placed their trust in him; in short, if he fails to provide effective leadership—they will look elsewhere for a leader in fact who does command their attention.

The reason for this should be self-evident: Effective leadership requires effective followship!!! No leader can be effective in a vacuum. Those in the leader's charge must buy into the leader's plan and work diligently and effectively in pursuit of his goals. And the only way for a leader to have people buy into his plan is through the power of persuasion, not force. A leader cannot be effective if his head is in the clouds, or if he listens with a deaf ear.

Attaining a position of leadership means accepting a job, and then doing that job to the best of his ability. That position is not a means of merely collecting a title and wearing it to show how important he is. The honor of the position/job comes after the job is successfully completed, and not before. Based on my observations, experience and study, here are what I believe are the core qualities of effective leadership.

Integrity, honesty and ethical conduct. These are qualities that a person brings to a leadership position. He has no ego, or he has left his ego someplace else. If a leader constantly demonstrates that he is a man of principle; honest and forthright in his dealings with others; and conducts himself with the highest degree of ethics, he will have earned the respect of his peers. For the followers to embrace these principles as well, they must see them in action from their leader.

Humility. An effective leader does not take himself too seriously. He is not afraid to admit mistakes because he knows no one is perfect and to make mistakes is human nature. An effective leader knows that there is no purpose in dwelling on mistakes, but in learning from them, showing remorse in a lesson learned, and taking corrective action and thereby make better decisions. In short, an effective leader knows how to admit error, correct where possible and move on toward the goal. People will generally forgive mistakes but will not tolerate being treated in an ill manner by a leader who spends valuable time trying to convince others that he did not make a mistake or that he is incapable of making a mistake or it's someone else's fault. Remember, people are a lot more perceptive than one might think; never underestimate the ability of a leader's subordinates to sense the truth and see through a charade.

Sensitivity and loyalty. An effective leader must be loyal to his charges and understand—and is sensitive to—their interests, wishes and opinions. He must be a good and effective listener. A leader who believes he has all the answers more often than not doesn't understand the questions. Similarly, a leader who believes he can establish a following by simply asking for or forcing loyalty is not going to be an effective leader. Demands don't work; at least, certainly not in the long run. Followship must be earned; it will not be given freely. An effective leader is one who is willing to learn from others and take those positive experiences and convert them into positive action.

Communication, Commitment, passion and determination. These principles are self-evident. What is important here is not to talk a good game. What is vital is that, to be an effective leader, he must demonstrate by word and deed that he is committed to a course of action, passionate in his pursuit of that action, and determined to accomplish his goals. If he is clear in articulating his vision, mission and directions; speaks with confidence, and the followers see their merits, they will buy into them much more willingly and freely. In short, it takes teamwork to demonstrate effective leadership.

Courage. It is important for a leader, to be effective, to set aside personal goals and desires for the betterment of the group. He must subdue his passion and personal desires, and work diligently to quell quarrels and piques if and when they arise. The ability to demonstrate the courage of conviction with the other principles set out here is the mark of an effective leader.

Preparation and organization. These two principles cannot be overstated. A leader must have a plan in place before assuming his position, inform others of that plan, get feedback, make adjustments where necessary, and generally perform all functions that one would expect from a leader. Remember, those who elected you to office look to you as one who can lead. You do not want to let them down. Yet, you must convince them to follow your lead. Faithful adherence to the principles highlighted here will assure that your leadership and their followship will go hand in hand. Once organized, however, a leader must follow through by careful preparation. If a leader fails to appear to be in command; if he struggles and appears uncertain; this will be quickly picked up by the organization and the leader will lose his followers.

Motivation. That effective followship is the hallmark of effective leadership is a given. To attain an effective following, however, requires that the leader be motivated. Motivation requires clarity of thought and expression, getting the right people into the right jobs, making sure everyone counts and that each one knows he counts, and instilling confidence in one another and in you as their leader. A key to motivation is convincing followers to treat your ideas as their own. A successful leader is one who carefully balances the flow of ideas so that the organization members are ready, willing and able to buy into his plan of action. Remember, success is more easily obtained if it doesn't matter who gets the credit. A leader will get the credit for success even when he points out that a particular idea came from elsewhere.

Confidence and positivity. A leader who continually emphasizes the negative will quickly lose his followship. Negativism deflates; positivism encourages. But positive words must follow positive action. People are willing to follow a leader who exudes confidence in his demeanor, words and actions, and is positive in his approach to things. Above all, an effective leader does not talk a good game; he knows that talk without action is meaningless. Therefore, he puts his words into effective action by developing effective teamwork and getting his subordinates to proceed on task.

Wisdom. Do not mix wisdom with intelligence. A leader may be very intelligent, yet fail to provide effective leadership because he doesn't have the wisdom to know what is right and what is wrong with a given approach. An effective leader knows people's strengths and weaknesses, and knows how to maximize those strengths while minimizing weaknesses. He knows that he has a choice: will he motivate others, as an effective leader must, or will he allow events to govern him? He knows that while he can delegate authority, he can never delegate responsibility. And he knows that he must never shy away from making decisions, but that common sense will more often than not dictate wise decisions. Far too often, the tendency is to let events dictate or control action, instead of the other way around. Followers appreciate decisiveness, and an erroneous decision will be more appreciated than inaction if a leader adheres to the principles set out above.

In sum, an effective leader is not attached to success nor afraid of failure. He works through others as much as possible, not caring who gets the credit for a project well-done. He is willing to compromise in order to meet the larger goals, is honest and humble in his approach to others, exudes confidence and positivity, is loyal and courageous, and is organized and prepared to move forward. He has no hesitation of getting in the trenches and leading by direct example.

21 Irrefutable Laws of Leadership-Addendum

Recently, I read a book that includes John C. Maxwell's 21 Irrefutable Laws of Leadership. Because I find them extremely helpful for those who are called upon to lead, I am sharing them with you.

1. **The Law of the lid.** Your leadership is like a lid or a ceiling on your organization. Your organization will not rise beyond the level your leadership allows. That's why when a corporation or team needs to be fixed, they fire the leader.

2. **The Law of Influence.** Leadership is simply about influencing people. Nothing more, nothing less. The true test of a leader is to ask him to create positive change in an organization. If you cannot create change, you cannot lead. Being a leader is not about being first, or being an entrepreneur, or being the most knowledgeable, or being a manager. Being a leader is not just holding a leadership position. ("It's not the position that makes a leader, but the leader who makes a position.") Positional leadership especially does not work in volunteer organizations. The very essence of all power to influence lies in getting the other person to participate. "He who thinks he leads, but has no followers, is only taking a walk."

3. **The Law of the Process**. Leadership is learned over time. And it can be learned. People skills, emotional strength, vision, momentum, and timing are all areas that can and should be learned. Leaders are always learners.

4. **The Law of Navigation.** Anyone can steer the ship, but it takes a leader to chart the course. Vision is defined as the ability to see the whole trip before leaving the dock. A leader will also see obstacles before others do. A leader sees more, sees farther, and sees before others. A navigator (leader) listens—he finds out about grassroots level reactions. Navigators balance optimism with realism. Preparation is the key to good navigation. "It's not the size of the project, it's the size of the leader that counts."

5. **The Law of E.F. Hutton.** Hutton was America's most influential stock market analyst. When he spoke, everyone listened. When real leaders speak, people automatically listen. Conversely, in any group or church, you can identify the real leaders by looking for those who people listen to. According to Margaret Thatcher, "being in power is like being a lady—if you have to tell people you are, you aren't." Tips for a Positional leader—like a newly appointed minister—who wants to become a REAL leader . . . look for the existing real leaders and work to have influence there. Factors involved in being accepted as a new real leader include character, building key relationships, information, intuition, experience, past success. and ability.

6. **The Law of Solid Ground.** Trust is the foundation for all effective leadership. When it comes to leadership, there are no shortcuts. Building trust requires competence, connection and character.

7. **The Law of Respect.** People naturally follow people stronger than themselves. Even natural leaders tend to fall in behind those who they sense have a higher "leadership quotient" than themselves.

8. **The Law of Intuition.** Leaders evaluate everything with a leadership bias. Leaders see trends, resources and problems, and can read people.

9. **The Law of Magnetism.** Leaders attract people like themselves. Who you are is who you attract. If you only attract followers, your organization will be weak. Work to attract leaders rather than followers if you want to build a truly strong organization.

10. **The Law of Connection.** You must touch the heart before you ask people to follow. Communicate on the level of emotion first to make a personal connection.

11. **The Law of the Inner Circle.** A leader's potential is determined by those closest to him. "The leader finds greatness in the group, and helps the members find it in themselves."

12. **The Law of Empowerment.** Only secure leaders give power to others. Mark Twain said, "Great things can happen when you don't care who gets the credit." Another point to ponder . . . "Great leaders gain authority by giving it away."

13. **The Law of Reproduction.** It takes a leader to raise up a leader. Followers can't do it, and neither can institutional programs "It takes one to know one, to show one, to grow one." The potential of an organization depends on the growth of its leadership.

14. **The Law of Buy-In.** People buy in to the leader first, then the vision. If they don't like the leader but like the vision, they get a new leader. If they don't like the leader or the vision, they get a new leader. If they don't like the vision but like the leader, they get a new vision.

15. **The Law of Victory.** Leaders find a way for the team to win. "You can't win WITHOUT good athletes, but you CAN lose with them." Unity of vision, diversity of skills plus a leader are needed for a win.

16. **The Law of Momentum.** You can't steer a ship that isn't moving forward. It takes a leader to create forward motion.

17. **The Law of Priorities.** Activity is not necessarily accomplishment. We need to learn the difference. "A leader is the one who climbs the tallest tree, surveys the entire situation, and yells "Wrong Jungle!" "If you are a leader, you must learn the three "Rs" . . . a) what's Required b) what gives the greatest Return c) what brings the greatest Reward.

18. **The Law of Sacrifice.** A leader must give up to go up. Successful leaders must maintain an attitude of sacrifice to turn around an organization. One sacrifice seldom brings success. As he worked to turn around the Chrysler Corporation, Lee Iacocca slashed his own salary to $1 per year. "When you become a leader, you lose the right to think about yourself."

19. **The Law of Timing.** When to lead is as important as what to do and where to go. Only the right action at the right time will bring success.

20. **The Law of Explosive Growth.** To add growth, lead followers. To multiply growth, lead leaders. "It is my job to build the people who are going to build the company."

21. **The Law of Legacy.** A leader's lasting value is measured by succession. "Leadership is the one thing you can't delegate. You either exercise it—or abdicate it."

If you are ever called upon to lead, or just want to have a grasp on what constitutes effective leadership, I hope this brief narrative will be of assistance to you.

NOT-SO-FINAL FINAL THOUGHTS

Let me start this entirely free-form narrative wrap-up by letting you in on one of the great value of having a legal education, and it's not that it allows you to practice law. I'm referring to its value as a red tape remover. Quite often, I hear from non-lawyer friends who vent their frustration at being stonewalled or, even worse, ignored by private companies and government agencies when a complaint is made. They call to complain, and they're met with the recorded numbering system such as "For our business hours, press one; for our location, press two"—you get the point. Then, when they finally get the number they want, they're greeted with "All of our representatives are currently assisting other customers. Your call is important to us. Please remain on the line and someone will assist you in the order in which you called." After waiting for what seems like forever, all-too-often they hang up. Do the folks who run these companies/agencies really expect us to believe these impersonal recorded messages? And I know you've heard the recorded message that you should please listen to the entire message as the system was recently changed to provide you with better service. Of course, if you call this number often, you'll get the same recording even though the "system" may have changed more than a year ago. These recordings become disingenuous when they're not changed more often. I suppose not enough people complain about silly recorded messages, so companies continue to use them ad nauseam.

I know a few people who work in this type of setting and they tell me they can set the phone to deliver these messages while on a coffee break, away from their desks, etc. Sure, there are times when these messages are legitimate, but try getting the bedraggled customer to believe that what they hear is always truthful. What I do to avoid this is to persist in getting a phone number that's not the one generally given out, or go online and write to the consumer affairs office. If I can get a name, I want that, too. I don't want a front-door receptionist; I want an interior operator who can put me directly in touch with a live person. This is not as hard as it may seem; when talking to a live person and I get a name, or I'm face-to-face with someone, he/she generally wants to help, if for no other reason than to get rid of me. Perseverance is vital here. When a written record is made via an online contact, a rapid response is more likely assured. No company wants a negative paper trail. This is one example of red tape removal—the ability to make direct contact and create a paper trail, with the contact knowing that I'm a lawyer. Putting a little fear via intimidation in the contact doesn't hurt. It's unfortunate that it has to come to that, but there are occasions when there is no other option.

A second one is not to threaten a company with a lawsuit when you think you've tried everything else to get positive action. That's too easy. Companies are used to these threats; they face them quite often, and they usually have either staff lawyers or a law firm under contract to represent them. Lawyers are good at obfuscating and using delaying tactics, the purpose of which is to frustrate the consumer into giving up. What I do to overcome this is that I gently but persistently let them know that I know they're licensed and regulated by government; and I also know that government hires investigators who are just waiting to be handed a consumer complaint so they can justify their continued employment by doing their jobs and investigate; and if these investigators find probable cause to believe there's a violation, a company could have its license suspended or revoked. You'll be amazed at how quickly the company will respond when its ability to remain in business is on the line. Ideally, it shouldn't have to take a person with a law degree to cut through red tape; however, I've led a red tape-proof life by casually letting company representatives know I'm a lawyer who's intimately familiar with the governmental regulatory scheme.

There is a downside to this that the consumer must be aware of and also needs to be addressed. After more than 32 years in state government, and working around both federal and local governments, I know that "the bureaucracy" is set up in such a way as to diffuse responsibility and accountability. If you use the telephone, far too often what you get (usually through a voice message, but even if you can get to a live person and then get through the secretarial blockage that a bureaucrat conveniently sets up) is a response that it's not his/her job to do whatever you ask; that you need to contact someone else. To best demonstrate this, take your arms, cross them at the wrist, and extend your index finger. You should now have both fingers pointing in opposite directions. This is how government diffuses responsibility.

To overcome this, I will persist either via the phone or website until I get a name, title and phone number. If I don't get the information, or the person doesn't take my call and talk to me, then I write a letter and copy whoever I believe ought to know about this lack of citizen response—usually a consumer advocacy group or the media. Pressing the issue with someone who doesn't want to give out this information usually works; the last thing these bureaucrats want is a paper trail created by a persistent pursuer. Eventually, I'll get what I want if for no other reason than to get rid of me as a nuisance. The short of it is that persistence and perseverance pays off in results. There are times, however, when it's necessary to use the bureaucracy game to your advantage. Locating the responsible and authoritative source and putting that person in the position of either responding or having his/her nonfeasance broadcast to the community will smoke out the recalcitrant. After all, they want to keep their jobs—especially in a tough job market—too.

Hollywood has made numerous movies—especially in the 30s to 50s—portraying news reporters and lawyers as hard-drinking, chain-smoking go-getters functioning on that blurred line between honesty and corruption. Early TV shows often created the perception that these two professions were less than honorable. I simply don't fit the hard-drinking, chain-smoking image. I don't particularly like the taste of liquor. I keep beer in a small refrigerator in my garage for guests. Harriet and I still have a couple of bottles of liquor that were given to us as wedding gifts. We keep these 40+ year-old bottles as conversation pieces. We have a few bottles (vodka, gin, rum) in our pantry for guests. This doesn't mean we're teetotalers by any means. We'll have a bloody Mary or gin and tonic now and then just to be sociable, and we might drink a glass of red wine every so often (for its medicinal value, of course). But that's it in the liquor department. I did smoke a cigarette now and then while in college because it was the cool thing to do; and had a very infrequent cigar while in private practice, but that's it in the nicotine department. I believed early on that taking smoke into your lungs can't be a healthy experience.

The subject of Hollywood brings to mind the impact of role models in our lives. Whether they're called role models, heroes, idols, etc., the significance is the same. The World English Dictionary defines "role model" as "a person regarded by others, especially young people, as a good example to follow." I think all of us had at least one role model at least one time in our lives, particularly in our youth. There's something in us that makes us want to be like someone else; someone to look up to, to in effect emulate. Because publicity seems to drive role model choices, most generally come from the sports and entertainment fields. A young boy, interested in sports, most likely will choose a famous athlete. A young girl, interested in style, most likely will choose someone from the entertainment world. As a boy growing up in New York City and with the New York Yankees so popular during the 1950s, it was natural for me to choose as my first role model Yankee great Mickey Mantle. He was big, strong, fast, and could hit the ball a "country mile" (one of baseball's great expressions, when uttered by southern-born announcers). I know I could never do what he did on the baseball field, but I wanted to be like him. I think an idol or role model is usually someone whose life is beyond reach. In the 1920s, bigger-than-life sports figures like Babe Ruth and Jack Dempsey were national idols. More recently, Michael Jordan was the dominant role model. Harriet would tell me how some many of her African-American students were going to grow up and be just like Michael Jordan. Of course, no one can be "just like Mike;" he was that rare athlete who transcended his sport.

As I got older and learned that my sports hero had taken "greenies" or amphetamines, during his career. I began to realize that these idols are all-too-human. Because Mantle's father died at 39, he didn't believe he would live long and lived on the edge, not thinking or planning for a tomorrow. Mantle didn't take care of himself and neglected his family. After he retired at 38 because of serious injuries sustained playing baseball, he led, shall I say, less than an exemplary life. He developed cancer and died in 1994 at 63. Often, he said that had he known he was going to live that long, he would have taken better care of himself. In his last interview, this once-great athlete—now a shadow of himself—pointedly said that he should never have been considered a role model. He was human and made more than his share of mistakes that hurt his family and himself. It takes a man to admit to such failures; that only endeared him more in my eyes. I was sad for him, but I fully understood who and what a true role model must be.

The point here is that too often we learn that our role models are all too human. Whether it be Elvis Presley, Michael Jackson, Whitney Houston, etc., we find that life in the goldfish bowl takes its toll. Nevertheless, when these idols pass, fans still hold them in reverence. This is probably because they did nothing to harm others; only themselves. And they never told their fans to live like they did; they never said they were examples of all that is good and right. It's an entirely different story when a supposed role model who claims to be virtuous, honest and completely above-board turns out to be entirely different. As previously discussed, the most recent glaring example is the late Penn State coach Joe Paterno. His reputation is shattered, his status as a legend destroyed—all because he remained silent when he should have spoken loudly. But he wasn't the first and, unfortunately, won't be the last who engages in self-immolation of reputation. Once those who held someone up as that kind of role model finds that the emperor has no clothes, the vilification comes fast and furious.

To his credit, basketball great Charles Barkley often said that he is not a role model; he wisely said that a parent or teacher is the real role model. Unfortunately, it's not up to the standout athlete, etc., who decides whether or not he/she is a role model; this is a status conferred by others. New York Yankee great Derek Jeter knows he's considered a role model and has said repeatedly that he tries to live his life with this understanding. I give him credit for understanding how others look to him and how he works to live his life accordingly.

It was when I was in my 20s that I realized that my true role models were my dad and grandpa. I also realized that these were the two men who I most admired all along. Neither tried to be anything but who they were. When they hurt, they cried. When they laughed, they made me laugh. I took note of the sacrifices they made so that I could live the American Dream. And they gave me lessons that have served me well throughout my life; lessons that I've made every effort to pass onto my daughters. I know they will pass them on to their children and, hopefully, on and on.

I don't have much of a recollection of my daughters having pictures of the star du jour on their walls, but one of my granddaughters has pictures of Justin Bieber on her wall, but in a negative fashion, writing "Sneezer" over his name. With social networking expanding by leaps and bounds, it is possible for fans to actually make contact (perhaps) with an athlete or movie star. Reading some of the blogs or tweets, quite frankly, I find many of them very difficult—if not impossible—to understand. It's as if blogging, tweeting, Facebooking, etc., has led to the creation of an entirely new way of expressing oneself—a way that's alien to the English language as I learned it.

I did a Google search on the factors that should be considered in choosing a role model. There are six and are as follows:

1. Choose someone who has a lot of confidence in themselves and their abilities. These people know who they are and won't pretend to be someone they're not.

2. Choose someone who thinks it's alright to be unique, even if it means accepting some ridicule. This type of role model makes you feel good about being yourself and don't make you compare yourself to them.

3. Think about someone who interacts well with others, and someone who is kind and can communicate well with others; like a teacher.

4. Look for someone who's living life the way you would want to. The younger a person is, the more difficult this is. But as a youngster approaches high school and must begin to think about life decisions, this decision becomes more and more important. If a youngster wants to be an author, look for someone who's a successful author. This applies to any choice of profession or vocation.

5. Find someone who doesn't always take credit for what he/she does. Humility is a critically important quality; it focuses more on the performance rather than the performer.

6. Finally, find a role model who has done something that is admirable, such as raising money for charity, helped people in need or was instrumental in a medical breakthrough.

To these six, I would hope those who seek a role model would add a seventh—who should really be at the top of the list—and be able to look at their parents. I can't find a greater statement about a role model than "I want to be like my dad (or mother or grandfather, etc.) because he's (she's) the best."

Ok, now it's time for me to wrap this up.

I would describe my work habits as focused, without panic. I never burned the midnight oil as a student, reporter or lawyer; didn't cram for exams as a student; only worked undercover as a reporter once; and didn't slave away at a desk day and night as a lawyer. I guess you can say I am the opposite of how these professions were and perhaps still are portrayed, at least in some instances. This explains why I wasn't exactly a top student. Academically, I was a solid student—solid B as an undergraduate and a solid C as a law student. The comment I often heard while in law school was that an A student became a professor, a B student became a judge and a C student practiced law and became the millionaire or multimillionaire. I suppose that, being a C student, I made a conscious decision to work for state government and thereby removed myself from this description of the usual C student category. Of course, I don't know whether this explanation of A, B and C students is actually true or not; what is true is that I never fit into category C above-for whatever reason.

Now, because I'm a lawyer, I must admit a detailed familiarity with lawyer jokes. In fact, I'm far too familiar with them. I hear them all the time, usually told by those who've either had a bad experience with one, or are simply passing along someone else's perception of the legal profession with which they might agree. It's as if the jokes take care of the joke-teller's perceptions of the legal profession, allow him to vent his spleen, and serve as an emotional catharsis of some sort. When I do hear one, however, I simply tell the jokester that the next time he (I've never been told one by a female) gets into hot water or needs help, to call his chiropractor; let him try to bail you out. That usually stops the joke-telling—at least until the next get-together. Some of the jokes are funny; some mean-spirited. I usually find, however, that those who tell them are the first to call a lawyer when facing a problem he/she can't handle. I certainly would like to meet the person who writes these lawyer jokes and ask why he doesn't do the same for architects, engineers, etc. I suppose that lawyer jokes are derived from the nature of the profession itself—the way lawyers write and speak. "Help, aid and assist," "aid and abet," etc. Lawyers tend to use many words instead of a few. There is a reason for this, however. I use the phrase that what a surgeon does with a scalpel, lawyers do with words. It's vital that, in communicating with one another, we are on the same page insofar as the subject matter is concerned. I've heard more than my share of arguments in which the people wind up eventually at least understanding where the other side is coming from because, after much squabbling, they were talking about the same subject, although using different words. The first order of business in any discussion is define what the subject is. Words must be chosen that "cut" exceedingly close and exceedingly fine. Each chosen word has a specific meaning, and one word may not fully cover a point, while two or more will. Hence, the need for precision in choosing words that appear to the layman to be duplicative.

There is one other thing that I suppose I should list under pet peeves, but this one has nothing to do with medical matters. Ordinarily, I wouldn't mention this subject if I didn't notice a disturbing—and growing—pattern. I simply don't understand why people don't return phone calls or respond to email—especially those who I know are on their computers because they're posting on Facebook, playing Scrabble or doing some other kind of activity that requires a computer. I can recall a time when a letter begat a responsive letter and a phone call begat a return phone call, and responses were prompt. These days, it's rare that I get a returned phone call the same day as my call—if at all—and it's equally rare for me to get a response to an email where one is expected. If I send an email asking for information, and the recipient receives it and, whether he/she has the answer not, simply fails or refuses to respond, what does that say about him/her? Here's the real rub: some of the people I know who complain about not getting responses within a reasonable time are the biggest offenders. Another side of this is when a person sends out an invitation with an RSVP and fails to get a response. This is especially important when one is planning a reception or dinner and needs to know how many will be in attendance.

Unless someone has an emergency situation in which they can't respond, I fail to see a single legitimate excuse for not doing the courteous thing and send off a timely response, especially since so many carry cell phones now. Usually, when I see a person to whom I sent an email, placed a call or sent an invitation, and ask whether they received my message, they'll say they have. But when I ask why he/she didn't respond, I'll get a "deer in the headlights" look as if there's something wrong with me for asking, following which I'll get some lame excuse such as "I tried to call you" or "I meant to get back to you" or the real bummer: "I forgot." My thinking in silence runs along this line: You "tried" to call me? What did you do, press the first five numbers? Wait for the first ring and then hang up? You "tried" to get back in touch with me? What did you do, fill out the RSVP and throw it in the garbage? Simply put, you don't "try" to call someone; you either succeed by getting the person or his/her voice message system, or you simply didn't call back. You don't "try" to get in touch with someone; you either do or you don't. And if you "forgot," this certainly tells me how reliable someone is. I believe it's a matter of attitude; those who don't respond are usually unreliable, inconsiderate, and have little appreciation for common decency. People will remember the only big letdown over the 100 punctual actions. A person is either reliable or dependable, or he/she isn't. And it only takes one or two instances for someone to be tagged as unreliable or not dependable. And inconsiderate. And that one or two occasions can ruin a reputation—if the person truly cares about his/her reputation.

Throughout this book, I've discussed what I perceive to be some serious societal problems that seem to be festering. There are those who say things will get better; there's no need to worry. I don't buy into this do-nothing approach. People create problems and it will take people to solve them. Doing nothing is not a solution. Two questions arise from my discussion: Do we have the ability to work toward addressing what appear to be insoluble problems implicating our health, safety and welfare? Do we have the will to overcome growing political intransigence and intolerance, and sacrifice selfishness in order to fully and substantively address issues of jobs, entitlements, government waste, education, health care, crime, immigration, war, international relations, infrastructure repair and rebuilding; etc., etc., etc.? We Americans are a competitive lot. We want to play the game and win. Losing is not something we ever want to experience, let alone deal with. But losing is a part of life; and it's not so much the loss that should be of paramount concern, it's what a person does after losing that counts. To be able to pick oneself up, dust oneself off and start all over again is an admirable trait. Indeed, it's the only one that truly makes sense.

There is absolutely nothing wrong with this desire to win, so long as we all play by the same rules. Problem number one is that because all of us don't play by the same rules—and for the most part, we don't even have the ability to set up the rules—there is no level playing field from which to launch programs and activities designed to work through our myriad of problems. The intransigence of "I'm right, you're wrong and it's my way or the highway" solves nothing. As I said throughout my personal observations, there must be moderation, negotiation and compromise. Government simply can't function on extremes; balance is the be-all and end-all of successful governance. There is no alternative to coming together as one nation, rolling up the sleeves and getting to work across party lines. The emphasis must be on what's in the best interests of the nation as a whole; not what's best for an official's party or his/her economic bottom line, and not what's in the best interests of his/her financial backers.

I am deeply concerned that it will take a cataclysmic event to force us to come together as one again. We had this unity right after 9/11, but it far-too-quickly vanished in the muck of the juvenile and unprofessional behavior by our government officials that can only be called nearsighted partisanship. I'll soon be 70. Harriet and I are enjoying our retirement years, but who's to say what conditions will be like in five or 10 years, maybe even sooner? I tell Harriet that all we can do is the best we can do for one another and hope that our government officials have the brains and will to rise above the perils of human nature and think about the people they're supposed to represent. That should be their sole focus.

My daughters read the newspapers and listen to the news every day. Both have young children who will someday—too soon for their parents—take their place in the world. They ask what's in store for them. I ask myself that same question quite often. And that's where my worries really lie What kind of nation and world will my daughters face in 10, 20, 30 or 40 years from now? What will my grandchildren experience 30 to 80 years from now? As a positive, if the last 50 years are any indication, they will see unimaginable technological advancements, as well as advancements in medicine and science that are the subject of science fiction today. I remember when the notion of a man on the moon made for some good science fiction movies. Fiction has become fact. These types of advancements will continue at a rapidly accelerating rate. My children and grandchildren can expect to live into the triple digits with technology making life's activities much easier to navigate.

As a negative, however, these advancements presume that disease is under control and war is avoided. Lethal forms of cancer, as well as incidences of heart attacks and strokes must—and to some degree, will—be conquered. These advancements, however, will necessitate personal responsibility for a healthy lifestyle. Food that is appealing to the taste buds far too often leads to unhealthy living, such as obesity, high blood pressure, etc. Consumption of certain products similarly are not indicative of a healthy lifestyle, such as tobacco, alcohol and drugs. Even as we find more ways to combat disease, new strains of life-threatening viruses and bacteria are born. We must remain ahead of that curve. In short, we have the tools; will we know how to effectively use them for the greater good of all?

Today, many nations either have stockpiles of nuclear and biological weapons, or are in the process of developing and stockpiling them. The risk, of course, is that with so many nations with these weapons, and with more and more becoming capable of producing them, a single mistake can send the world into an apocalypse from which we can't and won't escape. Treaties are worthless unless followed to the letter. International agreements must be made and kept. It is absolutely necessary to rise above human nature's drive for selfish self-promotion and its ego-driven counterpart of superiority and answer YES to the question posed by the late Rodney King: "Can't we all just get along?".

I hope will all my heart that it won't take a cataclysmic event in our country to bring us together as one. This is a teachable moment in our history. Politicians must stop whipping their supporters into a frenzy by demonizing those they oppose and by instilling in their respective bases a deep sense of fear and suspicion. The only kind of nation that can be governed by fear is a dictatorship run by a despot or demagogue—and that can last only so long. For any nation to endure, it must be by the will and pleasure of the governed. By the way, I hope that by this time you realize that I'm a moderate Democrat; they really do exist. I only wish I could say the same for Republicans. Whether it's called compromise, negotiation, moderation, it's all directed to The Center—this is where meaningful governance takes place. Government by extremes has never worked—and will never work—in a republic or democracy. It's all about moderation, moderation, moderation.

To be sure, there is no single, simple solution to the multiplicity of problems besetting our country. But doing nothing is not an option because the ultimate reality is that events will control us, or we will control events. The latter gives us hope; the former gives us . . . well, you can easily figure out the cost of non-action or inaction. As I said at the beginning of this narrative on the future, we have the ability; we must also have the collective will. The answer to these Solomon-type problems may not come in my lifetime. But they are going to have to come in my children's lifetimes, if at all. I have my family and close friends with young children who are literally betting their lives on our world leaders' ability to make wise choices for the hundreds of millions in our country, and the billions around the world.

By now, it should be obvious that my story is not a rags-to-riches tale. I didn't accumulate great wealth the old-fashioned way—by inheritance. Just kidding. I think. I didn't accumulate wealth through work. Neither did I strike it rich in the oil, minerals or securities market. I never had the kind of inside information that members of Congress have. Mine is more of a "khaki slacks-and-polo shirt to sports-coat-and-tie-or-dark-suit" success story. However, I did what I did honestly and I'm eternally grateful for all the wonderful things that have happened to me in my life, and all the people who helped me along the way. I can truly say that if I had to do it over, I can't think of a single thing I would change. In this narrative, I'm mentioned repeatedly the honors I've received and awards I've won in my chosen profession. To those who might view this as bragging, I'm reminded of what boxing great Muhammad Ali said about bragging: "It ain't braggin' if you can do it." I believe I did it. But awards are mere objects; what really matters are family and friends. A loving family and true friends are rewards for a life well-lived.

Several years ago, I read a book about the passages each one of us go through in life. As a teenager, we tend to believe we have the solutions to all of the world's problems, and that our parents are out-of-touch and don't "understand" today's world. I know I felt that my dad and grandparents didn't understand what it was like as a teenager. But what happened is that as I grew older—finished college, went to law school, got married, had a family, was responsible for putting food on the table and a roof over our heads—in short, actually acting as a responsible adult, my father and grandfather became smarter and smarter. Actually, they didn't; but what I didn't take time to realize is that they actually lived through each of the phases of life that I had yet to experience. In my youth, I rejected their efforts at giving me the benefit of their experience; I more than willingly embraced my dad's experiences as I got older.

I've been most fortunate in that my daughters actually asked what my childhood was like, and how important my experiences were—and are—in ultimately making wise decisions. Harriet and I taught our daughters to make wise decisions by thinking through the action they planned on taking, and what the consequences were of each potential action. Our girls are raising their children the same way. I believe children learn better and faster when they're taught to make decisions by thinking through the possibilities and consequences. This learning process takes more time, but the results are more than worth it. I think that if more parents taught their children to think through their actions, many of our problems with today's youth would certainly be less consequential.

One of the first things I'm asked after I tell someone I'm retired is "What do you do to keep busy?" I tell them I'm very busy, and then, when asked "Doing what?" recite the following courtesy of the famous country music stars the Statler Brothers: "counting flowers on the wall, that don't bother me at all. Playing solitaire till dawn with a deck of 51. Smoking cigarettes and watching Captain Kangaroo. Now, don't tell me I've nothing to do." I always get a kick out of their reaction. The other question I'm asked is "Do you miss it?" I assume (correctly) that they mean whether I miss the practice of law. Before retiring, I thought I certainly would, since I'd been doing it for so long. But to my amazement, in the more-than-two years since leaving the workforce, I haven't had a single day that I wish I were still on that treadmill. So, my answer is quick, short and categorical: NO. I find that my current laidback lifestyle is far more comforting and healthier than the helter-skelter life of a lawyer who makes his living in the courtroom.

In addition to hoping you enjoyed my story, I hope that by this time, you've convinced yourself that you, too, can write a book about your life. When I began this exercise, I wondered how I could possibly find enough to write about that would fill even a small book. I've certainly read enough autobiographies, biographies and memoirs, but they all had one thing in common: they were about famous or infamous people who, by definition, lived (or are living) interesting, fascinating, exciting—or treacherous, notorious, criminal or even murderous—lives. Either way, these writings appeal to our inquisitiveness or emotions, or both.

The vast majority of us, however, aren't known to millions of people; we're just ordinary citizens going about our daily lives who are known by comparatively very few. We work to put food on our table, provide a home for our families, provide for our children's education so that they can become productive members of society—in short, we're just trying to live the American dream, or at least our concept of it. But history is, in the last analysis, about people and how they lived their lives. I find nothing objectionable about letting others know about my life; what is objectionable about letting others know about your life through your own eyes?

In the interest of full disclosure, however, I must give a word of caution. In undertaking writing an autobiography/memoir, you will go it alone. You won't have a staff of researchers or ghostwriters like some famous writers do. While you can ask family members and friends for their recollections, what you write will be your words and yours alone. This book has more than 123,000 words.. Except for the column by Charlie Reese, a few quotes here and there, and the lists of six role model points and 21 leadership points, I am responsible for every word. Period. Nothing in this book will tell you how to accumulate incredible wealth; become a famous entertainer; start a business that becomes a multi-national corporation with you as CEO; how to hit or pitch a baseball; kick a field goal; throw touchdown and after touchdown; make dozens of consecutive free throws; score a Stanley Cup-winning goal; or become heavyweight champion of the world. All this book does is tell the reader about me. And hopefully motivate you to tell about you.

As I wrote this book, I had decisions to make. My first reaction was how I could possibly find enough to say that would fill a book. But then I began to frame an outline, asking such questions as: should I tell about my medical history? How much detail should I provide? Should I take on controversial issues? How much controversy do I want to create? The point here is that when a person sets out to write this kind of book, to be faithful to the project, the writer has to be willing to disclose personal matters. Life is, after all, a personal, individualized journey and each person takes a unique path. No two people live the same life. The most important decision for me was whether I should include so much of my personal views, thoughts, etc., about a broad spectrum of issues. But since lawyers and news reporters are steeped in thinking about and dealing with controversial issues, I couldn't be faithful to myself if I had chosen to ignore this aspect of my life. I also decided to include some thoughts on positive thinking, values and leadership because they are so important in shaping one's life. Positive thinking forms attitudes; values form personal conduct; leadership allows for inspiring others. A person doesn't have to run any organization to have the ability to inspire others. It really doesn't matter, however, what one's journey through life entails; we all have opinions and there's nothing wrong with expressing them. Therefore, I decided to express some of mine in a rather free-form manner. As I wrap up my writing, I can't say with absolute certainty whether my wife, daughters, sons-in-law or grandchildren (when they get around to reading this or if they get around to reading this) will agree or sharply disagree with many of my observations. But I think it's safe to say that Lani and Brian, with their small business backgrounds (and Brian's law enforcement background), and Amy and Frank, with their forensic and law enforcement backgrounds, probably won't agree with much of what I say. Harriet might be more inclined to agree with some of my points, if only because her background is not to dissimilar from mine.

One's background plays a very heavy role in the formation of opinions and views. I lived in apartments, government-funded housing projects, efficiency apartments occupied primarily by senior citizens, and dorm rooms until I lived in a home for the first time at age 33. I've lived in two homes in my entire life. I didn't drive or own a car until I was 22. My daughters, however, never knew an apartment until they moved out on their own. They were driving at 16, and had acting and dance lessons. Harriet's family are Holocaust survivors and she watched her parents scrimp and save as much as they could to give her and her brother what her parents missed out on. The point here is that, in my own family, Harriet and I were of different upbringings, and our daughters never had the harsh experiences that Harriet and I had.

My childhood gave me sensitivity to those less fortunate simply because I was around and interacted with so many of them, and I've never lost that sensitivity even though I was told that as I grew older and accumulated more money, my attitude would change. This hasn't happened, and I really don't know why. While I know I certainly don't fit into the wealthy upper class, I don't think I can be classified as a pure middle class member either.

As I said at the very beginning of this endeavor, my first thought was about my wife, children and grandchildren. With this book, I have now given them a permanent record of my life, including as much of my early childhood as was passed down to me and that I can now recall. My daughters are aware of my effort; I'll get their reaction after they read this. I don't know whether, years from now, my grandchildren will care one way or the other about what I've said here. But I care enough to leave it to them to decide. I believe all of us want to leave something—call it a legacy—for our children and grandchildren; something that says I was here. This is my contribution to them. I strongly recommend that you consider doing likewise. I think you will find the writing surprising, illuminating and rewarding. We all have a story to tell. I've told mine; you should tell yours. And whether you believe you have a story to tell or not; you do. If I do, you do. I must caution you, however, that there will be those who will try to dissuade you from doing this. When I told a few of my friends of my intention, I was given such encouragement as "Who the hell are you to write an autobiography or memoir? Nobody gives a @#^&$* anyway." Oh, ye of little faith, I told them. You can see how much effect their reaction had on me.

When you read an autobiography or memoir, it's usually a self-serving book extolling the virtues of the rich and famous with the ulterior motive of putting the author in a historically favorable light. And earn a few dollars to boot. Not so for me; I don't need to alter the opinions of those who know me, and I certainly didn't write this to feather my economic nest. My potential audience can't compare with those of the rich and famous, or notorious. But I can try to convince you the reader to do the same thing and give your family, friends, etc., something special in the form of your story in perpetuity.

Let me explain how easy it is to write a book about your life. I'll start with an easy question: who knows your life better than you? Once I decided to write my life story, I wrote down a few notes recalling my earliest times, and then proceeded along what seemed to me to be a decent chronological path. Once I had my outline, I started writing on my home computer. By the third day, I had written almost 12,000 words. Just about each day, I would think of a point, make a note of it and add it to my narrative. What you have read was never written in longhand and has taken me less than four months of a reasonably focused effort from start to finish. This type of writing is far different from the type associated with news reporting or law; I tried to write this as if I were talking directly to you. I'm told this is the best type of writing and with an autobiography/memoir, this conversational style works best for both writer and reader. So, get your paper and pen, make an outline, sit down at your computer, and you'll be amazed how quickly the words will flow.

There is yet another wrinkle to the consideration that went into the writing of this book. As I've already said, those who write autobiographies and memoirs fall into one or more of the categories of the rich, famous, notorious, or otherwise interesting and intriguing. But the vast VAST majority are none of these. This book, in addition to my family, friends, colleagues and acquaintances, is also for those who just might be interested in writing about their lives. Perhaps like you. So, what's stopping you? I know I'm repeating myself, but I never thought I would enjoy this effort as much as I have. And I firmly believe that if you put your mind to it, you will find—in a few short months—writing your life story to be one of the most exhilarating experiences you will ever have.

There is one final point of a deeply serious nature that requires comment. It is a theme that is woven throughout this narrative, but not stated directly. Until now. You see, whether we like it or not, we are dependent on others for our survival as well as progress. You don't believe me? Look in your refrigerator, pantry, kitchen shelves, etc., and notice where your food products, appliances, furniture, etc., come from. Get into your car. Do all parts of your car come from the United States? I'd be shocked if they did. Is everything in your residence made in the USA? When you need service, do you call on a phone made in America? Is the person answering your call even in America? How many foreign-born workers are in your business, agency, etc.? We're in a rapidly changing and growing global economy. We need oil and other products manufactured in other countries, and those countries need our money, food and other resources and supplies that are uniquely ours.

At home, we have government stalemate unless both political parties agree to work together. It takes two branches of our government to get things done; the legislature can pass laws until hell freezes over, but unless they're enforced by the executive branch, the laws mean nothing. The executive branch can only do what the legislature authorizes; if that branch exceeds its legislative authority, the courts will tell it so. And if the courts overextend themselves, the legislature will pass legislation that addresses the infirmity. This is called checks and balances, and our system's success depends on the faithful adherence to this remarkable arrangement created by the brightest minds of the 18th century.

As much as we talk about independence, liberty and freedom, the fact is there is a very real dependency on others in order to assure success in any venture, domestic or international. Individuality and freedom must be considered in tandem with communities of interest. Living together and working together on this one planet we have is really not an option.

Although this obvious reality came to me later in life, I make a conscious effort every today to have a positive attitude. This isn't an easy thing to do; there are stresses in everyday life that can block positivism. I try not to give in to them. I still have aches and pains from arthritis; the most painful areas now are my lower back and thighs. This is the stenosis, or narrowing of the area where the nerves pass through the spine. When you see an older person, especially a man, having difficulty walking, getting in and out of a car, etc., chances are you are looking at someone who has lumbar spinal stenosis. Frankly, my fear of immobility is very real, and I am seeing specialists—my orthopedic surgeon, physical therapists, and pain management physician—to deal with my condition. Hopefully, they will eliminate or at least stave off this prospect and allow me to enjoy my retirement years without debilitating pain and relatively free movement. I readily admit that it's not easy to always be positive. Talk is cheap, and when I'm hurting, it's hard to see a silver lining. This, however, is precisely the time when positivism must be paramount. One thing is certain, however; I will do everything I can to avoid giving in to negativism; I refuse to let my condition identify me in any manner. Here's a great line that I follow that's worth repeating: growing old is unavoidable; growing up is an option.

For me, retirement also signaled a stark reality: I'm getting older. I'm getting old. Old!! Of course, all of us are getting old; we're not meant to live forever. But I realize that I have far fewer years left than I've already lived. However good a person may feel at, say 50, chances are he/she has lived more years than are left. I think that in our 20s, 30s, and maybe even into our 50s, we tend to feel indestructible. We can do pretty much what we want, with no major difficulty. I pretty much felt this way until I reached 62 and needed knee replacement surgery. The previous surgeries I had took care of pain, and I generally felt good. Then, the pain level increased and was not fully taken care of by subsequent orthopedic surgery. This is where I am now as I reach 70 on my next birthday.

I think we have this retirement thing backwards. Right now, if a person retires at 67 like I did, he/she has about 10 years left, according to life span studies. Of course, depending on one's lifestyle, that person can expect to live well into the 80s. But let's face it, an older person can't do what a younger person can. Travel in retirement can be a painful experience. Generally, hiking, swimming, sightseeing on foot, etc., are harder to do when a person is past 70. So here's my plan. What our government should do is give every person $1 million at age 21 to use as he/she sees fit. A married couple would get $2 million. Each person could also work, but that would be an individual choice. They could raise a family, but again, that would be an individual choice. The point here is that this money could be used for all the things people want to do when they retire. But they would be young enough to do all those things with the great enjoyment born of vigorous youth. Then, after 20 years of living as a retiree, they would have to go to work and pay off that million-dollar loan at a low interest rate (like a student loan, for example). If they have to work 20-40 years to pay it off, it really doesn't matter. After all, they wouldn't be looking forward to retirement anymore.

They could work into their 80s without the pressure of saving for retirement because they had the option of working full—or part-time and could have opted to buy a home and provide for a nest egg very early on in their lives and used some of what was left for travel, etc. This plan would alter the current pension, Social Security and medical benefits, the amounts of which could potentially pay for this plan. If a person dies before the amount is paid off, I have no doubt the government can find a way to secure some measure of reimbursement. Of course, consideration would have to be given to those people and families who are already multibillionaires and multimillionaires who actually don't have to work and can live the life of a retiree now. There are numerous factors that would need to be considered, but the primary goal would be to make retirement years of 21-41 far more appealing to the healthy and vigorous, and the workaday world of 41-71 or 81 more appealing because it requires less physical strength and the nation gets an experienced, well-traveled and more relaxed workforce.

Ok, back to reality now. Although I don't have the neck mobility I once had—the nine-vertebra fusion took care of this—my focus is on what I can do, and that will continue to be my focus. I certainly won't try to do what is now physically impossible or hurtful to me. I'd like to think that I'm not stubborn enough to deliberately do anything that will cause me injury or self-inflicted pain. After all, I'm not 30 anymore—or 40, 50 or 60 for that matter. I can't avoid getting old; I can control how to make the best of my life. With chronic pain syndrome (that what doctors call it now), there are days when I feel like crawling in bed and staying there, or just sitting in my recliner and not getting up. But I also know that these are the times when I must move and engage in some activity, even if I have to force myself. I know that chronic pain will always be with me; but I don't have to let it define me, and I won't. I will take my own advice that I've given to my daughters over the years—I will persevere. I have a loving wife who looks after and protects me, mostly from myself. I have the best daughters any father can have, and two marvelous sons-in-law who look after and protect my children and theirs as well. My three granddaughters are very loving and can't wait to visit with their grammy and grampy; and I know my grandson will be no different because his parents will take care of that, and Harriet and I will make him laugh and play silly funny games with him, too.

Since I retired in 2010, I force myself to concentrate even more than ever before on two important things that are necessary to be successful in any venture. They are positivism and direction. While there are inevitably going be events that I can't control, or at least can't control fully, I realize that my attitude and response to these events are largely within my control. As I said previously, it's the old "glass half—full vs. glass half-empty" view. I can choose to see the negatives in any event that is bothersome, stressful or aggravating. I can also take a deep breath and make every possible effort to take a lemon and turn it into lemonade. I can then turn my full attention to those things that will put a positive spin on the otherwise negative event. Arthritis is an age-impacted condition. I am all too aware that exercise is a vital part of maintaining mobility. By being positive and faithful to an exercise regimen, while keeping my weight in check, I can do a lot to help myself.

This takes more time and effort; but it certainly beats dwelling on the negative, which only worsens the situation. I find that, on occasion, I must either be reminded—or remind myself—that I am the master of my fate,

I am the captain of my soul (ok, so I'm being overly melodramatic here, but you get the point.) I believe that, in the long run, this will help me deal with my arthritic condition and any other stressor that will come my way. Of course, not having to deal with job-related or finance-related stress also helps a great deal in daily living.

One aspect of retirement didn't really hit me until after I left the workforce: I never took stock of how much older I was than many of my co-workers. When I was working with them—ranging in ages from about 25 to the 50s—it never dawned on me that I was anything other than a peer. Now, when I go back for a retirement party and see so many familiar faces, I realized that they were the young sailors and I was the ancient mariner. Perhaps it's for the best that I didn't focus on age differential; it didn't seem to matter while I was working (except for the evaluations the merits of which I discounted); and it's too late to matter now.

There is yet another aspect of retirement that is most enjoyable. You may recall me mentioning that at my retirement reception, I was given as a gag-gift a clock with the numbers jumbled and placed in one corner. A short time later, my daughters gave Harriet and me a clock that has the days of the week, but no hours. There is a simple reason for this. When you're retired, every day is Monday . . . or Tuesday, or Wednesday, etc. At the risk of repeating a truism, retirement is a most liberating experience. No longer is there literally a daily struggle to meet deadlines. The great shift is from external to internal control of one's life. Days and hours are of far less significance when a retiree controls his activities.

There are occasions when time is important—catching a flight, being at a particular location (mostly to meet family or friends), having lunch or dinner—again with family, friends, etc. The reality is that the stress and anxiety of meeting deadlines is virtually extinguished when the deadline is not imposed by someone who has authority over you; and in the workaday world, someone almost always has such authority, even if a person owns his/her own business, where the customers or clients exercise the power of the wallet. Now, we check when our pension and Social Security payments are dropped into our accounts, and we review our quarterly statements to see how much interest we've earned on our DROP funds and other investments. Tough job, isn't it?

Going to the movies or shopping takes on a whole new meaning. No lines to purchase tickets. Harriet and I catch matinees when we literally have an entire movie theater to ourselves. No giants sitting in front of us, forcing us to crane our heads to see the screen. Uh, uh. Now, no one is in front—or behind—us. No more crowded malls or supermarkets, either. We go in, do our shopping, and wait on short lines—if we have to wait at all—and then head home. This kind of freedom to choose what we want to do and when we want to do it is a wonderful thing considering this didn't exist for us when we were working, raising our children and just generally trying to make it to the weekends to get everything done. The rush-rush pace of life is now history.

There is one minor drawback, however: since the days of the week hardly matter, Harriet and I frequently have to ask each other what the day of the week is, but that's ok. At no time before—or since—retiring, has a single retired person told me that he/she isn't enjoying life. In fact, it's just the opposite. I thought people who made this observation to me before I retired were simply trying to make me feel good about myself and my future. Now I know how right they were. If a person has all the time in the world to do what he/she pleases, and is happy with this freedom, then what more can anyone ask for? If I had known retirement was this good, I would have done it 40 years ago.

There is one other thing that retirement allows you to do; and by now this one should be obvious to you. I have all the time in the world to write a book. I'm not sure I could have done this while working; in hindsight, I could have easily convinced myself that there wasn't enough time to focus on my life and that I was too busy living it to write about it. I think for me, writing this involved a confluence of timing and focus. Whether in hindsight I could have written this while still working and were motivated to do so, is now quite beside the point. I had reached the point in my life where I had the time, was focused to write, and motivated to do so. Remember, life is about making memories so that, when you grow older, you have moments to remember. Life is what happens when you're busy making those memories. If you can look back and be proud of what you've accomplished, then you've lived a productive life. It's really that simple.

Retirement gives me time to pause and reflect, to gather thoughts and put them on paper. This has both a genealogical and cathartic impact. In this book, I've praised a few by name, and was somewhat critical of some but didn't mention their names. I don't believe I needed to do that; those people know who they are, and I have friends with whom I worked and otherwise associated with who know who I'm talking about. The simple fact is with no one holding anything over me, I am free to speak my mind with impunity and, so long as I am honest with myself, that's all that really matters here. If you are retired, there really is nothing preventing you from doing what I've done; if you're not, you have something else to add to your to-do or bucket list, if you have one. I don't for one simple reason: there is nothing more meaningful or important as family. As I sat in the hospital room on August 8, 2012-a day after Connor's birth—and watched as Lani, Hailey and Kelsie came to visit Amy, Avery and her newborn son, I realized that this was the very first time I had my wife, children and grandchildren together at one time. Needless to say, the cameras clicked as pictures of this historic family moment were taken. I realized that all of the material things that I have in my life are quite insignificant when compared to having my family all together. I'm told I have all the time in the world to visit tourist sites here and those in foreign lands as well. I'd rather spend the time with my family. If I never see the white cliffs of Dover, the Aurora Borealis, or the Great Wall of China, so what? If I get to see some sites, fine; but this isn't my passion. Being with family and good friends beats sightseeing any day.

Allow me to give share with you some words of wisdom. Our country is special because we have certain rights that we deem are inalienable; they're generally set out in our Bill of Rights. They must be exercised or suffer atrophy. Always be willing to stand up for what you believe, but do so with an open mind. Don't blindly accept as true what you are told by others. Do your own reading, inquiry and analysis. Engage in introspection or self-examination of your views; I do, and find this very helpful. And above all, be true to yourself. When you look in the mirror, you must like what you see. If you don't, see my previous comments.

My primary focus is on family, and I am accountable only to them. I have a quote on my desk in my den that says "A hundred years from now, it will not matter what my bank account was, the sort of house I lived in, or the kind of car I drove. but the world may be different because I was important in the life of a child." Then there's that wonderful line from the Wizard of Oz: "It's not how much you love, but how much you are loved by others" that counts. I try to live every day of my life with these thoughts in mind.

Then there are my Masonic brothers and activities, and travel; plenty of travel to both foreign and domestic exotic spots. The past is gone, the present is the only time to enjoy life and plan for the future; and this is precisely what I'm doing. I've been blessed with a great wife, great children and grandchildren, a successful professional life, and many wonderful friends, colleagues and fraternal brothers. And if I'm repeating myself, that's ok, too. I like to remind myself again and again how lucky I am. If however many more years I have are anything like the ones I've already had, then I consider myself a very lucky and fortunate man. As I said previously, it's important to see the bright side of things; humor, laughter and a positive attitude equal good mental health, which leads to good physical well-being.

Just remember the sage advice set out in the song above and "accentuate the positive, eliminate the negative, latch on to the affirmative, and don't mess with Mr. In-Between." The important thing is to find personal fulfillment in anything you do; I've certainly found this in my life.

Who can ask for more?

POSTSCRIPT

I wonder if this book will make the New York Times best-seller list. While I'm waiting to hear from the Times, I think I'll check with the Pulitzer Prize committee. Hmmmm, Nah, that's too presumptuous. I wonder when the bidding wars will start for the film version.

And for those of you who may still be wondering why I wrote this book, my final, final answer is, Why not!!!

About The Author

George Waas is a retired Florida government lawyer who spent 32+ years in state government practice, 24 years with the Florida Attorney General's Office. He was born in New York City and grew up on Miami Beach. He graduated from the University of Florida with a degree in journalism and spent two years as a news reporter before attending Florida State University College of Law. He was editor of the FSU student newspaper while attending law school. He worked as a lawyer for several state agencies, and spent seven-plus years in the private sector. He served on several Florida Bar committees and sections, serving as chairman for a number of them; has written and lectured extensively on constitutional law, administrative law and practice and procedure; and is a Mason, Scottish Rite (32nd degree) Mason, as a member of the Grotto. George has held high offices in all Masonic organizations. He has received numerous awards for his legal work, including the Claude Pepper Outstanding Government Lawyer Award and appears in several Marquis Who's Who, including Who's Who in America. He is married to Harriet Issner Waas, and has two daughters, Lani (Hudgins) and Amy (Kinsey) and four grandchildren, Hailey and Kelsie (Lani) and Avery and Connor (Amy). He lives in happy retirement in Tallahassee with his wife and two cats, Sandy and Mandy.

CPSIA information can be obtained at www.ICGtesting.com
Printed in the USA
LVOW040217081112

306400LV00003B/10/P

9 781477 262559